The Ends of Utopian Thinking
in Critical Theory

Historical Materialism Book Series

The Historical Materialism Book Series is a major publishing initiative of the radical left. The capitalist crisis of the twenty-first century has been met by a resurgence of interest in critical Marxist theory. At the same time, the publishing institutions committed to Marxism have contracted markedly since the high point of the 1970s. The Historical Materialism Book Series is dedicated to addressing this situation by making available important works of Marxist theory. The aim of the series is to publish important theoretical contributions as the basis for vigorous intellectual debate and exchange on the left.

The peer-reviewed series publishes original monographs, translated texts, and reprints of classics across the bounds of academic disciplinary agendas and across the divisions of the left. The series is particularly concerned to encourage the internationalization of Marxist debate and aims to translate significant studies from beyond the English-speaking world.

For a full list of titles in the Historical Materialism Book Series available in paperback from Haymarket Books, visit: www.haymarketbooks.org/ series_collections/1-historical-materialism.

The Ends of Utopian Thinking in Critical Theory

Nina Rismal

Haymarket Books
Chicago, IL

First published in 2023 by Brill Academic Publishers, The Netherlands
© 2023 Koninklijke Brill NV, Leiden, The Netherlands

Published in paperback in 2024 by
Haymarket Books
P.O. Box 180165
Chicago, IL 60618
773-583-7884
www.haymarketbooks.org

ISBN: 979-88889-0-219-6

Distributed to the trade in the US through Consortium Book Sales and
Distribution (www.cbsd.com) and internationally through Ingram
Publisher Services International (www.ingramcontent.com).

This book was published with the generous support of Lannan
Foundation, Wallace Action Fund, and the Marguerite Casey Foundation.

Special discounts are available for bulk purchases by organizations and
institutions. Please call 773-583-7884 or email info@haymarketbooks.org
for more information.

Cover art and design by David Mabb. Cover art is a detail from *Painting
41, Rhythm 69, (William Morris Block Printed Pattern Book, with Hans Richter
Storyboard, developed from Richter's Rhythmus 25 and Kazimir Malevich's
film script Artistic and Scientific Film – Painting and Architectural Concerns –
Approaching the New Plastic Architectural System)*. Paint and wallpaper on
canvas (2007).

Printed in the United States.

Library of Congress Cataloging-in-Publication data is available.

When you walk through a storm
Hold your head up high
And don't be afraid of the dark
At the end of a storm
There's a golden sky
And the sweet silver song of a lark
Walk on through the wind
Walk on through the rain
Though your dreams be tossed and blown
Walk on, walk on
With hope in your heart
And you'll never walk alone.

'You will never walk alone', OSCAR HAMMERSTEIN II

⁖

Contents

Acknowledgements

This book is a result of my doctoral study at the University of Cambridge during 2014 and 2018, which was made possible by financial support I received from the Public Scholarship, Development, Disability and Maintenance Fund of the Republic of Slovenia, the Alfred Toepfer Stiftung and the Tiarks German Scholarship Fund at the Department of German and Dutch, University of Cambridge. I am very grateful for having had the privilege to dedicate four years of my life exclusively to trying to understand what the world is about.

I finished the book towards the end of the first year of the Covid-19 pandemic while working at The New Institute Foundation in Hamburg. From the Foundation I would specifically like to thank Erck Rickmers and Wilhlem Krull for enabling me to take all the time I needed for finishing this book project.

Sincerest thanks go to my PhD supervisor Martin A. Ruehl, whose support and advice have been unfaltering over the course of my studies. I am grateful to a number of other people who have helped me immensely at various stages of my project. I am grateful to Cat Moir, Eva von Redecker and Lukas Kübler for their interest in my work and their invaluable feedback on it. I would further like to thank Daniel Weiss, Ruth Levitas, Ivan Boldyrev and Johan Siebers, with whom I had valuable discussions on various shorter sections of my manuscript. I would like to deeply thank Johan also for his unwavering support in turning the dissertation into this book. In this process I also benefited greatly from the comments I received from Peter Thompson, James Ingram and two anonymous reviewers of my manuscript. I would also like to extend my thanks to Ulrike Balser from the German and Dutch Department and to all the staff at the University Library in Cambridge.

I am lucky to have had a host of dedicated friends on whose willingness to discuss my ideas and to offer moral support I have been able to rely. Above all I have in mind the communities built around the house on Mawson Road in Cambridge and in Mesendorf. Thank you especially to Aurelie, Lucy, Matthias, Eva and Pascale for keeping my spirit high during the difficult last year of my PhD.

Last but not least, many thanks to Brill Academic Publishing for selecting my manuscript for publication. Above all, thank you to Danny Hayward whose help and support I will never forget!

Note on Translations

The citations of the original German texts in the body of the text I have translated into English. I have indicated all consulted translations in the Bibliography. Where necessary, I have modified the consulted translations to bring them closer to the original. Where no translated edition was available, translations are my own.

Introduction

Over the last fifty years utopian thinking has been dispossessed of its political purpose. At its inception, in Thomas More's novel *Utopia*, this activity of imagining an infinitely more desirable society of the future carried both a political and an artistic value. The detachment of utopian thinking from politics has been acknowledged by many social observers and scholars. In his introduction to the edited volume on the *Political Uses of Utopia* from 2017, James Ingram notes that the gap between the two domains of politics and utopia, which began to open up five or six decades ago, has now become firmly entrenched.[1] In 2016, the Marxist philosopher Fredric Jameson noted that '[w]e have seen a marked diminution in the production of new utopias over the last decades', and the social psychologist Harald Welzer talked of 'the loss of utopian thinking'.[2] In the same vein, Russel Jacoby, the author of *Picture Imperfect: Utopian Thought for an Anti-Utopian Age*, published in 2005, observed that 'countless individuals – writers, scholars, politicians, and ordinary people' share the sentiment about the decline of utopian thinking.[3] For them, Jacoby writes, 'utopian thinking is finished'.[4]

Even in the sphere of left-wing activism, utopia's home, politics seems to have been deprived of utopia. As Bini Adamczak argues, what marked the most significant anti-capitalist movements in the 1990s and the early 2000s – the Zapatistas in Chiapas in 1994, the anti-globalisation protests in Seattle in 1999, and in Genoa in 2001 – was that their appeal to the wider public stemmed from the mere slogan 'another world is possible', with no thought for what this other world could be, what it would look like, and when it might arrive.[5] By the end of the 2000s, according to Erik Olin Wright, one of the most prominent theorists of utopian thinking of the twenty-first century, even the very possibility of a different world did not seem tenable anymore: most people in the world today, Wright wrote in 2009, no longer believe 'that a fundamental alternative to capitalism was possible'.[6]

The Great Recession triggered by the financial crash in 2008 and its backlash that reverberated throughout the 2010s may have somewhat shifted the tide.

---

1 Ingram 2017, p. 15.
2 Jameson 2016, p. 1; cf. Amjahid and Randow 2016.
3 Jacoby 2005, p. 6.
4 Jacoby 2005, p. 6.
5 Adamczak 2014, p. 76.
6 Wright 2009, p. 1.

Utopia once again changed its meaning, becoming a rallying cry for movements like those of Occupy, which in its disillusionment with capitalism reignited a search for a radically different socioeconomic system. Dauting ecological emergency, paired with a dwindling confidence that elected officials are going to resolve it, has prompted the formation of vigorous national and international climate movements advocating for a more sustainable and just society. The attention of movements such as Fridays for Future and Extinction Rebellion, however, seems to be primarily focused on increasing public awareness and understanding of the ongoing environmental deterioration and on demands for action from governments, and less on spelling out a vision of the future society they seek. On the back of an overwhelming scientific consensus, millions of activists are recognising that an alternate social system is in fact *necessary* – for even humanity's own survival – rather than merely *possible*.[7] Utopianism, whose historical task has been to propose more elaborated versions of desirable social arrangements and structures and not only to argue the need for one, therefore remains to be truly revived in today's politics.

How can this decline of utopian politics be explained? Since their very beginnings, criticism and controversy have hovered over all kinds of utopian projects. Utopia's name has become so tarnished that it has been used almost interchangeably with its evil twin, dystopia. Another twin of utopianism, anti-utopianism has also been there since its birth, trailing in its shadow. In fact the two '-isms' cannot be neatly separated: very few defenders of utopia advocate this concept blindly, and even its most fervent critics sometimes acknowledge its positive potential. Recent decades nevertheless present a distinct turn within the history of utopian thinking. Although utopian thinking already acquired its strongly negative connotation in the nineteenth century, when revolutionary uprisings were surging through Europe, it was not until a century later that such thinking started to lose its impetus. What has been put in jeopardy now is not merely utopia's name but also that which lies behind it – the very act of imagining and pursuing a better society, the practice of utopian thinking.

History, with a capital H, is commonly offered as an explanation of the decline of utopian thinking. In 1986, the Polish poet Czesław Miłosz reminded his audience that '[i]nnumerable millions of human beings were killed in this century in the name of utopia'.[8] Within historiography, it is the Soviet communist regime that is seen as the main culprit of the death of utopia. As became increasingly apparent during the Cold War, especially in Hungary in 1956 and

---

7 Hagedorn et al. 2019.
8 See Anderson 2004.

Czechoslovakia in 1968, this regime degenerated irretrievably, lapsing into an oppressive and totalitarian form, with horrific consequences for its citizens. Nazi Germany, Communist China and Pol Pot's Cambodia are cited as further proofs that, as the French economist and futurist Bertrand de Jouvene's famous line reads, '[t]here is a tyranny in the womb of every utopia'.[9]

This explanation of the decline of utopian thinking has by now become common knowledge. Even among the scholarship, this explanation is taken for granted. For instance, Russel Jacoby finds it unnecessary to explore this explanation further in his account of the history of utopian thinking, saying that he 'can add little to this story.'[10] The fact is that '[t]he failure of Soviet communism entailed the end of utopia', he writes, adding that such end is simply 'the verdict of history.'[11]

History, its lessons and verdicts, however, have never been self-standing entities; they have instead have been written up by historians, intellectual historians and other thinkers. This is the case also with utopian thinking. The explanation for its decline is founded on ideas advanced foremost by the philosophers Isaiah Berlin, Karl Popper and Friedrich Hayek, alongside those of the historians Jacob Talmon and Norman Cohn. In a dozen years, a liberal anti-utopian consensus took shape that has not only endured but gained strength with each passing decade. Its major writings include Hayek's *Road to Serfdom* (1944), Karl Popper's *The Open Society and Its Enemies* (1945), J.L. Talmon's *The Origins of Totalitarian Democracy* (1961), and several essays of Isaiah Berlin from the 1950s, including 'The Decline of Utopian Ideas in the West', published in his book *The Crooked Timber of Humanity* (1959). Together, these texts make an inclusive case for the dangers of utopian thought, providing the intellectual foundations to the existing popular explanation of the decline of utopian thinking.

The thrust of the anti-utopian arguments of these thinkers is the idea that utopianism and totalitarianism are fatally intertwined: every utopian vision leads to totalitarian politics, which in turn is always premised on a utopian ideal. '[T]he tragic paradox of Utopianism', writes Talmon, is that instead of leading to freedom, 'it brought totalitarian coercion'.[12] Similarly, Popper finds that utopia brings 'only the familiar misery of being condemned to live under a tyrannical government', and Berlin claims that for a utopian society to be real-

---

9   See Kapur 2016.
10   Jacoby 2005, p. 6.
11   Jacoby 2005, p. 6.
12   Talmon 1957, p. 12.

ised, 'no amount of oppression, cruelty, repression, coercion will be too high'.[13] The underlying justification of these arguments is grounded in a distinct ethics of value pluralism and subjectivity of values, norms and ideals, namely that people have differing and incompatible utopian visions that cannot be rationally reconciled. Given this plurality of conflicting visions, these thinkers argue, a political leader or a political party who wants to realise their own utopian vision is compelled to use violence.[14] The critical achievement of this liberal discourse, which was later reinvigorated in writings like *Black Mass: Apocalyptic Religion and the Death of Utopia*, a book by John Gray from 2007, is that utopian thinking lies at the very core of the past political terrors and that it therefore needs to be discarded once and for all.

This reasoning about the intertwinement of utopian thinking and totalitarian politics is not without its problems. The critics, mostly of a more left-leaning political persuasion, highlight ideological generalisations and assumptions entailed in this position, such as the assertion that *any* intervention by the state necessarily slides into totalitarianism, and point, moreover, to an ideological rationale of this position: construing utopia as dangerous in this way simply supports, and thus empowers, the conservative position of opposition to change and newness. Critics of the liberals further agree that the liberal position hinges on a very specific definition of utopia as 'a static, perfect and harmonious whole, at odds with the complexity of the real world', and in turn point out that visions of a desirable society can also be worked out over time, in a dialogue with practice and adjusted in line with experiences.[15] These more dynamic notions of utopia cannot be blamed as easily for utopia's supposedly intrinsic dangers as the static one can be. Instead of assuming that a certain utopian vision must be realised in its original outline – under all circumstances and by whatever means – the original vision could also be informed by the experiences which its realisation brings – and consequently corrected for. The allegedly logical link between utopia and violence is thus valid only for a very narrow definition of utopian thinking and not for other, equally plausible understandings of this concept.

13   Popper 1986 [1963], p. 8; Berlin 2013 [1959], p. 49.
14   See Talmon 1957; Popper 1986 [1963]; Berlin 2013 [1959].
15   Levitas 2013, p. 7.

1   The Blow to Utopia from the Left

It is easy for the left-wing critics to defend utopia against its conservative
attacks. This criticism might leave the impression that the Left has always been
on the defensive when it comes to utopia and has perceived the role of utopian
thinking as a positive one. Yet, as I argue in this book, this is not the case. Within
the theoretical heritage of the Left too, utopian thinking has had an ambivalent
status. In fact, as I show in the ensuing chapters, criticism of utopian thinking
by left intellectuals might even have been more decisive for its death than the
liberal attacks have been.

Utopian thinking, for sure, lives on both extremes of the political spectrum.
From Hitler to Breivik, various far-right ideologues have envisaged a society
that certainly is radically different from the existing one. Yet, the very demand
to institute a different society is more typical of the Left than the Right and historically overlapped significantly with the intellectual heritage of the former.
This overlap is located in the idea of a classless, stateless society based on the
communal ownership of property and wealth. Although in Western thought
this idea stretches back all the way to antiquity and early Christianity, it culminated in the socialist and communist movements of the mid-nineteenth century,
of which Karl Marx was a key creator and representative. As such, Marx can
hardly be held directly responsible for the death of utopia. Despite his objections to utopian thinking, it was very much alive in his own writings. Marx
and Engels's *Communist Manifesto*, one of the most influential works from the
period of the latter half of this century, clearly sets out the principle features
of a communist society. In the form of communism, utopia endured and utopian thinking thrived. Many parties and movements identified themselves with
this label. Indeed, communism was far more than a label at this time: revolutionaries attempted to realise it in practice in the Revolutions of 1848 and 1849,
the Paris Commune in 1871, the 1917 revolutions in the Russian Empire, and the
1918 November Revolution in Germany.

Then the tide turned. In one sense or the other, all these revolutions are
perceived to have failed. The French and German communists were crushed
within months of their occurrence, whereas the Russian Revolution – even if it
appeared to have succeeded at the time – resulted in a social order far removed
from the conceptual ideal of communism. Today, communism has basically
disappeared as a state-level political regime. Stalinist Russia is gone, Maoist
China has transformed into a nakedly capitalist country, and the prospects of
communism in places like Cuba are darkening.

In contrast to the intellectual space of the Right, where the historical failures
of communism simply cemented the death of utopian thinking, thinkers on

the Left were challenged to reconsider its place and role anew. From their perspective, it was far from clear whether utopian thinking was indeed destructive, or whether the opposite might actually be the case. The historical conditions around the Second World War opened up a space in which novel understandings of the role of utopian thinking could have been accepted and proven lasting. By that time, communism was losing its popular and intellectual base as an alternative to the ever more powerful capitalism. Those opposing capitalism had no 'ready-made' alternative to turn to. It could be said that, on the one hand, these conditions called for a new, third alternative to be proposed, or, at least, for the idea of communism to undergo a substantial revision. On the other hand these conditions raised the more fundamental question of whether a conception of such an alternative should be available in the first place. If Marx himself did not face this question, his twentieth-century followers did.

Given the influence Marx's writings exercised on later Marxist thinkers, his objections certainly contributed, indirectly, to the ensuing decline of utopian thinking. Marx, however, played a very direct role in making this question worth entertaining at all. First, as I have already suggested, Marx's thought is marked by a certain paradox as far as utopian thinking is concerned: on the one hand he was vocal in his criticism of those communists and socialists he considered to be preoccupied with outlining and describing the nature and features of the social systems they advocated; on the other hand, Marx himself, to a certain extent, participated in creating these outlines. If Marx was a utopian thinker himself, why was he also critical of such thinking? The political battles Marx fought with the competing communists and socialists, as well as his own idiosyncratic usage of the label 'utopian', begin to explain this paradox entailed in his thought. Yet they explain it only partially, and all those who adopted his philosophical framework were forced to confront it in one way or another.

The other way in which Marx elevated the relevance of utopian thinking for his followers concerns one specific aspect of his philosophical framework, namely his theory of social transformation. This theory has many different formulations, offered both by Marx himself and by subsequent scholars. For reasons which I consider in the first chapter of this book, one very viable generalisation of this theory is the following: social transformation is determined *primarily* by objective or economic factors. Whereas history does not change by itself, but instead by the means of individual and collective actions exercised by individuals on their objective conditions, the scope, direction and effect of these actions are dictated, enabled and limited by the objective environment itself. The failed communist revolutions in the early twentieth century – or rather, the failed attempts at revolutions – showed that something was not quite right with this theory. Raymond Geuss describes most succinctly the theoretical problem facing Marxists in the period following the First World War:

> If Marx was right about the economy, why were the workers so docile? Could it be that capitalism was more flexible than Marx had anticipated; could it reach to providing at least for the immediate future something rather more ample than declining starvation wages for its slave labourers, the proletariat? Could it, furthermore, be that the power of the status quo resided not simply in its police force, army, and prison system, or even its factories, railways, and merchant ships, but in the power of its control over the human imagination? If that were true, then the realm of consciousness, culture, and 'ideology' could be an important potential arena of political struggle in a sense not clearly envisaged by Marx himself.[16]

This latter premise – that consciousness, culture and ideology, as opposed to the economic or objective factors, played a very significant role in social transformations – is a position that most aptly characterises a specific branch of Marxism that was first devised at the Institute for Social Research in Frankfurt in the 1920s.[17] The members of the Institute rejected parts of Marx's theory of social change, positing that it did not adequately account for the potential of bourgeois ideology to co-opt and control the ideas and actions of those with clashing objective interests, namely the proletariat. In making the assertion that certain ideas, rather than material circumstances, were preventing workers from acting, the Frankfurt scholars opened up a more general question concerning the role of ideas, thought and thinking in social transformations. As a type of thinking, utopian thinking also emerged as a factor that could influence social change. In a way, utopian thinking was a ready-made option, offered by Marx himself when he supplied some vivid and memorable comments on what a communist society could be. But Marx never seriously considered utopian thinking as a viable method of revolutionary theorising. He preempted this theoretical consideration by prioritising the economy. This was very different for the later generations of Marxist thinkers. As the economy failed to deliver the desired social changes that Marx had promised it would, questions of the possibility, necessity and desirability of utopian thinking became negotiable.

---

16   Geuss 2004, p. 132.

17   See Jay 1973, pp. 41–85.

In a radio interview in 1964, two associates of the Institute, Theodor W. Adorno – the leading member of its inner circle – and Ernst Bloch – its prominent
outcast – debate these very questions. Adorno doubts the possibility of utopian thinking as such, claiming that people have lost 'the capability to imagine
the totality as something that could be completely different'.[18] In addition, he
endorses 'the commandment not to "depict" utopia'.[19] Bloch counters Adorno
on both claims, positing that our capacity to imagine a world radically different from ours has endured, and that if this world cannot be displayed 'in the
picture', it can be represented 'in the process of being'.[20] Moreover, Bloch under-
scores a point which reaches beyond these disagreements: utopian thinking
should not be disposed of.[21] The two thinkers, however, also share lots of common ground. On numerous occasions in the conversation Bloch agrees with
Adorno's arguments against portraying utopias. In turn, Adorno, as the critic
of utopian thinking, sometimes sides with its defender, in particular regarding
the detrimental loss entailed in the prohibition of depicting utopias. This prohibition, Adorno claims:

> also has a very confounding aspect, for something terrible happens due
> to the fact that we are forbidden to cast a picture. To be precise, among
> that which should be definite, one imagines it to begin with as less defin-
> ite the more it is stated only as something negative. But then – and this is
> probably even more frightening – the commandment against a concrete
> expression of utopia tends to defame the utopian consciousness and to
> engulf it. What is really important, however, is the will that it is differ-
> ent.[22]

The central issue Adorno sets out concerns the relation between the prohibition of depicting utopias and the will for change. Adorno contends that the
absence of a positive image of utopia could 'defame' the utopian consciousness, which would in turn engulf that which really matters, namely the will to
change the world. The presence of the will for the world to be different has
consequences, presumably, for the actual realisation of utopia.

Between Adorno and Bloch, there might have been no clear winner to this
debate. Yet, more widely, within their intellectual circle, that of Critical The-

---

18   Adorno in Bloch 1977 [1969b], p. 353.
19   Adorno in Bloch 1977 [1969b], p. 361.
20   Bloch 1977 [1969b], p. 366.
21   Bloch 1977 [1969b], p. 366.
22   Adorno in Bloch 1977 [1969b], p. 363.

ory, Adorno's prohibition on utopian thinking prevailed and thereby made an additional contribution to the overall decline of utopian thinking. Adorno's prohibition, which I call 'Utopieverbot', became part and parcel of today's dominant strand of Critical Theory. Although some of its leading figures, including Amy Allen, Eva von Redecker and Axel Honneth have over the last few years, in different ways turned against the tide, the *Utopieverbot* endures.[23] Among the writings by contemporary critical theorists, there is a marked absence of texts explicating alternative social arrangements, structures and systems.[24] For example, Rahel Jaeggi, a prominent member of the Frankfurt School, firmly maintains Adorno's position, and instead defends a different philosophical praxis, namely that of social critique, and, to be more precise, of metacritique. Critique, which was a much employed tool of the first generation of critical theorists, is targeted at specific aspects of the existing society. In contrast, metacritique goes beyond this intention, and aims to establish the normative criteria which are then to constitute the practice of critique. It was this turn towards metacritique, also known as the procedural or Kantian turn, which cemented the death of utopian thinking in Critical Theory.

Whilst Adorno's preoccupation with the negative and the false represented a step towards the removal of utopian thinking from Critical Theory, the concern with the metacritique and procedures was another step towards this removal. Utopian thinking retains its place in Adorno to the extent that the good and the positive present merely the other side of the false and the negative. This, however, is not the case in the context of theories of metacritique, where the concerns of both the good and the false are of secondary importance. Jürgen Habermas, the Frankfurt School figure most responsible for the creation of this 'two-step removal' of utopian thinking from Critical Theory, superseded the question of the right and wrong *norms* with the question of the right and wrong *procedures* – procedures for establishing the norms.[25] Whereas this question of how norms are to be justified – that is, why we should conform to this and not to that normative principle – did already trouble Habermas's predecessors, including Marx and Adorno, it certainly did not become the focus of their theories. The theories of Marx and the early generations of the critical theorists remained strongly normative, that is, containing ideas of the good and the wrong. Habermas, in contrast, disposed of this kind of normativity, positing that no legitimate explanation exists as to how a theorist could extend the legitimacy of his or her personal, subjective norms into universally valid ones. He

---

23   See Honneth 2015.
24   See Chrostwska 2019.
25   See, e.g., McNay 2013, pp. 138–54.

has suggested, instead, that all a theorist can achieve is to propose certain procedures and conditions on the basis of which individual members of a society could reach an agreement on the universal norms and values guiding a genuinely progressive and just order. In Habermas's own words, a theorist can only establish

> the necessary but general conditions for the communicative practice of everyday life and for a procedure of discursive will-formation that would put participants themselves in a position to realise concrete possibilities for a better and less threatened life, on their own initiative and in accordance with their own needs and insights.[26]

In this articulation of the procedural turn, the emancipation of political theorising from utopian thinking comes is clearly apparent.[27] Conceiving and realising the concrete possibilities of a just and good society becomes the occupation solely of the participants of society, and not of the philosopher. Seyla Benhabib refers to the socio-epistemological perspective adopted by participants as the standpoint of 'intersubjectivity'.[28] This she distinguishes from the perspective of 'transsubjectivity', which reflects the view of the observer who is also in the position to 'analyse and judge social relations'.[29] This second perspective has been traditionally taken by social theorists, and it is in this capacity that theorists have been robbed of any right to say anything of content about a good society.

---

26   Habermas 1985, pp. 161–2.

27   In two respects Habermas too could be interpreted as a utopian thinker, specifically in that his theories of ideal speech situation and communicative rationality do propose a set of *ideal* norms, and moreover, in the sense that these norms are often deemed to be unrealistic and unattainable in practice, on the grounds that they fail to take into account unequal intrasubjective power relationships. However, these are not the meanings of utopian thinking I am primarily interested in this book. I am instead concerned with more substantive social ideals, those that concern social life itself, and not those that merely regulate its communicative practices. I perceive the descriptions of an ideal society that consider only its communicative ethics as too barren and abstract to call utopian thinking. I am also not concerned with understandings of utopian thinking that emphasise the inherently impossible nature of the word utopia, which seems to be the case with those scholars who tend to see Habermas's theories of theories of ideal speech situation and communicative rationality as instances of utopian thinking. For an extended definition of how I use the term utopian thinking, see the section '(Political) utopian thinking' in this introduction.

28   Benhabib 1986, p. 12.

29   Benhabib 1986, p. 12.

If Habermas, through his procedural turn, established the *Utopieverbot* as a significant structure within Critical Theory, its foundations had been laid down by his mentor, Adorno. The *Utopieverbot* is a much more complex theoretical structure than liberal anti-utopianism. The arguments against utopian thinking espoused by the liberal ideologues are centred above all on its inherent danger, and in turn hinge on perceiving it as a form of totalitarianism. References to the totalitarian regimes of Nazism and Stalinism are common in this literature. Adorno's own arguments were equally embedded within and affected by the historical catastrophes of the first half of the twentieth century. Born into a bourgeois Jewish family in 1903, Adorno witnessed and was personally affected by the atrocities of National Socialism. However, Adorno's utopian critique reaches beyond this specific history and the perils which the liberals perceive as being inherent in utopian thinking. The *Utopieverbot*, in contrast, stems from Adorno's view that utopian thinking is impossible. By this I mean that Adorno contended that it was impossible to conceptualise the 'good' society of the future. In the radio conversation with Bloch he put it in the following words: it is impossible to know 'the right' ('das Richtige'), that is, the shape and features of a genuinely better society.[30] The alternative social systems one might conceive at any given moment, in Adorno's view, can be simply a variation on the present society, and are thus not radically different from it. In Chapter 2 I explore the reasons and theoretical conditions that sustain Adorno's view. In particular, I argue that it cannot be fully understood in terms of influences exerted on Adorno by Marx and the idea of the Jewish *Bilderverbot*, but is in fact corroborated by Adorno's conception of time, and by his ideas about the 'culture industry' and 'identity thinking'.

Another prominent aspect of Adorno's thought – namely negative dialectics and determinate negation – in turn explains why Adorno's own influence on the dissolution of utopian thinking in Critical Theory, as well as more broadly in Western political thought, has so far not been adequately accounted for. An underlying idea of this theory is that the exclusive task of philosophers is the explication of 'the false', that is the wrong, negative or false features of the existing society – its problems, ills and wrongs, the sufferings and injustices it causes.[31] In contrast to the good society, it is possible, Adorno believes, to precisely know the false society.[32] This way of describing negative dialectics, however, conceals something crucial. As the name of this theoretical tool suggests, Adorno does not understand reality in the binary 'either or' fashion. The

---

30   Adorno in Bloch 1977 [1969b], p. 362.
31   Adorno in Bloch 1977 [1969b], p. 362.
32   Adorno in Bloch 1977 [1969b], p. 363.

ideas of the false and the good society are not, in his view, completely independent of each other, as if each could exist for itself.[33] Instead, he claims that the vision of the good, that is of the utopian society, is always already implied in the exposition of the false one, an exposition which is achieved through determinate negation ('bestimmte Negation').[34] In that determinate negation always entails or points to the vision of a utopian society, Adorno's theoretical tool has itself been interpreted by majority of his scholars as a form of utopian thinking, which I, in this book, refer to as 'negative utopian thinking'.

But can negative thinking, as some thinkers like Rahel Jaeggi contend, in fact be taken as a form of utopian thinking? Is not this negative utopian thinking perhaps misinterpreted and its value overestimated? Can we simply accept Adorno's contention that a positive projection of a utopian society is subsumed in its negative counterpart? In fact, at some points Adorno argues that a positive projection is not merely subsumed by, but results from, an identification of what a wrong society is. How can this identification of the old at the same time also produce something new? And, furthermore, is not such a subsumed projection fundamentally different from a more explicit, ad hoc one? Is negative utopian thinking not a fundamentally depreciated variety of utopianism?

2   The Road Not Taken

Some of the clues to these questions lie in the philosophy of Ernst Bloch. Bloch, a Marxist thinker of hope, utopia and futurity, in many respects presents an anomaly among critical theorists. A contemporary of Adorno and other members of the Institute for Social Research in Frankfurt, his work is non-contemporaneous, substantially removed from the kind of thinking and writing involved not only at the Institute but more broadly in his times. This isolation of his thought continues to the present day and partly explains why his views of utopian thinking never exercised a broader influence, and in turn, why Adorno's position prevailed. Be that as it may, Adorno's position is not unquestioned and, as I have already indicated, contains certain unresolved puzzles and questions. These, as I show in this book, can be put into focus only if we

---

33   See Jaeggi 2005. The reading of Adorno that Jaeggi defends in this article is the dominant one in the existing scholarship. One exception is Fabian Freyenhagen, who holds that, apart from in a few instances, Adorno does not possess a prior positive conception of the good society, and proceeds with his critique of the modern capitalist society independent of this standard. See Freyenhagen 2013, pp. 13–14.

34   Adorno in Bloch 1977 [1969b], p. 362.

also examine Bloch's fundamental revision of the notion of utopian thinking and his defence of its place within Critical Theory. This parallel conceptual history, Critical Theory's road not taken, however, not only highlights potential faultlines of Adorno's arguments. It also offers some valuable answers to the broader issues of the role of utopian thinking in politics. Bloch's thought in fact represents a fully fledged philosophy centred around utopian thinking, setting out what kind of utopian thinking can have a productive role in political processes and arguing that, in the first place, utopian thinking is vital to achieving any far-reaching political change.

Bloch's philosophy counters both of what I argue are two essential contributions by Adorno within the interface of utopian thinking and Critical Theory. These are *Utopieverbot* and the replacement of the positive kind of utopian thinking by the negative one. Bloch opposes Adorno and contends that critique, the negation of the existing adverse conditions, the explication of the wrongs prevailing in our society, cannot be directly equated with the positive expressions of utopia. More specifically, Bloch argues that:

> In the negative of objective dialectics (sickness, crisis, imminent decline into barbarism) there is doubtless some association of annihilation, thus not only of the Not, as the active motive force, but also of nothingness, as merely effacing negation, which of itself by no means automatically has the negation of its negation within itself.[35]

The utopian society to which Bloch refers here as 'the negation of the negative' does not automatically follow from negation. In his view, 'negativity by itself [...] bears no fruit historically, that is, the negation of the negation is by no means capable of developing itself from its own objectivity alone'.[36] Whereas determinate negation does in itself include the utopian society as one possibility, it includes another one, the dystopian one. Bloch calls this possibility 'annihilation', which can be understood as the total destruction of the existing system, or its descent into the worst imaginable dystopia. In order to prevent such annihilation, and moreover to pave the way for the realisation of the true utopia, Bloch argues that 'a subjective-active countermove against the annihilation' is necessary.[37]

But what does Bloch mean by this 'subjective-active countermove'? Is this a positive utopian vision, to which Marx, and then Adorno objected? And, does

---

35   Bloch 1977 [1962], pp. 515–16.
36   Bloch 1977 [1962], pp. 515–16.
37   Bloch 1977 [1962], pp. 515–16.

it represent a reversal of Adorno's *Utopieverbot*? To a certain extent, it indeed does. In Bloch's philosophy, utopian thinking remains primarily a form of positive thinking – it includes images of what a desired society would look like. Moreover, such positive thinking remains a necessary element of revolutionary philosophy, if the latter is to play a role also in *changing*, and not merely understanding, the world. For Bloch, utopian thinking, and hoping which is an activity he sees as constitutive of the former, correspond to going *beyond* that which already is, beyond Adorno's negative thinking. Due care, however, needs to be taken when interpreting Bloch's position as a reversal of that of Adorno. As I have already indicated, Bloch and Adorno had common grounds, and these need to be seen side-by-side to their differences. It is my objective to specify where exactly these differences lie, what exactly they are, and why exactly they matter.

3   (Political) Utopian Thinking

I have opened this introduction by pointing to the well established phenomenon of the decline of utopian thinking within politics that started emerging about half a century ago. I have consequently argued that there are two missing pieces to the understanding of this phenomenon. First, contrary to the established view, I argue that the ideas which initiated this decline come not only from the liberal-conservative tradition, but also its polar opposite, a strand of Marxism known as Critical Theory, and in particular from one of its most influential figures, Theodor Adorno. The second piece of the missing history has to do with transformations of utopian thinking within Critical Theory itself. While the first part of this book delineates the dominant current of these transformations, which contributed to the overall decline of utopian thinking, the second part shows that this Adornian current presents only one side of Critical Theory's internal relationship to utopia, and shows that the other, Blochian side, despite being marginalised so far, also offers many valuable contributions to our understanding of utopian thinking,

A difficulty in making any kind of contribution to our understanding of utopian thinking is a great ambiguity in what is meant by this phrase in the first place. This ambiguity becomes even more pronounced when talking about utopia in the realm of politics. Utopia is itself a term that has been ill-defined since Thomas More first used it in 1516 in the title of his depiction of a society of a fictional island, in which he elaborated on its religious, political and cultural customs. More employed the word to mean both a 'good place' (*eutopia*) and a 'non-existing place' (*outopia*). This dual meaning laid the basis for the contested question that haunts utopia to this day. The contestation focuses specifically on the nowhere of utopia: is the nowhere simply a result of some specific historical conditions, or is it inherent to the idea of the good society?

The term utopia accrued additional meanings as More's neologism filtered through into spoken language and was used more widely. Whereas in More's title the word utopia is the name of an island – that is, it designates one concrete object – in the first half of the seventeenth century the concreteness of this island was abstracted from, and utopia evolved into a more general concept. One of the first lexicographically documented meanings of the word utopia as a concept, instead of as a name, is found in a French-English dictionary compiled by Randle Cotgrave (1611), who recorded utopia as the noun 'Vtopie' and defined it as 'an imagnerie place, or countrey'.[38] But by the late sixteenth century, utopia did not only mean an imagined place, a place beyond this world, but rather came to indicate a work of fiction analogous to More's. That is, the word utopia by then corresponded to a specific literary genre – utopian fiction. In German encyclopaedias of the early twentieth century, the works of fiction most frequently classified as utopian, besides More's book, include Campanella's *The City of the Sun* (1602), Cabet's *Voyage to Icaria* (1840), Morelly's *Code of Nature* (1755), Harrington's *The Commonwealth of Oceana* (1656) and Mercier's *The Year 2440* (1771).[39]

Mercier's work marks another shift in the meaning of utopia, which Reinhart Koselleck famously labelled as 'the temporalisation of utopia'.[40] Utopia by and large stopped referring to a perfect state of affairs that was supposed to exist already somewhere in the present, as on More's fictional island, and instead began to exemplify the conception of a perfected arrangement of society, to emerge at some point in the future, as in Mercier's Paris of the year 2440. The transplantation of utopia from space to time is significant, as it facilitated the use of this word in the realm of politics. Utopia was now used above all in two senses. One usage, corresponding to the term's more common usage today, prioritises the aspect of utopia as an unrealisable or an impossible society. As such, utopia has a strong pejorative undertone and has become widely used as a more general expression of disparagement, indicating one's hostility to someone else's political views. Records of this meaning of utopia exist since the time of the English Civil War in the 1640s, when it was often employed to describe any constitution that one party would regard as unacceptable.[41] More

---

38   Hölscher 1996, p. 7.
39   Hölscher 1996, pp. 15–16.
40   Koselleck 2002, p. 85.
41   Hölscher 1996, pp. 18–19.

recently, it has been evoked in a Marxist critique of the existing regime, when Slavoj Žižek described late capitalism as utopian.[42] The use of utopia as a derogative term is best known in the context of disputes between various socialist movements of the mid-nineteenth century, although this is not indicative of that period of history's monopoly on utopia. The most notorious of these was Karl Marx and Friedrich Engels's critique of, above all, Saint-Simon, Fourier and Owen, whom they labelled 'utopian socialists'.[43] According to Fritzie and Frank Manuel, 'utopian' for Marx and Engels served simply as an 'epithet of denigration to be splashed onto any theoretical opponent'.[44] Martin Buber, similarly, remarked that it presented them with 'the last and most pointed shaft' employed in 'the internal political action' to be waged 'against the other so-called – or self-styled – communist movements'.[45]

These political movements have also been referred to as utopian in another, non-derogatory sense in which the word utopia has been used in the political discourse, which emphasises the side of utopia as a good society of the future, as opposed to being inherently unrealisable. In this second sense, which I argue is most relevant to what is currently meant by utopian thinking in politics, the term utopian was first employed by Louis Reybaud in his 1864 study, in which he identified as utopian not the figures of contemporary socialism and communism but their intellectual forerunners, who included, in addition to the More and Plato, a list of social movements, mostly of Judeo-Christian roots. Very soon the theories and as well as practical undertakings of the contemporary socialists and communists themselves became known as utopian.[46] What was common to these intellectuals and social movements is that they were advocating a system of social relations that was fundamentally different from the dominant order. It was this aspect of their activities that was implied in their designation as utopian. What was further novel about this usage of the term utopian was that these ideas and projects for social reforms were meant to be actual political proposals and not fictive exercises. Utopia became a vision to be pursued, a projection to be envisaged, a goal to be chased, an idea to be engendered with an actual will for political change. The precursor to utopian thinking that was at the same time also an intentional kind of thinking was in fact a work of fiction itself, namely *Oceana* by James Harrington, published in 1656, which, contrary to Thomas More's novel *Utopia*, was meant to

---

42   See Žižek 2010.
43   Marx and Engels 1977 [1848], pp. 489–92.
44   Manuel and Manuel 1979, p. 11.
45   Buber 1958, pp. 11–12.
46   Hölscher 1996, pp. 24–5.

present an actual proposal for a new English constitution.[47] Yet, by the time of the mid-eighteen century, it became more prevalent to articulate even very radical proposals for political change also as explicitly political, and not present them as a work of art. This development thereby gave rise to utopian thinking as a distinctly political practice, designating ideas, plans and proposals for social and political change that were sufficiently different from those already existing.

This affirmative meaning of utopian thinking as a political practice, as opposed to the ideologically-critical one, was further strengthened through the transformations that the concept of utopia underwent in twentieth-century philosophy, advanced by thinkers such as Karl Mannheim, Gustav Landauer, Ernst Bloch, Otto Neurath and a few others. These philosophers increasingly started considering utopia not as an individual work, be it literary or political, but as an expression of collective mentality, as a dimension of human thinking. Imagining, wishing and hoping for a fundamentally better future, constituted also by ideas of a fundamentally better form of social-political organisation, are understood by these philosophers simply as an attitude of humans towards their environment. This reconceptualisation of utopian thinking is responsible for some further confusions regarding utopia, by enabling an controversial expansion in the application of this concept, rendering any, but especially any creative human activity, as utopian. Not only fiction but other fields of the arts such as music, poetry, painting, design and architecture present possible domains of utopian thinking. Yet, this reconceptualisation also provided new theoretical justifications to seeing utopia as an idea that is inherently desirable, and not unrealisable. This shift in the emphasis certainly contributed to, if not directly enabling, the affirmative meaning of utopian thinking in the political discourse with which I am concerned in this book.

To be clear, by this meaning I understand conceptual visions for a radically better social future that are engendered with a political purpose, that is as visions that are intended to also be implemented, and not merely expressed. Expressions of these visions can take different forms, from those that are concerned with particular aspects of a society, such as plans for social reforms or descriptions of specific social arrangements, to more general ones, like core organising principles of these alternative social arrangements. These latter ones include forms such as political manifestos or philosophical treatises focusing on fundamentally different social structures and relations, in contrast to its individual parts. What all these forms have in common, however, is that they are affirmative and expressed through concepts. The best example of such uto-

---

47   Hölscher 1996, p. 19.

pian thinking is indeed 'socialism', even if one needs to be more precise in what is meant by this concept in this context. I contend that it is specifically the early socialism, in its Marxian strand as well as the non-Marxian ones, which emerged in the early nineteenth century in response to the failure of the French Revolution to solve the problem of poverty and the onset of industrialisation, that is of most pertinence here. The initial two sections in Chapter 1 explore this early socialism, and its various conceptions of an alternative future society, in more detail.

Whereas this meaning of utopian thinking presents only one possible and existing meaning of this notion, I argue it is the one that is most relevant to my investigation. It is the meaning of utopian thinking that exists within the discourse of its decline in the political realm. In turn, even if that might in the first instance appear methodologically unsound, it is not the meaning of utopian thinking that has been established within Critical Theory. My interest in this book is to show how Adorno and Bloch respectively enabled and halted the discourse of the decline of utopian thinking, and not to investigate their understandings of utopia in general.

Critical theorists were above all interested in artistic expressions of utopia. In fact, critical theorists themselves substantially expanded the overlap between art and utopian thinking, by seeing art, rather than concepts, as more suited to the task of expressing utopia.[48] A reason for this better suitability of art was its supposed greater independence from existing material conditions. As one of the critical theorists, Herbert Marcuse, put it: 'by virtue of its aesthetic form, art is largely autonomous *vis-a-vis* the given social relations. In its autonomy art both protests these relations, and at the same time transcends them'.[49] Adorno and Bloch furthermore considered that art, especially music, can express utopia more fully and more truthfully.[50]

This historical relegation of utopian thinking to the arts, however, does not and should not prevent us from examining the critical theorists' views on utopian thinking purely as a conceptual enterprise. There are at least three additional reasons for my original belief that it is valuable to focus on conceptual expressions of utopias. First, most of the available literature on the relation between Critical Theory and utopian thinking in fact considers the latter primarily in the form of art.[51] Second, my focus on utopian thinking in the

---

48   See their writings on aesthetics, e.g.: Adorno, 1990 [1970]; Bloch 1977 [1954/55/50]; Marcuse 1977.

49   Marcuse 1977, p. ix.

50   For Adorno see Jarvis 1998, pp. 90–147; for Bloch see Boldyrev 2014, pp. 10–11.

51   E.g. Korstvedt 2010; Paddison 1993; Huhn and Zuidervaart 1997; Howells 2015.

form of concepts will in turn complement this literature by explaining why critical theorists shied away from conceptual utopian thinking. And last, I consider that conceptual expressions are immanent to the project of Critical Theory. As theory, Critical Theory is nothing but a conceptual project, and if critical theorists are themselves to employ any form of utopian thinking it needs to be its conceptual form. In this sense I follow Ruth Levitas, who considers utopian thinking as a method, that is, as a tool that lies at the disposal of theoreticians.[52] But whereas Levitas focuses on the field of sociology, the domain of my investigation is that of Critical Theory.

Utopian thinking as descriptions of what a better future society looks like needs to be distinguished from another utopian concept that has become well engrained within Critical Theory. This is the notion of 'utopian consciousness', to which Adorno refers in his 1964 conversation with Bloch, and which in his words corresponds to the will to be different.[53] This will for something different is akin to the collective notion of utopian thinking, an expression of collective attitude towards the world. Some philosophers, Bloch foremost among them, interpret 'collective' in the broadest sense, that is as the whole of humanity. As I will elaborate in the last two chapters, desire, longing and will for a fundamentally better future is according to Bloch innate to being human, it makes us human. The notion of a collective can, however, also be interpreted in a narrower and less controversial sense, such as by designating certain communities of people with shared views and aspirations. Critical theorists certainly represent such a community that is in fact defined by deep-seated utopian aspirations. According to Max Horkheimer, one of its founders, the aim of this theoretical project is 'emancipation from slavery', transformation of the existing society into 'the community of free people'.[54] In other words, it is indisputable that the realisation of a certain utopian society is an objective of Critical Theory; and this is what defines the utopian consciousness or desire inherent to it. Questions of just how much the critical theorists were committed to this objective, and how radical their utopian aspiration was, can of course be legitimately posited, and indeed have been. They do not, however, constitute the focus of my study here. The potentially more consequential question I pose

---

52   Levitas 2013. In considering utopian thinking as a tool or means of Critical Theory I further follow Maeve Cooke's account of 'means' in *Re-Presenting the Good Society*. Cooke contends that since the conceptual project of Critical Theory is not sought for its own sake but for the sake of achieving a superior perception and materialisation of the society in which it is supposed to result, this conceptual project and its various conceptual practices cannot be goods in themselves but only means. See Cooke 2006, p. 13.

53   Adorno in Bloch 1977 [1969b], p. 363.

54   Horkheimer 1968, p. 550.

concerns expressions of manifestations of this utopian desire, and more specifically, to what extent and in what forms critical theorists were willing to
articulate these expressions.

4   Critical Theory

The term 'critical theory', just as that of utopia, is unstable and contested,
and entails a wide range of meanings. In its most narrow usage, often indicated by capitalising the initials, 'Critical Theory' refers to the German tradition of interdisciplinary social theory inaugurated in Frankfurt in the 1930s,
and carried forward today in Germany by such thinkers as Jürgen Habermas,
Axel Honneth, and Rahel Jaeggi, and in the United States by theorists such
as Thomas McCarthy, Nancy Fraser, and Seyla Benhabib. In a more capacious
usage, often recognised by its non-capitalised initials, 'critical theory' refers to
any politically inflected form of cultural, social, or political theory that has critical, progressive, or emancipatory aims. Understood in this way, critical theory
encompasses much if not all of the work that is done under the banner of feminist theory, queer theory and postcolonial theory. A third distinct but related
broader usage of the term refers to the body of theory mobilised in literary and
cultural studies, often simply known just as 'theory'. Here 'critical theory' refers
mainly to the French intellectual traditions spanning from poststructuralism to
psychoanalysis, and includes thinkers such as Michael Foucault, Jacques Der-
rida, Gilles Deleuze, and Jacques Lacan.
    In my usage of the term I mean, above all, 'critical theory' in its most nar-
row sense, that is as Critical Theory. Furthermore, in my considerations I do not
cover Critical Theory in its entire historical range, but roughly over the interwar
and early postwar era, between the early 1930s and late 1960s. I thereby consider
the representatives of Critical Theory who are commonly labelled as its first
generation. Thus, when I say that I am investigating utopian thinking from the
perspective of Critical Theory, I have in mind the perspective of the members
of this German tradition of interdisciplinary social theory, which is also known
under the term 'the Frankfurt School'. Sometimes these two are merged into a
third – 'the critical theory of the Frankfurt School'. The three descriptors are
more or less synonymous and I will stick to using only that of Critical Theory.[55]

---

55   From a historical perspective there exist substantial differences in the work of the Insti-
      tute. In the first decade of its functioning from 1923 onwards, during which the Institute
      was directed above all by Grossman, Grüneberg and Pollock, economics and empirical
      research were its two focal points. This focus gradually shifted towards more philosoph-

This choice also has to do with the fact that my book features Ernst Bloch who is not usually counted amongst the representatives of the Frankfurt School. Whereas this name was first applied to this group of German-Jewish intellectuals by their commentators, pointing to their common institutional roots, that of the 'Institut für Sozialforschung' in Frankfurt, the critical theorists referred to their own theoretical project as Critical Theory, after its leading figure Max Horkheimer, originally employed this term in 1937 in his article entitled 'Traditional and Critical Theory'. In this article Horkheimer provides the first explicit definition of this body of theory, including in terms of its aim as a practical one, which he explicated even more succinctly in a later article as 'man's emancipation from slavery'.[56] By slavery Horkheimer refers to the social relations prevailing under the then existing capitalist system. For theory to aim at 'emancipation from slavery' thus means thus nothing other than to contribute to a liberation of society from its existing repression, that is, to transform an existing society into a radically better one, beyond exploitation and alienation, and free of class oppression. By positing this practical aim of facilitating the attainment of such utopian society as the ultimate objective of a theoretical pursuit, Horkheimer breached the traditional divide separating the activities of theory and practice and converted Critical Theory into a form of practice itself. In this sense, Critical Theory overlaps with an earlier revision of theory, namely that made by Karl Marx in his eleventh thesis on Feuerbach in 1845. In this text Marx inaugurated his type of theory or philosophy – the foundation of numerous theoretical projects known today under the label of Marxism – as one that aims at a transformation of the world, and is opposed to the hitherto existing philosophy which, in Marx's view, aimed only at an explanation of the world.[57] The name of Marx was, besides G.W.F. Hegel, Sigmund Freud, Georg Lukács and Max Weber, acknowledged by the critical theorists themselves as the thinker who shaped their own ideas most substantially.[58] In fact, Critical Theory can be best understood as a revision of Marx's thought in the light of new historical developments. Marx's ideas did not simply influence those of the critical theorists: they presented the very basis of Critical Theory's project. Critical Theory is thus often classified as a current of Marxism, more specific-

---

ical and abstract questions when Horkheimer assumed the directorship in 1930 and when Adorno became a more active and respected member towards the end of 1930s. The name Critical Theory tends to be associated more closely with this later period, and less so with the inaugural decade of the Institute.

56   Horkheimer 1968, p. 578.
57   Marx 1978 [1888], p. 5.
58   See Jay 1974, pp. 42–3.

ally as a representative current of Western Marxism, a term coined by Maurice
Merleau-Ponty to designate those versions of Marxism which emerged in Western Europe, primarily in Germany, France and Italy, but in the post-war period
also in Yugoslavia, as an alternative to the 'Eastern', i.e. Soviet, Marxism.[59] In
the early twentieth century, this Soviet Marxism established itself as the dominant variety of Marxism, i.e. orthodox Marxism, and was heavily influenced by
Friedrich Engels and Karl Kautsky's interpretation of primarily those works by
Marx in which his deterministic and materialistic side is accentuated, i.e. the
'mature' Marx. Western Marxism, by contrast, gives priority to early Marx, and
thus favours the subjective and dialectical elements of Marx's theory. These latter dimensions of Marx received their hitherto clearest articulation and highest
degree of elaboration in Georg Lukács's *History and Class Consciousness* and
Karl Korsch's *Marxism and Philosophy*, two texts which laid the foundations,
in the early 1920s, for the interpretation of Marx contained in Critical Theory. By the early 1930s, however, in addition to the theoretical inadequacies
of the Soviet Marxism, its practical defects also crystallised. Although various
communist and socialist sympathisers, from the aftermath of the Bolsheviks's
seizure of power in 1917 onwards, became sceptical of the Soviet Union as offering a real progressive alternative to capitalism, it was not until the 1930s, when
the Moscow purges became publicly known, that its flaws were recognised as
definite, including in the eyes of the critical theorists.[60] Critical theorists thus
constructed their own theoretical project not only as an alternative to Soviet
Marxism but as a criticism of it, which partially explains why they refrained
from describing themselves as Marxists, in any sense of the word. The specific playing down of their debts to Marxism, the reasons for which can also
be found elsewhere – for example in the fact that, in their exile prior to and
during the Second World War, the critical theorists were dependent on the
support of American institutions – constitutes the more general toning down
of the political language employed by the critical theorists. Since conceptualisations of a utopian society are clearly highly political, a reason for critical
theorists' apparent apprehensiveness to supply them might thus also be found
in these very pragmatic considerations. Thus, whereas the ensuing chapters
seek to reconstruct the arguments of critical theorists against utopian thinking that are internal to their body of theory, these arguments need to be seen
in their historical context, which I thus also appropriately highlight.

---

59   See Kellner 2005; Jacoby 1981; Anderson 1976.
60   See Jay 1974, p. 20.

5   A New Perspective on Contemporary Critical Theory

There is no book-length examination of the place of utopian thinking in Critical
Theory. The closest existing study is probably Vincent Geoghegan's monograph
Marxism and Utopianism from 1987. Geoghegan, however, considers solely
those thinkers who were either favourable towards utopian thinking and/or
possessed a certain positive conception of utopia, whereas I look at both the
pro- and anti-utopian current in Marxism. This book moreover contributes to
the field of the intellectual history of utopian thinking by considering the latter in a very specific, political sense, as a tool of contributing to desirable social
change. The existing field of literature of the intellectual history of utopian
thinking, which comprises seminal texts such as Manuel and Manuel's *Utopian Thought in the Western World* (1979) and Gregory Claeys's *Searching for
Utopia: the History of an Idea* (2011), and more popular ones like Eric Reece's
Utopia Drive: A Road Trip Through America's Most Radical Idea (2016), in contrast focuses on two other meanings of utopia, namely as a literary genre and
as an intentional community. A typical characteristic of such literature is its
form, that of historical overviews, and moreover of rather predictable overviews. As an influential utopian scholar Krishan Kumar notes, these overviews
construct a fixed storyline in the course of which 'one is bounced through the
ancients [...] served up with More, Campanella and Bacon [...] and finished
off with the nineteenth-century socialists: often with a coda which proclaims
or laments the death of utopia in our own century'.[61] While these overviews
leave a reader with a strong sense of the depth and extent of the European and
North American utopian imagination, their intention is primarily descriptive
– providing descriptions and interpretations of various past instantiations of
utopian thinking.

   As an alternative, this book aims to make an argument about utopian thinking as a political practice. Whereas I do offer close readings of the individual
engagements with utopian thinking, I do so, ultimately, in order to explain how,
as well as why, the discrepancies among them affected and changed the existing
conception of utopian thinking in the realm of politics. The death of utopia in
the twentieth century is the most prominent transformation that such utopian
thinking experienced, and while often acknowledged, very limited scholarship
actually takes as its central subject. In his books *The End of Utopia* and *Picture Imperfect*, Russell Jacoby illustrates this phenomenon, making a case that

---

61   Kumar 1987, p. vii.

utopian thinking has indeed been marginalised in contemporary politics.[62] Russell, however, does not supply an explanation as to how and why it has been marginalised, which he does consider elsewhere, in his contribution to the volume *Temporalisation of Utopia*.[63] Russell's account is typical of the sole explanation that has been advanced so far, namely that the main culprits of anti-utopianism are the libertarian thinkers of the mid-twentieth century, such as Hayek, Popper and Berlin, who associated utopian thinking with totalitarianism.[64] This stance has also been taken recently by Ruth Levitas in her *Utopia as Method*, where she refers, in addition to the Hayek-Popper-Berlin triumvirate, to Judith Shklar, Jacob Talmon and Norman Cohn, as well as to some more contemporary defenders of anti-utopianism like John Gray.[65] Apart from this liberal discourse, the existing literature does not refer to any other influence which might have facilitated the death of utopia. In my book I point to another strand of anti-utopianism which, despite arising at around the same time as the right-wing one, emerged from a competing political domain, the radical left, and more specifically from one of its constituent discourses, that of Critical Theory. I not only point to the anti-utopian current in Critical Theory as an additional determinant of the existing status of utopian thinking, one which has thus far been neglected, but also comprehensively examine it by spelling out its conceptual rationale and historical conditioning.

This book also contributes to scholarship on Critical Theory. With some exceptions, such as Gerhard Richter's *Thought-images: Frankfurt School Writers' Reflections from Damaged Life* (2007), none of the better known works on Critical Theory discusses Bloch's ideas in any significant detail. In contrast to this literature, my book considers Bloch as one central figure of Critical Theory. A reason why Bloch has so far not been considered as part of the core of Critical Theory does not have to do so much with irreconcilable differences between his philosophy and that of the others, but rather more with the lack of physical proximity to the Institute and its members: besides the fact that he was never a member of the Institute, Bloch remained relatively removed from it, both during the interwar exile in the United States and after his return to the postwar Germany. The existing literature is, however, inconsistent in applying this reason as a criterion for determining who does and who does not belong to the core of Critical Theory. In the core of Critical Theory it includes Benjamin, who was never a formal member of the Institute, and moreover, while

---

62   Jacoby 1999 and 2005.
63   Jacoby 2011.
64   See also Davies 2001.
65   Levitas 2013, p. 7.

he might not have led a life isolated in the same fashion as Bloch, he was nevertheless, due to his premature death in 1940, also removed from the rest of the critical theorists. Benjamin's ultimate inclusion is thus justified differently, namely on the basis of his involved relationships with the Institute's members, especially with Adorno. But this very same observation can be made for Bloch as well. Correspondences between Bloch and several members of this group show that Bloch's work unfolded in a constant dialogue with that produced by others. Bloch, for his part, wrote his early expressionistic work *Traces* (1930) in the context of frequent discussions with Benjamin, who was then writing *One-way Street* (1928), also a work influenced by Expressionism. The latter work was subsequently reviewed by Bloch for the Institute's journal, one of a number of reviews he submitted to this publication. Remarks made by Adorno and Benjamin also point to substantial interlinkages between their and Bloch's thought: as early as 1919 Benjamin observed that despite all the reservations he had with respect to Bloch's work, *Spirit of Utopia* is 'the only book which I can compare myself with'.[66] The significance of this work is also acknowledged by Adorno many years later when he notes that he does not believe he has ever written anything without commemorating the motifs of *Spirit of Utopia*.[67] As another case in point, we may recall another letter by Adorno from 1937 in which he expresses his desire to officially involve Bloch with the Institute.[68] These comments invite a closer and more balanced study of the mediations between Bloch and Adorno, and also Benjamin's writings, than has been supplied so far.

Finally, this book intervenes also in the field of contemporary Critical Theory. Whereas it investigates the generation of critical theorists active up to until 1970s, its findings also prove relevant to the contemporary representatives of this tradition. By reconstructing the underlying reasoning of the arguments advanced by Adorno against utopian thinking, and the marginalised pro-utopian ideas of Bloch, I provide a new angle on one of the commonly accepted, sympathetic conceptions of Critical Theory. In addition, through the reconstruction of these reasons, I directly challenge the implicit adherence to the *Utopieverbot* by contemporary critical theorists. As I have pointed out above, these thinkers refuse to engage in any kind of affirmative utopian thinking, and instead insist on negation or criticism as their main and only vehicle of theory, often founding their approach directly on Adorno's own emphasis

---

66   Benjamin 1996, p. 46. For a brief description of the degree of mutual influence between Benjamin and Bloch, see Geoghegan 1996, pp. 16–18.

67   Adorno 1996 [1965], p. 557.

68   Adorno 1994, p. 537.

on negativity.[69] This approach has been challenged over the last decade by theorists from other fields, including by Bruno Latour, who in his article of the same title enquires whether 'critique has run out of steam'.[70] Some other scholars, like Nikolas Kompridis, have directed their call for the embrace of some form of affirmative utopian thinking specifically at the practice of contemporary Critical Theory.[71] Kompridis, however, does not tie his arguments in favour of utopian thinking to the tradition of Critical Theory, that is, he does not explain why it is the task of Critical Theory in particular to restore the forgotten practice of envisioning concretely a better society. Kompridis, moreover, does not provide convincing reasons as to why the negativity of contemporary Critical Theory should indeed be complemented by a more explicit affirmation. By considering Bloch's thought I show why negation on its own is an insufficient tool for Critical Theory, and highlight those forms of utopian thinking which overcome some of the problems and aporias with which it has been traditionally associated, such as its authoritarian inflections and its need to make some presumptions about the essence or telos of human being. Thereby my book informs contemporary Critical Theory of a new direction in a more substantiated way than existing scholarship has done so far.

The broad objective of my book is threefold: first, to delineate the relationship between Critical Theory and utopian thinking; second, to substantiate the contribution critical theorists made in the decline of utopian thinking within politics; and third, to lay out their ideas which carry a potential to defy this anti-utopian trend. This book is divided into five chapters. The first chapter considers Marx, the following two Adorno, and the final two Bloch. I present Marx's attitudes towards utopian thinking as highly ambivalent, and present the reasons to see him both as a utopian thinker and as a critic of utopian thinking. Marx's views are taken into account not merely because of the great influence that they exerted on Adorno's and Bloch's own views. They are also relevant because their inherently unclear and contradictory nature partly initiated, together with the changed historical circumstances, the later split between Bloch's and Adorno's positions. The objection posed by Marx to utopian thinking that I examine in detail is that it is impossible and unnecessary for progressive social change. Chapter 2 examines Adorno's objections to utopian thinking. At first this chapter shows that Adorno indeed instituted the *Utopieverbot*, for which the subsequent sections then offer various explanations. I argue that the rationale for the *Utopieverbot* has so far been poorly

---

69   See Jaeggi 2004.
70   Latour 2004.
71   Kompridis 2005.

understood and confined mainly to the influences of the Jewish *Bilderverbot* and Marx's own thought. I advance three other explanations for Adorno's idea that utopian thinking is impossible, which have to do with his philosophy of history, substantially shaped by Benjamin, and his understanding of late capitalist society and of the then prevailing form of conceptual language. Chapter 3 offers a critical commentary of the view that is shared by much of the scholarship on Adorno, which reads his writings as strongly utopian. One of the readings of Adorno I criticise is the one offered by Rahel Jaeggi. By investigating the two other strands of the existing argumentation as to why Adorno's negative dialectics is at the same time also a display of a utopian society, I make evident that something fundamental to utopian thinking remains missing within Adorno's approach, and suggest that this lack is related to positive thinking. Chapter 4 serves as an introduction to the centrality of utopian thinking in Bloch's work. By touching on some of the basic concepts of Bloch's philosophy, such as the 'Not-Yet', 'Heimat' and the 'Invariant of Direction', this chapter delineates Bloch's rejection of the *Utopieverbot*, as well as his notion of 'concrete utopia' that represent one alternative to Adorno's negative one. My final chapter looks more generally at those aspects of Bloch's philosophy which illuminate why in his view utopian thinking is a possible, indeed a necessary, element of Critical Theory. These aspects of his thinking are largely ontological. Through a brief illustration of how Bloch radically revised the then existing conception of materialism into one he called 'speculative', the chapter paves the way for an account of 'processual utopian thinking' as an alternative form of utopian thinking and as an element of Critical Theory.

CHAPTER 1

Marx's Two Utopian Paradoxes

1   The Deployment of the Label 'Utopian' and Its Consequences

Marx used the term 'utopian' in a highly idiosyncratic way. As a political activist, most notably as the founding member of the First International Work-
ingmen's Association, Marx applied this label to his opponents only to convey
his general disagreement with their politics.[1] The French visionaries of socialism Charles Fourier and Henri de Saint-Simon and the English social reformer
Robert Owen were the most frequent targets of Marx's criticisms of what he
called 'utopianism'. Marx did not apply this term only to the individual conceptual or practical schemes devised by Saint-Simon, Fourier and Owen, as well
as their disciples, but also used it interchangeably with their names as such.[2]
Thus, thanks to Marx and Engels, Saint-Simon, Owen and Fourier are today perhaps best known jointly as 'utopian socialists'.[3] Next to the utopian socialists,
Marx designated as utopian some other of his French-speaking adversaries. For
example, Pierre-Joseph Proudhon, an influential spokesman of the Paris workers' movement of the mid-nineteenth century and a pioneer of anarchism, was
also recognised as a representative of those thinkers who were 'merely utopi-
anists'.[4] Moreover, Marx denounced the actions of the Paris proletariat itself
as 'utopian nonsense'.[5] Similarly, in the context of the revolutionary upheavals
in Germany, which was then still divided into multiple large and small states,
Marx considered an 'a priori' call for 'one united German Republic' as a 'utopian
demand'.[6] Finally, towards the end of his life, in the 1870s, Marx also described
as utopian the demands instituted by the German socialists, specifically the
Socialist Workers' Party of Germany (Sozialistische Arbeiterpartei Deutsch-
lands, SAPD).[7]

---

1   See Buber 1958, p. 11; Claeys 2014, pp. 1–2; Manuel and Manuel 1979, p. 698; Ollman, 2007, p. 7.
2   See Marx and Engels 1977 [1848], pp. 68–72. The term 'utopian socialists' was appropriated
    and popularised by Engels later in his life, in a 1880 article entitled 'Die Entwicklung des Sozi-
    alismus von der Utopie zur Wissenschaft'. See Engels 1987 [1980].
3   The term 'utopian socialists' was actually not coined by Marx and Engels, yet it was their use
    that firmly entrenched it in the register of socialist thought. See Stedman-Jones 1991, p. 561.
4   Marx 1977 [1885], p. 143.
5   Marx 1960 [1852], p. 121.
6   Marx 1959 [1848], p. 42.
7   'Marx to F.A. Sorge, 19 October 1877', in Marx 1979, pp. 319–20.

Marx's habit of using the term utopian in this pejorative and very general-ising way has obscured his actual views on the activity of utopian thinking. By Marx's actual views, I mean his view on the activity of envisaging the ideal future society at the more substantive or theoretical level. The fact that Marx used the term utopian in this way does not by any means need to be reflective of his views of utopian thinking in the sense of the currently established meanings of this phrase, or in the specific sense in which I use it here. Yet Marx's seem-ingly indiscriminate usage of the term utopian, pitching it against seemingly anyone who, from his point of view, did not grasp communism quite correctly, has not been sufficiently distinguished from the very concrete objections he had against envisaging the future society. In the most extreme case, Marx's use of the term utopian is seen as indistinguishable from what he thought about the functions of utopian thinking. Many misguided conclusions can be derived from conflating these two perspectives. One, represented by Bertell Ollman, among others, has been that Marx in fact did not hold any objections to uto-pian thinking.[8] The fact that Marx's explicit denunciations of utopian thinking and utopian thinkers were motivated by strategic reasons is supposed to dis-credit any view of Marx as a critic of utopian thinking. This conclusion, to be sure, misses other possible ways in which Marx could have, and indeed did, express his opposition to utopian thinking.

My focus in this chapter does not centre on Marx's rhetorical usage of the term. By this I do not mean to dismiss the possible repercussions this exerted on the later developments of the status of utopian thinking in Critical Theory. I simply want to emphasise that when it comes to Marx and utopia, it can be equally important to put the consideration of this usage aside. My objective in this chapter is instead to reconstruct Marx's actual views on the activity of utopian thinking, which I do by looking at some aspects of Marx's theoretical framework. I show that Marx can justifiably be perceived both as a critic and as an advocate of utopian thinking, and moreover as someone who had an under-developed view of this topic. I argue that this is the most important view to have if we are to better understand the later developments of the status of uto-pian thinking in Critical Theory. Rather than judging whether it is the pro- or the anti-utopian tendency that carries greater weight in Marx's thought, the first argument of this chapter is that the critical issue is to recognise the simul-taneous presence of both tendencies, as well as what we might describe as an element of indifference in Marx that lies between his pro- and anti-utopianism. I argue that, in part, the question of utopian thinking was for Marx not the

---

8   See Ollman 2007, p. 8.

most relevant question to consider *comprehensively* and *in detail*. It is crucial to recognise this third side of Marx, because it implies that the views he held on this topic should not be regarded to be conclusive and definite, as the later Marxist thinkers and scholars have often considered them to be.

My second argument concerns the interplay between these three sides of Marx. To some extent these sides can be neatly separated, which is also reflected in the structure of this chapter: the section on the communist society emphasises Marx's pro-utopianism; the following section, which deals with the impossibility of utopian thinking, unleashes his critical side; and the final section on its irrelevance offers reasons as to why utopian thinking was not among Marx's central concerns. The separation of the three sides is, however, not completely neat. They sometimes intersect, producing certain paradoxes which, even on a further examination, cannot be entirely resolved. One paradox I investigate concerns Marx's view on the possibility of utopian thinking: in his criticism of the utopian socialists he claimed that the future cannot be envisaged, yet in some instances this was precisely what he was doing himself. I argue that the existence of this and one other paradox of the irrelevance of utopian thinking facilitated the closer engagements with this question by the critical theorists. In fact, the very existence of these paradoxes in Marx's thought is the reason why his views on utopian thinking need to be spelled out before we can turn to investigate them in Adorno and Bloch.[9]

2   Marx's Vision of the Communist Society

Some of Marx's most memorable statements deal with the content of a communist society:

> This communism as completed naturalism is humanism, as completed humanism it is naturalism. It is the *genuine* resolution of the antagonism between man and nature and between man and man; it is the true resolution of the conflict between existence and essence, objectification and

---

9   My argument about Marx's influence on the thought of Adorno and Bloch does not primarily concern the direct affinities that exist between their individual viewpoints on utopian thinking. That is, I am not concerned so much with tracing the causal linkages between the specific statements that Marx made regarding utopian thinking, and those of Adorno and Bloch. Rather, I argue that in adopting Marx's general theoretical project as one fundamental to their own approaches, Bloch and Adorno also inherited its problems, ambivalences and inconsistencies, and furthermore, that the utopian paradoxes I discuss in this chapter present two of these problems.

self-affirmation, freedom and necessity, individual and species. It is the riddle of history solved and knows itself as this solution.[10]

The scholarship is, however, united in that Marx did not supply a fully fledged and spelled-out vision of a communist society: he neither followed early Enlightenment utopians such as Locke or Rousseau who derived a specific institutional structure of a society from an account of what they considered the human needs, wants and passions to be; nor did he ponder on the details of the ensuing institutional structure like the utopian socialists had done before him.[11] For example, questions such as how Marx's favoured social decision-making processes, namely those of direct democracy, would actually be set up and run, remain unaddressed in his writings. Or, given his insistence on the international character of the revolution, he never gives us any details on the international character of the post-revolutionary globe. Yet this is not to deny that Marx did not advance a handful of highly significant theoretical principles underlying the idea of a communist society; moreover, it is true that he alluded to various aspects of this society from a more practical perspective, even if only by way of shorter and sporadic remarks.

Most of Marx's widely known remarks about how he envisaged the communist society originate from his early works, specifically the 1844 'Economic-Philosophic Manuscripts' (also known as the 'Paris Manuscripts') and *The German Ideology* (1846). Some foundations of the ideas presented there, however, Marx had drafted earlier, in his slightly lesser known notes on James Mill (1844).[12] As Daniel Brudney notes, in this text Marx 'gives a self-realization account of the human good'.[13] For in these notes Marx implicitly contends that having certain relationships to other human beings and to the world, as well as engaging in a particular kind of activity, would realise one's human nature. From this, a certain conception of a life that is in accord with human nature, that is, of the good human life, can be derived.[14]

The core of this theory of human nature consists in Marx's concept of 'species-essence' ('Gattungswesen'), namely that the essence of human beings

---

10   Marx 1968 [1932], p. 536.
11   Partial exceptions to this view are the positions of Bertell Ollman and Peter Hudis. While agreeing that Marx did not provide a systematic and detailed conception of communism, Ollman and Hudis contend that such a vision can be reconstructed from his overall corpus. They attempt such reconstruction themselves. See Ollman 2007 and Hudis 2012.
12   Marx 1992 [1932], pp. 428–72.
13   Brudney 1998, p. 146.
14   For a more detailed account of Marx's conception of human nature see Brudney 1998, pp. 143–91; Chitty 1993, pp. 23–31.

is their community, as opposed to the individual self, the self which could, at least hypothetically, exist autonomously to others.[15] The idea here is not so much that individuals could not live independently of each other in terms of their mere survival, as in living on an isolated island, but rather that the mere notion of the independent self, of my own self, the 'I' of the Cartesian subject, is intertwined and dependent on other human beings to such a degree that it is, as such, bereft of any meaning. The easiest way to grasp this idea is to relate it to the concept of needs, which also, in Marx's view, constituted the essence of human beings. Marx argued that more complex needs, like the need for diverse, balanced, aesthetically appealing, high quality nutrition, as opposed to food as such, can only be satisfied by others, by their labour. In that others fulfil my needs which in turn define who I am, these other people too define my 'own' self. Whereas this thought is often misinterpreted as denying the existence of individuals and as giving a categorical precedence to society over individuals, it means, in the first instance, that the self of an individual emerges and exists only in the context of a society; only in an interaction or relation with others. In other words, a Robinson Crusoe type of character is a purely mythical construction.

The other important idea that Marx introduces in his early works relates to the type of activity that would allow for one's self-realisation. Marx calls this activity 'species-activity' ('Gattungsakt') and means by it the activity characteristic of a species-essence.[16] This activity is generally better known under the name of non-alienated labour and is used to designate the type of work that would prevail in a communist society. It is also known as the activity that would prevail in 'the realm of freedom', as opposed to those occurring in 'the realm of necessity', phrases that Marx introduces in *Capital* to distinguish between communist and capitalist societies.[17] Although connected to each other, there are three key aspects to understanding what non-alienated labour is. First, through this activity human beings 'relate to themselves as the present, living species', which means producing things for other human beings and enjoying the products of other human beings.[18] Second, the activity of non-alienated labour is in a certain sense free or directed, that is, human beings not only act on nature, but they act on their own actions. This characteristic is for Marx what distinguishes human species-activity from the activities of animals. Since, according to Marx, 'The animal is immediately one

---

15   Marx 1968 [1932], p. 515.
16   Marx 1968 [1932], p. 545.
17   Marx 1964 [1894], p. 828.
18   Marx 1968 [1932], p. 515.

with its life-activity. It does not distinguish itself from it; it *is* that activity'.[19] In contrast: 'Man makes his life-activity itself into an object of his willing and consciousness. He has conscious life-activity. It is not a determination with which he immediately merges'.[20] The third characteristic of non-alienated labour is its diversity. As opposed to capitalism, which through its division of labour confines individuals to one single activity, communism allows for a more diverse working day. This third characteristic Marx formulated most succinctly not in the 1844 Manuscripts, in which he discusses the first two in terms of the species-activity, but in *The German Ideology*, where he famously observes that in a communist society 'nobody has one exclusive sphere of activity but each can become accomplished in any branch he wishes'.[21] Moreover, such a society 'makes it possible for me to do one thing today and another tomorrow'.[22]

The significance of Marx's ideas of individuals as social beings and of non-alienated labour is that they supply the central institutional characteristic of a communist society – common ownership of the means of production – with a rationale. Thus, in Marx's account of communism, common ownership of the means of production emerges not as a dogmatic demand, but rather as the implication of a theory about the nature of human beings; it is not a goal on its own terms, but merely a means to achieve the ultimate goal of realising the very essence of human beings:

> The positive transcendence of private property, as the appropriation of human life, is therefore the positive transcendence of all estrangement – that is to say, the return of man from religion, family, state, etc., to his human, that is social existence.[23]

Marx did, however, also discuss common ownership itself and referred to some institutional features of communism. These thoughts are generally contained in his critical reactions to the various then existing political proposals in which concrete institutional characteristics of communism were indeed drafted, such as for example in *The Communist Manifesto* (1848), and in his response to the so-called 'Gotha Program', the first manifesto of the Socialist Workers' Party of Germany (SAPD), devised in the town Gotha in 1875. The members of the SAPD

---

19   Marx 1968 [1932], p. 516.
20   Marx 1968 [1932], p. 516.
21   Marx and Engels 1978 [1932], p. 33.
22   Marx and Engels 1978 [1932], p. 33.
23   Marx 1968 [1932], p. 535.

called for 'the abolition of the wage system', that is, a remuneration system in which the pay of the workers simply equals the amount necessary for their survival, and for its replacement with 'the collective regulation of the total labour with a fair distribution of the proceeds of labour', a system in which workers' pay would be proportionate to the work they expend.[24] Although Marx, in his response to the manifesto, known as the 'Critique of the Gotha Program', concedes that the system of wage labour should indeed be abolished, he derides the alternative proposed by the SAPD.[25] Marx contends that the proposed system would also be unfair, although in a different sense than the capitalist one is. The unfairness of the SAPD alternative, Marx argues, would stem from failing to take into account the difference in predispositions, skills and needs of different individuals, instead of from rewarding the idle, non-working class, as is the case under capitalism. For example, a young, physically stronger worker would in principle be able to carry out a larger share of physically demanding work than an older, frailer one, but these capacities, which are to some extent biological, should not entitle the former worker to a higher pay. It might actually be the case that a more just remuneration would result in the older worker being paid more, since, for instance, he is likely to need more resources to take care of his ill health. After he thoroughly scrutinises the faults marking this specific SAPD policy, Marx discloses his principle on which the compensation system for one's work should be based instead. This principle is contained in the famous slogan of 'from each according to his ability, to each according to his needs'.[26]

Besides the character and organisation of work, Marx elaborated on another aspect of the communist society to a slightly greater extent: its political institutions. The political system that Marx advocated and discussed in most detail in relation to the Paris Commune, in the pamphlet entitled 'Civil War in France', is closest to what we nowadays understand under the term direct or radical democracy. The underlining characteristic of such a system is a fundamental overhaul of the state. As Engels once observed: 'The state is not to be "abolished"'.[27] Instead, it is to be converted from an organ superimposed upon society into one completely subordinate to it.[28] In the *Manifesto*, Marx and Engels provide a few more clues as to the nature of the communist state: it would be stripped of all regulative, legal, judiciary and other functions maintained by the

---

24   Marx 1987 [1891], p. 24.
25   Marx 1987 [1891], p. 21.
26   Marx 1987 [1891], p. 21.
27   Engels 1975 [1878], p. 262.
28   Marx 1987 [1891], p. 27.

liberal state and these would be replaced by the management and coordination of production.[29] The *Manifesto* lists some further, not strictly political parameters of the communist society, shared by most of the existing socialist and communist movements, from the precursors of the SAPD to the utopian socialists, including the abolition of child labour, abolition of the distinction between country and town, dissolution of the bourgeois family, and free education for all children.[30] In *Capital* Marx makes another remark regarding education, from which it is evident that he does not consider it should be pursued in an isolated fashion. Commenting on Robert Owen, Marx suggests that the most desirable form of learning and instruction would be one that is combined with productive activity, as well as with play.[31]

Marx, however, never expands on any details of life under communism. For example, he does not explain how the disappearance of differences between urban and rural areas is to be achieved, and what kind of settlement would eventually replace the two: small, in part self-sufficient, in part agriculture-based communities; or whole regions, continents transformed into one great highly urbanised environment; or cities in the forests or 'forest-cities', settlements which retain the modern structure of densely planned high buildings, but now covered with a thick horizontal blanket of vegetation? This lack of concrete detail in Marx's vision of communism is striking, especially when compared with accounts drafted by some of his contemporaries. Fourier, for example, assembled a very specific plan for an ideal type of settlement, the basic unit of which was a specific type of dwelling he called the 'phalanstery', designed after the configuration of a 'phalanx', a military formation in Ancient Greece. For a phalanstery Fourier specified the number of inhabitants (between 1,600 and 1,800, who would live in families of around four members), how much time each inhabitant would devote to different activities (three-quarters to agriculture, and one to manufacturing), how its democratic institutions would be ruled, how profit would be distributed, etc.[32] Other such examples of detailed institutional accounts include Owen's outline of various divorce procedures, complete with carefully specified 'cooling off' periods, and Saint-Simon's sketch of the membership rules of the maritime council, which would be responsible for the naval budget of the forthcoming new industrial order.[33]

29   Marx and Engels 1977 [1848], p. 481.
30   Marx and Engels 1977 [1848], p. 481.
31   Marx 1962 [1867], pp. 507–8.
32   Fourier 1983, pp. 240–2.
33   Owen 1993.

This degree of detail in describing utopian communities is indeed, as Marx contended, unprecedented, not only from his perspective, but also from that of our time, if we compare the level of detail provided by the accounts of some of the twentieth-century utopians.[34] However, the kind of utopian thinking practised by the utopian socialists should not have presented for Marx the only possible way of devising a more concrete plan of a communist society. Giving a name to the building of utopia and specifying the number of its floors (the phalanstery is to have four) is not the only alternative way of discussing communist residential arrangements. Yet Marx remained silent on this and on other aspects of communism. In fact, over the course of his life he became increasingly silent about the future: most of his self-standing comments regarding the communist future are clustered in his earlier writings. The 'Critique of the Gotha Programme' and his manuscript 'The Civil War in France' might present two possible exceptions. While they belong to Marx's later writings, the utopian references contained within them should be perceived as his reaction to the immediate political events, that is, as corrections of the communist visions implicit in these events. As such, when we attempt to evaluate the presence of utopian thinking in Marx's writings, these references carry less weight than the ideas Marx advances more independently, that is, in developing his own theoretical corpus. Marx's largest body of theories is, as is widely recognised, contained in his three volumes of *Capital*. However, as Bertell Ollman contends, judging from an 1851 outline of this work, Marx was initially planning to include in it a more systematic outline of communism.[35] The fact that the plan later changed could suggest that in the later stage of his life Marx developed more definite objections to utopian thinking, objections which outweighed the reasons he initially had for *Capital* to encompass his outline of the future.

Marx's historical context strengthens the idea of him as an utopian thinker, simply in that he belonged to what can be most broadly designated as the political movements of communism and socialism. This movement was very much alive in Marx's time. As he illustrates himself in the memorable opening line of the *Manifesto*: 'A spectre is haunting Europe – the spectre of Communism'.[36] Although the word communism only came into use in the early 1840s, by the end of this decade it had become a commonplace, designating a real-

---

34   Cf. Paden, 2002. Paden argues that the accounts offered by the utopian socialists and Marx
       are indistinguishable in terms of their level of detail.
35   Ollman 2007, p. 8. Note that Ollman does not provide a reference for this Marx's manu-
       script, and that I have not come across this observation in any other secondary literature.
36   Marx and Engels 1977 [1848], p. 461.

istic alternative to the existing social and political order.[37] This is seen both in terms of the fear it caused amongst the ruling aristocracy and bourgeoisie, and in terms of the support it drew among the workers. Despite the differences that divided the broad movement of communism and socialism into separate factions, this movement was undergirded by the positive ideas of radical equality and freedom, and the abolition of private property. Marx, as a founder of this movement, subscribed to and advocated these ideas.

Thus, even if utopian visions are sometimes only implicitly present in Marx's writings – as in the case of his discussion of species-being – or are presented only in the form of unelaborated comments, or as part of his critical reactions to other socialists and communists, often motivated by strategic political reasons, utopian thinking nonetheless does have a place in Marx's thought that is often under-appreciated. With the exception of Bloch, all other critical theorists downplay the significance of the utopian dimension in Marx and never examine it thoroughly. Yet it would be a mistake to simply portray Marx as a utopian thinker. Above I have already pointed to a few reasons why the depiction of Marx as a utopian thinker needs to be treated with caution. The most crucial qualification of the portrayal of Marx as a utopian thinker is, however, that he was a critic of utopian thinking, holding certain objections against it. Similarly to utopian thinking itself, Marx's critique of utopian thinking is not advanced in a sustained and thoroughly argued fashion. Yet a strong implicit critique is contained in his writings, which I reconstruct in the remaining two sections of this chapter.

However, as suggested in the introduction to this chapter, Marx's critique of utopian thinking is not to be conflated with his own pejorative use of the term 'utopian', which was very general. By focusing on his more substantive criticism of utopian thinking I am not, however, contending that his rhetorical use of the word is irrelevant to our interests here, that is, to the subsequent development of the relationship between utopian thinking and Critical Theory. That this is in fact the case is proven not least by the fact that the derogatory use of the term had increased in Marxist circles by the end of Marx's life, and has continued to increase ever since. Frank and Fritzie Manuel contend that the later Marxists attached this label to any theoretical opponent whom they considered to be misinterpreting Marx and Engels's original message.[38] Lenin too used this term in the same negative sense: prior to the October Revolution of 1917 he described as 'utopian' the proposals of the

---

37   Stedman Jones 2015.
38   Manuel and Manuel 1979, p. 698.

two political adversaries of his Bolshevik Party.[39] In contrast, the critical theorists themselves did not adopt this usage of utopian thinking, perhaps also
because of the lesser degree to which they were involved in political activism,
which was the context in which this label would have been primarily used.
However, they must have been familiar with this strongly negative connotation of utopian thinking. It is thus plausible to think that their understanding
of utopian thinking too would have been affected negatively, that is, that they
would have perceived the pursuit of utopian thinking as being fundamentally
at odds with the intentions of Marx's and, by extension, their own intellectual
project.

Yet this conjecture about how the critical theorists might have been affected
by this original *usage* of the term utopian by Marx does not undermine the need
to examine Marx's substantive, that is, his 'actual' objections to utopian thinking. The critical theorists, as Marx's close readers, must have been influenced
by Marx's more specific objections, as well as by the usage of the term in the
wider culture. Marx often articulated these objections without any reference
to the term 'utopian', or in any other immediately evident way. Instead, Marx's
arguments against utopian thinking are mostly implied in his own viewpoints
and assumptions about fundamental categories such as history, knowledge and
human beings. I suggest that Marx's criticism of utopian thinking can most
effectively be grasped in two senses: first, as an impossible and, second, as a
redundant endeavour, each of which can be justified from two standpoints
internal to Marx's thought.[40]

3   Utopia Cannot Be Envisaged

The first objection by Marx to utopian thinking is that it is impossible. What this
might mean is not immediately obvious. The suggestion is presumably not that
we are unable to draw up plans for an ideal future society; after all, Marx and
Engels were familiar with a wealth of past and present examples that suggest
otherwise. The objection is, rather, an epistemological one, namely an objection concerning the nature and sources of knowledge contained in descrip-

---

39   Lenin 1975, pp. 355–9.
40   Cf. Leopold 2016; Webb 2000; Paden 2002; Geoghegan 1987; Lukes 1984. One argument
        that this literature mentions, but which I omit, is Marx's so-called 'anti-democratic' cri-
        tique, namely the idea that affirming a certain society of the future restricts the future
        individuals to self-determine their existing conditions. See, e.g., Leopold 2016, pp. 118–22.
        I find that this argument lacks the necessary primary textual evidence.

tions of utopian societies. More specifically, it is an objection to whether the ideas contained in these descriptions bear any resemblance to reality, that is, to whether these ideas could correspond to objectively valid, accurate knowledge, to something we could call truth. In this epistemological sense, Marx refuted the possibility of utopian thinking and argued that it was impossible to construct any kind of objective account of the future society. Thus, utopian thinking practised by the utopian socialists and others does not, in Marx's view, qualify as *knowledge* about the future. Whatever conceptions of the future these thinkers came up with, they had nothing to do with the future, for knowledge of the future was, for Marx, an impossible kind of knowledge to have. Below, I explore two rationales for this position. The first is contained in Marx's adherence to materialism; the second in his understanding of how the human mind actually produces knowledge.

4   Historical Materialism as an Impediment to Creating New Ideas

In essence, materialism asserts the primacy of the realm of matter over that of thought; in other words, our material conditions determine our ideas and understanding of the world. Whilst in the materialist framework in the broadest sense, matter itself is a very broad category and amounts to all objects that have physical substance, like mass, Marx's concept of materialism, namely historical materialism, was more specific. He argued that there is a very specific set of material conditions that is primarily responsible for the changes of our ideas. This set corresponds to inputs into the production process, like machines, land, and water, as well as to relations of production which stand for the distribution of these inputs among different social groups, that is, who controls them and decides where and for what purposes they should be utilised. For Marx, relations of production of a society give a society its fundamental character and make it, for example, a capitalist rather than some other kind of society. In Marx's words:

> the social relations of production [...] in their totality form what is called social relations, society, and specifically a society at a determinate historical stage of development, a society with a peculiar, distinctive character. Ancient society, feudal society, bourgeois society are such totalities of relations of production, each of which at the same time denotes a special stage of development in the history of mankind.[41]

---

41   Marx and Engels 1961 [1849], p. 408.

For Marx, the major institutions of a historical epoch, specifically its legal and political systems, but more broadly the accepted ideas and knowledge of a society, are deeply conditioned by its relations of production. An implication of historical materialism relevant to our concerns here is that ideas of the future can only be engendered in the future itself, once the existing relations of production will have been reorganised; and, conversely, that the ideas engendered under the prevailing relations of production can never be ideas of the future. Even if they might appear to be different from the ideas of the present, they are still only ideas of the present and nothing else.

This implication is articulated very clearly in Marx's Gotha Critique. In this text, Marx argues that the SAPD manifesto is, in every respect, economically, morally and intellectually, still stamped with the birth-marks of the old society and hence that it cannot represent a socialist society.[42] The programme that was intended to be socialist, but that is phrased in the language of the old, bourgeois society, cannot actually imply a socialist programme. Marx contends that socialist programmes 'cannot allow such bourgeois phrases to pass over in silence the *conditions* that alone give them meaning'.[43] In this assertion the underlying materialist viewpoint is evident – it is 'the conditions', by which Marx means the material conditions of the relations of production, that provide phrases, or ideas more generally, with meaning in the first place. In the Gotha Critique Marx provides some illuminating examples of how ideas of the supposedly future society are still marked by this material character of the existing society. In his words, a socialist principle which the SAPD included in their manifesto was that an individual producer receives back from society exactly what he gives to it.[44] Whereas by adopting this remuneration policy the workers were supposed to be compensated fairly, in Marx's view, this policy was not radically fairer than that prevailing under the capitalist regime. As I have already suggested above, Marx contends that on the basis of the scheme proposed by the SAPD, due to differences in initial predispositions and skills, 'one receives factually more than another, one is richer than another'.[45] Marx identifies as the flaw of this policy the fact that it was underpinned by the principles of commodity exchange, and of workers seen merely as commodities: two key tenets of capitalist society, according to which 'the individual producer receives back from society [...] exactly what he gives to it'.[46] Marx

---

42   Marx 1987 [1891], p. 19.
43   Marx 1987 [1891], p. 15.
44   Marx 1987 [1891], p. 19.
45   Marx 1987 [1891], p. 21.
46   Marx 1987 [1891], p. 20.

argues that as soon as one attempts to address a specific aspect of the future society – in this case, of how that which workers produce, i.e., various goods and services, should be distributed – one unknowingly answers them in terms of the existing applicable terms, here in terms of exchangeability and commodification, and thereby does not specify anything about the properly future society.

This objection to utopian thinking presents a certain paradox. This paradox is the following: on the one hand, Marx's historical materialism implies that since the existing relations of production always condition the existing ideas, these ideas cannot be new, they cannot be indicative of the new relations of production of the future; on the other hand, however, this very same historical materialism does contain ideas that have to do with the future – it not only posits what the relations of production in the past were, but also what they will look like in the future. Marx does not only analyse the ancient, the feudal and the capitalist forms but also the communist form of the relations of production. So, does Marx think we can possess knowledge of the future or not?

This paradox can be partially reconciled if we distinguish between different types of knowledge we could hold about the future: for example, between more and less specific or detailed ones. This differentiation is common in the scholarship on the relationship between Marx and utopian thinking which emphasises that Marx was opposed to writing plans, programmes or blueprints of the future. Amongst others, David Leopold argues that the key to understanding this relationship is to understand that what Marx was hostile to, above all, were '*detailed* descriptions of the ideal society'.[47] In this account, the idea of common ownership and management of the means of production is not classified as specific knowledge of the future. This differentiation can be justified from Marx's own perspective. One possible explanation could be that since relations of production present the most fundamental aspect of society, knowledge of these relations necessitates a privileged status, including a privileged epistemological status. Another, more plausible explanation is related to the deterministic nature of Marx's historical materialism. Here I do not mean the deterministic relationship between the relations of production and the superstructure, but the determined character of the relations of production themselves. I consider this highly disputed Marxian topic in more detail in the final section of this chapter, as it presents a distinct critique by Marx of utopian thinking related to its redundancy. In brief, however, it can be said here that Marx did accept a certain deterministic philosophy of the future. According to

47   Leopold 2016, p. 114.

Marx, the form of each set of relations of production for subsequent historical epochs is subject to certain objective laws of history. These laws are independent of time: whilst some forms of relations of production, like communism, are not yet realised, their existence is nevertheless already warranted by these laws. These laws can be perceived as a justification of why, from Marx's perspective, knowledge about the future relations of production is more tenable than knowledge about other aspects of the future.

Another possible way to reconcile this paradox of (im)possibility of knowledge about the future would be to weaken Marx's claim that such knowledge is indeed impossible at all, by saying that it can only be engendered in a very specific manner, for example through a process of close *reflection* on this knowledge. What I mean by this process of reflection is illustrated by Marx himself when he criticises the ideas of a communist society put forward by those whom he perceived as his political adversaries. In this chapter I have outlined one such illustration, namely Marx's criticism of the claim in the Gotha programme concerning the remuneration scheme of workers proposed by the SAPD. Marx takes the suggested idea of such a scheme (that one's wage should be proportional to one's output) as his starting point and concludes with his own positive idea ('from each according to his ability, to each according to his needs'). The process of how Marx moves from his starting to his concluding point entails considering how each individual concept, such as the notion of the wage itself and of one's output, is mediated by existing material conditions, and by attempts to find alternative, more adequate concepts. The process moreover corresponds to identifying how and when these ideas emerged, and to a consideration of whether they might not have been discredited by the events that occurred since then. This latter part of the process of reflection appears, as well as in Marx's Critique of the Gotha Programme, in Marx and Engels's criticism of the so-called utopian socialists. Whilst, according to Marx and Engels, the central figures of utopian socialism were indeed Saint-Simon, Fourier and Owen, they are more critical of the followers of the latter, that is, the groups and social movements that advanced the ideas of the original triumvirate. Marx and Engels find the greatest fault with the Owenites, Fourierists and Saint-Simonians in that they were dogmatically applying the policies proposed by their forerunners and strictly adhering to their theoretical systems, without considering whether these ideas are still applicable to the current historical circumstances.[48] Once ideas are subjected to this process of reflection, Marx might recognise them as a certain knowledge of the future. We could then say

---

48   See Marx and Engels 1977 [1848], p. 491; Engels 1987 [1880], pp. 189–201.

that a better way of formulating Marx's view on the possibility of the know-ledge of the future is that it is not absolute but dependent on this condition of reflection.

Although the second approach to reconciling the paradox seems quite plaus-ible, especially when compared to the first one, recognition of which requires us to accept the existence of those objective laws of history, a strong tension remains between Marx's various ideas on the question of whether we can know the future. In fact, this tension is exacerbated and further complicated once we look at Marx's other rationale for why knowledge of the future is impossible, which, just like his rationale for materialism, is rather problematic.

5   Imaginary vs. Rational Ideas

The other rationale behind Marx's contention that utopian thinking is impos-sible stems from his conception of the human psyche or mind. Unlike some other disciplines, like political economy, socio-economic history or even philo-sophical anthropology, psychology was not systematically developed by Marx. To approach the understanding of how people and societies function in and comprehend the world from a psychological point of view was in fact a central development of Marxist thought advanced by the critical theorists: not only in the narrow sense of critical theory, as I employ it here, as more or less synonym-ous with the Frankfurt School, but as corresponding to Western Marxism more generally. The contribution to a psychologically richer Marxism made by the Frankfurt School thinkers themselves centres on their incorporation of Freud's psychoanalytic insights into Marx's understanding of ideology.[49] Yet, even if there are many psychological treatises to be found among the collected works of these later Marxist thinkers and none in Marx's own, underlying his thought is a certain conception of the human psyche, one aspect of which grounds one criticism he makes of utopian thinking.

This aspect can be usefully conceptualised in terms of a dichotomy that Marx appears to have drawn between two cognitive faculties, namely between reason and imagination. For Marx, the two seem to differ in terms of their rela-tion to external reality: whereas reason is fundamentally reliant on inputs from external reality, that is, on our observations, our sense perceptions of this real-ity, imagination is not. Instead, Marx viewed imagination as a process purely internal to the human mind, not dependent on or influenced at all by what happens in the outside world.

---

49   See, e.g., Whitebook 2004.

This distinction between reason and imagination informs several writings by Marx and Engels. In *The German Ideology* they contrast their type of materialism to that of the Young Hegelians in that theirs is premised on conceptions of individuals 'as they *really* are', by which they mean that these conceptions are merely conceptual articulations of the material or objective situation of individuals.[50] In contrast, the theories of the Young Hegelians stemmed from conceptions of individuals 'as they may appear in their own or other people's imagination'.[51] In *Poverty of Philosophy*, Marx criticises Proudhon along a very similar line, though not by employing the term 'imagination'. Marx dismisses Proudhon's ideas because they are not based on what is happening before his eyes but result instead solely from his mind.[52] Further, in his own late writings, Engels encodes this view of imagination most concisely. Compared to all other existing theories of communism and socialism, his and Marx's theory of communism is not a 'concoction', engendered by means of the 'imagination', but is instead derived only from observations of the external world, corresponding directly to 'an insight into the nature, the conditions and the consequent general aims of the struggle waged by the proletariat'.[53]

For Marx and Engels, this differentiation is also epistemological. Reason and imagination differ not only in whether they rely on the inputs from external reality but also in the sort of ideas they engender. In their view, reason is constitutive of scientific knowledge and imagination of imaginary ideas and phantasies. Scientific knowledge is supposed to be objectively valid and correspond to, or at least approach, truth as such. In contrast, phantasies have no objective relevance and pertain only to the subject which engendered it in the first place.

The designation of ideas as fantastical or imaginary needs to be treated with some reservation, as its meaning is probably also rhetorical. It probably functioned to some extent, as the very label of utopianism did, simply as a device for Marx and Engels to politically distance themselves from certain other thinkers. Marx and Engels did not consider all ideas and thoughts engendered by the utopian socialists, Proudhon and others, to be fantasies. They sometimes complimented these thinkers for their contributions to scientific knowledge. Engels in particular praised Owen for relying in his investigations on empirical inputs.[54] Moreover, utopian socialists themselves perceived their methods as scientific.

---

50   Marx and Engels 1978 [1932], p. 25.
51   Marx and Engels 1978 [1932], p. 25.
52   Marx 1977 [1885], p. 143.
53   Engels 1962 [1885], p. 212.
54   See Engels 1987 [1880], p. 198.

Saint-Simon claims that in his investigations of 'the best possible constitution' he 'will use only two principles which can be relied on to produce absolute proof: reason and experience'.[55] Similarly, Owen contrasts 'the inventive faculties' that had hitherto been used in 'this inquiry' into the nature of 'the good society' to 'experience', which he regards as 'the only true guide that can lead to true knowledge on any subject'.[56] This perception of their own approach is corroborated by today's view, especially of Saint-Simon, but to some extent also of Owen and Fourier, as being precursors of positivism, a methodological tradition that prioritises the use of empirical data above all else.

Marx and Engels were, however, very insistent that utopian socialists' visions of the future were fantastical or imaginary ideas. That is, whereas not all of their thoughts and ideas were engendered by the faculty of imagination, those that have to do with the future were. In 'The First Draft of *The Civil War in France*', Marx criticises the utopian socialists and their followers for trying to 'compensate for the historical conditions of the movement by phantastic pictures and plans of a new society'.[57] It is, in particular, the 'pictures and plans of a new society' that Marx perceives as phantastic.

We can now see how Marx and Engels's differentiation between reason and imagination served as a rationale for the claim that the knowledge of the future is impossible. The rationale does not lie only in Marx's view, as Roger Paden puts it, 'of the essential epistemological limitations of scientific knowledge'.[58] In addition, it lies also in Marx's view of the epistemological limitations of imagination. Whereas Marx ascribes to this cognitive faculty the ability to look into the future – as opposed to reason, for which insight forward in time was simply impossible, since empirical information about future states are not yet available – he contends that the ensuing thoughts and ideas are completely devoid of any objective validity. Grasping Marx's rationale of his critique of utopian thinking not only in terms of his conception of reason but also in terms of imagination, basically in terms of the differences between the two, is essential for our understanding of Bloch's stance on the possibility of utopian thinking. In contrast to Marx, Bloch insists on the possibility of knowing of the future, and a central tenet behind this claim is indeed his own conception of imagination, which, in his view, engenders knowledge not only of subjective but also of objective validity. Thereby Bloch advances not only a new conception of human mind, but also a new anthropological and ontological theory,

---

55   Saint-Simon, 1987, p. 87.
56   Owen 1971 [1813], p. 34.
57   Marx 1975 [1871], p. 499. Note that Marx wrote this text originally in English.
58   Paden 2002, p. 78.

in which the reason-imagination binary is no longer applicable. This dualism, however, cannot be sustained entirely even in Marx's own thought. This claim brings us back to Marx's materialism, which posits that *everything* intangible is conditioned by material forces. Where does the faculty of imagination fit in this scheme? Marx and Engels contend that the issue with imagination is that it does not take into account what happens in the objective world – but how could they see this subjective faculty as existing somehow separately of this objective world in the first place? We could say that Marx and Engels's notion of the imagination contains a certain remnant of idealism, which in its crude variety embraces the idea that the spiritual, ideal or conceptual reside in their own independent realm. This second rationale of Marx further complicates the paradox of the (im)possibility of utopian thinking. As with the first explanation, this second one too contradicts the rest of Marx's philosophical framework, thus leaving Marx's followers needing to revise his historical materialism so that it would result in a more consistent answer to the question of whether or not utopian thinking is possible.

6   Utopian Visions Are Insignificant

Marx's other central objection to utopian thinking is that he considers it to be unnecessary for facilitating desirable historical change: what one says about the future is completely irrelevant to what actually happens in the future. One argument supporting this objection follows from Marx's philosophy of history, and the other from another aspect to his psychological understanding of the human being.

7   Objectivity of Historical Change: Utopia Cannot Be Enacted

Marx's philosophy of history posits the process of historical change as both an objective and a subjective process. This means that whilst historical change does not occur independently of the intentions, consciousness and actions of individuals, it is also not fully under their control. As Marx puts it in *The Holy Family*, history is not an autonomous entity possessing its own agency:

> History 'does nothing', it 'possesses no immense wealth', it 'wages no battles'. It is man, real, living man who does all that, who possesses and fights; 'history' is not, as it were, a person apart.[59]

---

59   Marx and Engels 1962 [1845], p. 198.

Besides being shaped by individuals, history is conditioned by objective forces – forces that are by definition, at least partially, beyond the sphere of human influence. The objective and subjective factors in part constitute each other: technology, as one objective force, does not just progress on its own – humans devise and implement the idea of how to improve existing technological structures. On the other hand, the already existing technology greatly affects the scope of possible ideas for its own improvement. The relevant point of his critique of utopian thinking is that, for Marx, the objective forces are the more important ones in directing the course of history. This is not a straightforward point, as they are of greater importance only in a very narrow sense, namely in that the objective factors engender the 'critical' moments of history, such as revolutions. Although humans always play a role in bringing about these critical objective conditions and transforming them into different ones, they themselves cannot bring about a revolution itself if the objective conditions have not been already met.[60] If the objective conditions are not 'ripe', that is, not such as to necessitate a change in the economic and political organisation of a society, no protest, no strike, no *coup d'état*, no building of an anarchist collective, will actually set this change in motion.

An implication of this view of historical changes is that people's conception of the post-revolutionary society is, for Marx, actually wholly irrelevant to its realisation. This conception is thus also irrelevant to what he, in his capacity as the intellectual, philosopher, and member of the so-called intelligentsia of the revolution, thinks about this society. Instead, his task is only to 'prove concretely how in present capitalist society the material, etc. conditions have at last been created which enable and compel the workers to lift this historical curse'.[61] Marx posits here not only that a certain state of material conditions enables revolutionary action by the workers, but moreover that it *compels* them to take this action. In that the workers are compelled to act in particular way, a certain inevitability of historical change is implied. The progressive impoverishment of the working class will necessarily lead to their revolt, and, furthermore, to the realisation of communism. This realisation of communism is not a result of intentional human action. In writing about the Paris Commune, Marx famously insists that these intentions do not play a role in directing the actions of proletariat, that they:

---

60   The question of how prominent the degree of automatism or inevitability is in the development of the objective conditions is one of the most disputed points in scholarship on Marx and Marxism. There is a general agreement that the early Marx emphasises more the role of human agency, and the mature one that of objective forces.

61   Marx 1987 [1891], p. 17.

'have no ideals to realise', 'no ready-made utopias' to introduce by 'decree' – but rather that their task is 'to set free elements of the new society with which old collapsing bourgeois society itself is pregnant'.[62]

Another way of formulating this same view of Marx would be to say that the possibilities for a new society of the future are contained in the objective conditions themselves. We could imagine these possibilities as soap bubbles that are waiting to be burst. Human action is one of the factors that can prick these bubbles and release their content. As we will see, Bloch considers this view of Marx to be too narrow. For Bloch, the possibilities of the new are incarnated in human beings themselves, which renders the subjective side of historical change more significant than Marx thought. The role of human action is, then, not simply to set free the ready-made elements but to constructively participate in the production of these elements, including by creating visions of a desirable future.

8   Humans as Rational Beings: Understanding Leads to Action

In denying that workers can know the form and features of a society which could better meet their needs, demands and interests, Marx is not, however, claiming that they do not understand that the existing capitalist society is ill-suited to serving these needs – the workers eventually become aware of the negative effects that capitalism has on their lives. Awareness or consciousness, as one of the subjective factors, is dependent on the objective ones. This means that the crystallisation of the workers' interests is determined by the development of objective factors towards a critical point. This determination is not complete or automatic – the condition of the objective factors does not, on its own, translate fully into the allegedly corresponding state of consciousness of the workers. This incompleteness and lack of automatism allows the ideas of the workers to be influenced by other factors, such as by the ideas and theories of the intellectuals and philosophers who supposedly have a privileged access to the state of affairs. The kind of ideas engendered by philosophers that would play a constructive role in this sense was for Marx very specific: as he posits in the remark above, taken from his Gotha Critique, his task is to prove the existing state of the material conditions, and, as per his widely-known assertion in *Capital*, to critically analyse the actual facts.[63]

---

62   Marx 1975 [1871], p. 335.
63   Marx 1962 [1867], p. 25.

Entailed in this view is another presumption which further consolidates Marx's argument that utopian thinking is unnecessary. Because he thinks that *proving* the existing conditions and revealing *facts* are constructive activities through which consciousness and hence actions are influenced, Marx priorities the rational side of the human psyche. That is, Marx not only believes that the objectivity of reality can be comprehended through his own rational capacities, but moreover that this reality can be conveyed to others, and accepted by them merely on the basis of the coherency, logic, and consistency of the account of this reality. Once the workers *understand* their actual situation, they will take recourse to revolutionary action and transform the world into one that is more in accordance with their interests. The workers only need to see that they 'have a world to win', as the fine slogan in the *Manifesto* puts it.[64]

In this chapter I have argued that, from the point of view of Marx's theoretical framework, it is not evident why utopian thinking would be needed in processes of social change in general, and specifically in conceptual projects that aim to facilitate this social change. From his writings only one argument can be reconstructed supporting the opposite position, namely, the actual presence of utopian thinking in his writings. As discussed at the beginning of the chapter, a certain positive utopian vision is suggested by Marx's texts. This objection is substantial and poses the question as to why Marx elaborates the content of communism in the first place, given that he considers it to be unnecessary. I have highlighted reasons which make the presence of utopian thinking in Marx contingent on certain marginal factors: for example, that many of Marx's comments on communism can be comprehended as reactions to existing visions which he thinks need to be corrected. But it is implausible to think that these reasons can account for all of the utopian thinking that pervades Marx. We are thus left only with an impression or a suspicion that Marx appreciates utopian thinking in some positive way, but not with actual reasons, internal to his theories, as to why this might be the case.

This incongruence between the presence of utopian thinking and the lack of any theoretical justification for it is one puzzle that the critical theorists inherited from Marx. The other puzzle concerns Marx's paradox about the possibility of envisaging the future. Whereas Marx is clear in his claims that the future and thus also the utopian future cannot be known, he is less clear in his rationalisation of these claims. In fact, both rationales I have identified, one related to his materialistic worldview and one to his conceptions of imagination and

---

64   Marx and Engels 1977 [1848], p. 493.

reason, contradict many other aspects of his philosophy. The inheritors of his philosophy thus also inherited the confusions and unresolved issues that define Marx's relation to utopian thinking. In what follows, I look at the attempts by two critical theorists, Adorno and Bloch, to deal with these unresolved issues.

CHAPTER 2

The Origins of Adorno's *Utopieverbot*

1   Adorno and Marxist Theory in the Early Twentieth Century

Theodor W. Adorno (1903–69) was raised in a Jewish bourgeois family of trades-men.[1] In stark contrast to Marx he was never a socialist or communist act-ivist.[2] Nevertheless, he subscribed to the principles of such politics, even if in a highly abstract and uncompromisingly critical way. This critical side of his thought became evident most famously in the context of the events of 1968, in which Adorno quickly became implicated.[3] Adorno was by then an established left-wing intellectual, recognised as a thinker whose theories sub-stantially influenced the students' demands. His opposition to students was revealed especially clearly in December of that year when the students occu-pied the premises of the Institute for Social Research, where Adorno had resumed his post in 1949 upon his return from forced emigration in 1933, when the Nazi regime barred him from teaching.[4] Throughout this period Adorno, however, remained formally affiliated with the Institute, the operations of which never ceased, but were instead moved, first to Geneva and Paris and eventually to New York, at the premises of the Columbia University. After the end of the War Adorno also spent some time in California, dismayed by the then emergent popular culture, which he labelled the 'culture industry', a term intro-duced in the *Dialectic of Enlightenment* co-authored with Max Horkheimer, which was transcribed by his wife, Gretel Adorno, in Santa Barbara during the Second World War. This book, probably the most well known work today asso-ciated with Critical Theory, set the tone of the change in direction that this tradition underwent in the postwar era. This tone is most clearly exemplified in Adorno's widely cited remark from that era, namely that poetry after Aus-chwitz is impossible.[5] Many commentators interpret this tone as pessimistic with respect to the possibility of the social change that the critical theorists desired. In parallel to this change of tone in the postwar era, Adorno has been perceived as distancing himself further from activist politics, barricading him-self in 'the Grand Hotel Abyss'. This derogatory term was invented by Georg

---

1   This section draws on Claussen 2005.
2   See Demirović 1999.
3   See Kraushaar 1998.
5   Adorno 1977 [1951], p. 30.

Lukács to describe the activities of the critical theorists as self-indulgent, with at best no, and at worst damaging consequences for the real world. Adorno, however, defied such accusations. From his perspective, the integration of theory and political activism devised by Marx had been shown by history to be flawed, and his aim was to revise theory's connection to practice in such a way as to make its contribution more, rather than less, effective and relevant. Adorno developed this transformed approach to theory most extensively in *Negative Dialectics*, published three years before his death in the summer of 1969.

As discussed in my Introduction, the project of Critical Theory is best perceived as a continuation of Marxian philosophy. Adorno himself acknowledged that the need for philosophy or theory persists precisely because Marx's prognosis of the end of capitalism and the arrival of communism has not been realised.[6] The central question that thus motivated the establishment of the Institute in Frankfurt in 1923 and the activities of its members in subsequent decades was how to revise Marx's key insights so as to bring about their realisation in practice. That is, while Adorno and other critical theorists adhered to the overall thrust of Marx's project, namely to the conviction that the existence and the sufferings of the insulted and the injured is neither rational nor necessary, and thus need to be resisted and overcome, they perceived the then existing tendencies within Marxism to be essentially flawed. Critical theorists, but also two of their immediate intellectual predecessors, Karl Korsch and Lukács, believed that the Marxism of the early twentieth century had degenerated into yet another form of positivistic and scientific creed. A particular problem that the critical theorists identified in this so-called vulgar or orthodox Marxism was an insufficient stress on the Hegelian roots of Marx's thought, namely aspects such as consciousness, spontaneity and subjectivity. An objective of the Institute in Frankfurt was thus to recover Marx's Hegelian roots. Moreover, Marx's theory also needed to be revised in the light of certain vital social, political and economic conditions that separated the critical theorists from the concerns that Marx and his contemporaries faced in the mid-nineteenth century. By the time of the early twentieth century, capitalism had entered a qualitatively new stage, with its modernising effects being felt more intensively and widely across society. On the other hand, socialism had evolved from being limited to a few examples of rather isolated communities into a state-wide phenomenon – the Soviet Union. In addition, the critical theorists contested some of Marx's own basic premises. One of the most

---

6   Adorno 1996 [1966], p. 3.

highly contested was Marx's idea of the existence of a revolutionary agent, a particular section of the population that has a privileged role to play in the transformation of history. Critical theorists considered this idea to be both epistemologically problematic and one that can be utilised for authoritarian purposes.[7]

In their attempt to recuperate Marx's central insights into a body of theory, which would, on the one hand, stay faithful to Marx's Hegelian foundations, and, on the other hand, be suited better to the new historical situation, the critical theorists undertook a thorough re-reading of Marx's work. Whereas certain issues with Marx's theories, such as the alleged existence of a transcendental subject of history, initially motivated this revision, other problems and tensions cropped up as it was undertaken. One of these tensions was the paradoxical place of utopian thinking in Marx's thought.

2   What Is the *Utopieverbot*?

The argument of this chapter is that Adorno's response to Marx's confusions regarding the ends of utopian thinking strengthened the anti-utopian dimension of Marx's position. More specifically, I suggest that the strengthening of this anti-utopian dimension in Adorno took the form of imposing a ban on the practice of utopian thinking in Critical Theory. I call this prohibition on utopian thinking by Adorno the 'Utopieverbot'. Given that Marx too maintained his own objections against positively envisioning the future society, it might appear confusing that I apply this label only to Adorno. However, in contrast to Marx, Adorno actually respected this ban. By no means was Adorno's prohibition simply a rhetorical device: it was constitutive of his theoretical framework.

Adorno's clearest and best known articulation of the *Utopieverbot* is the following passage from his *Negative Dialectics*:

> The materialist longing to grasp the thing aims at the opposite [of idealism]: it is only in the absence of its images that the full object could be conceived. Such absence concurs with the theological ban on images. Materialism brought that ban into secular form by not permitting Utopia to be positively pictured.[8]

---

7   Jay 1973, pp. 41–2.
8   Adorno 1996 [1966], pp. 206–7.

In this passage, in which Adorno refers to Critical Theory as 'Materialismus', he asserts that the object of its longing – a utopian society – can only be thought without picturing it. Adorno then reiterates the *Utopieverbot* by claiming that materialism does not allow for a utopia to be positively imagined. In his epilogue to *Minima Moralia*, this prohibition is expressed in very similar terms, insisting that a critical theorist is reluctant to engage herself in 'positive images of the proper society, of its members, even of those who would accomplish'.[9] Perhaps less well known is Adorno's formulation of the *Utopieverbot* in the *Aesthethic Theory*, in which Adorno applies it not only to Critical Theory but also to art, contending that 'the wordless, imageless utopia [...] reigns also over artworks'.[10]

Just as clearly as Adorno himself, scholars of Adorno are unanimous in claiming that Adorno in fact imposed the *Utopieverbot*. Simon Jarvis notes that Adorno considers philosophy unable to address utopia 'positively and explicitly', and similarly, Susan Buck-Morss insists that Adorno refuses 'to delineate the nature of postrevolutionary society'.[11] Less explicitly, yet nonetheless pointing in the same direction, Rahel Jaeggi observes that, in Adorno's view:

> in a wrong society the good cannot be *done*, cannot be *known*, and, independent of its realization, does not *exist*, and is thus not available as an independent (counterfactual) standard for right action.[12]

Given the consensus on the *existence* of the *Utopieverbot*, it is curious that the existing literature offers no comprehensive *explanation* of this ban, especially of its underlying rationale – why did Adorno institute and adhere to this ban? Most commonly, what is given is a mere clue to an explanation. This clue points to the Jewish heritage of Critical Theory, in particular to the so-called *Bilderverbot* (image-ban) – a principal idiosyncrasy of the Jewish religion, demarcating it from its predecessors among the pagan creeds. It corresponds to a taboo on depicting or visualising God, and is encoded in the Bible as one of the Ten Commandments: 'You shall not make for yourself an image in the form of anything in heaven above or on the earth beneath or in the waters below'.[13] Gerhard Schweppenhäuser construes the link between the prohibition against envisioning a future society and the *Bilderverbot* by observing that 'Adorno gives us

---

9   Adorno 1980 [1951], p. 297.
10   Adorno 1990 [1970], p. 367.
11   Jarvis 1997, p. 7; Buck-Morss 1977, p. 130.
12   Jaeggi 2005, p. 123.
13   Exodus 20. 4.

no detailed picture of utopia. He refuses to conjure up images of the better condition. He stresses that the Old Testament prohibition on images remains philosophically and socially mandatory'.[14] In the same vein, Martin Jay draws no significant distinction between the *Bilderverbot* and the *Utopieverbot*, asserting that the latter is a mere 'reproduction' of the former.[15] This explanation of Adorno's *Utopieverbot* in terms of the Jewish ban on images is not surprising given that Adorno himself frequently discusses the two together, including in the longer passage I quoted above from *Negative Dialectics*. Here, Adorno not only claims that the prohibitions of Judaism and materialism resemble each other, but by evoking the process of secularisation, he implies that Critical Theory's aversion to utopian thinking is indeed derived from Judaism. In another instance, in his essay on 'Reason and Revelation', Adorno does not differentiate between the two prohibitions at all, contending that what Critical Theory adheres to is the *Bilderverbot* itself. He contends that he does not see any other possibility: 'I see no other possibility than an extreme ascesis toward any type of revealed faith, an extreme loyalty to the *Bilderverbot*, far beyond what this once originally meant'.[16] The idea that the *Utopieverbot* is not necessarily distinguishable from the Jewish *Bilderverbot* was shared by other members of the Frankfurt Institute. Towards the end of his life, in a 1970 interview with the magazine *Der Spiegel*, Max Horkheimer reflects on the Jewish heritage of Critical Theory, and contends that its care in dealing with the name of God is indeed of Jewish heritage. He claims that:

> this care has been incorporated into our social theory, which we call Critical Theory. 'Thou shalt not make unto thee any graven image of God', it says in the Bible. You cannot represent the absolute good. The pious Jew tries to avoid the word 'God' as far as possible; indeed, he does not write it out, but makes an apostrophe in its place. In a similar way, the Absolute is in Critical Theory cautiously called 'The other'.[17]

This chapter explores Adorno's argument for the *Utopieverbot*, which can, to a large extent, be perceived as a continuation of one of Marx's own arguments against the very possibility of utopian thinking. However, the actual reasons that Adorno provides for why utopian thinking is impossible differ significantly from those I have reconstructed from Marx's theories. This is one reason why

---

14   Schweppenhäuser 2009, p. 77.
15   Jay 1973, p. 56.
16   Adorno 1977, p. 616.
17   Horkheimer 1970, p. 81.

Adorno's *Utopieverbot* cannot be fully grasped in terms of influences that Marx exerted on Adorno. Nor can the *Utopieverbot* be explicated in terms of the Jewish *Bilderverbot*. As I contend in this chapter, these are two interpretations that have prevailed in the scholarship. I argue that in order to fully understand the origins and the meaning of the *Utopieverbot*, additional aspects of Adorno's philosophy need to be examined. The second half of this chapter is devoted to Adorno's conception of time, and to his ideas of the culture industry and identity thinking.

3   From the *Bilderverbot* to the *Utopieverbot*

If the *Utopieverbot* is merely a copy, a reproduction, or a slight permutation of the *Bilderverbot* – one is posited in theological terms, prohibiting the depiction of the divine, of God; the other is a secular claim, forbidding the depiction of a utopian society – then the underlying rationale, the reasons why Adorno considered the *Utopieverbot* to be a good idea, must lie in Judaism. These rationales of the *Bilderverbot* are, however, complex and highly ambiguous, just as is the *Bilderverbot* itself. In contrast to the image of the *Bilderverbot* that the critical theorists present us with, namely of the *Bilderverbot* as a single, easily interpretable statement, which is spelled out somewhere in the Hebrew Bible, this stricture in fact encompasses a set of diverse, often incompatible statements. Alongside the most widely cited in reference to the *Bilderverbot* – the Ten Commandments – the Bible contains at least five further allusions to it, each of which is phrased, and can thus be interpreted, slightly differently. For instance, the three references included in the book of Exodus proclaim respectively:

> You shall not make for yourself an idol in the form of anything in heaven above or on the earth beneath or in the waters below;[18]

> Do not make any gods to be alongside me; do not make for yourself gods of silver or gods of gold;[19]

> Do not make cast idols.[20]

---

18   Exodus 20. 4.
19   Exodus 20. 23.
20   Exodus 34. 17.

Contrary to the understanding of the *Bilderverbot* we obtain from Critical Theory, in none of these excerpts from the Bible is it actually God itself that is the object of prohibition. What is forbidden to be depicted are, rather, idols and gods in general, that is other deities than the Jewish God (Yahweh). The idea of an idol itself is complex. Besides corresponding simply to an object that simply *represents* the divine, the word idol refers also to an object that is *by virtue* of this representation accorded with a certain value, a status of worship. Such a reading of an idol would then imply that the *Bilderverbot* forbids not so much, or, at least, not only the mere depiction of the divine, but rather a certain kind of worship. These different formulations of the *Bilderverbot* also differ in the kind of representation they ban. Whereas the first one seems to ban any conceivable kind of representation: visual (e.g. pictures, icons, portrayals, sculptures, frescoes, engravings, illustrations, woodcuts), and phonetic or conceptual (e.g. name, discursive description), the other two talk much more narrowly about metal sculptures ('gods of silver or gods of gold', 'cast idols').

The Torah itself offers no explicit argument for the *Bilderverbot*. Theological scholarship has, however, in turn advanced a long list of explanations, two of which seem to have some relevance for the *Utopieverbot*. The most straightforward response to why God should not be depicted is that God is an *invisible*, non-corporeal, non-theophanous being.[21] The depiction is disallowed not so much because humans would lack the cognitive capacity to perceive it, but more due to God's inherent nature (being invisible). The other widely held reading of the *Bilderverbot*, influenced by the revisionism of Moses Maimonides, a prominent medieval rabbi, posits God's *unknowability* as the reason against its depiction.[22] The unknown nature of God is here, unlike its innate invisibility, not simply hypothesised, but grounded in view of God as a 'not completed' being. As Eric Fromm, a critical theorist with a particular interest in Jewish thought, elaborates:

> [God's] being is not completed like that of a thing, but is a living process, a becoming; only a thing, that is, that which has reached its final form, can have a name. [...] Only idols have names, because they are things. The 'living' God cannot have a name.[23]

There are, in fact, palpable parallels between these two rationalisations of the *Bilderverbot* (the invisibility and unknowability of God) and some of Adorno's

---

21   Ellul 1985, p. 115.
22   Maimonides 1963.
23   Fromm 1967, p. 31.

remarks. Just as there is a dimension to God which renders its depiction impossible, so too does Adorno's understanding of utopia insist on its unrepresentability. In *Negative Dialectics* he claims that philosophy is essentially concerned with thinking 'the ineffable of utopia', namely that which is intrinsically beyond the grasp of our senses.[24] He moreover uses the term 'the unsayable', which I take to be synonymous with the former Latinate word.[25] Similarly to the way in which Judaism argues that God, as becoming, cannot be expressed by passivity of words and concepts, Adorno too opposes the description of different aspects of a utopian society, such as freedom, contending that such a description entails an impermissible reduction of a utopia:

> The intelligible character as subjective possibility, like freedom, is a thing that comes to be, not a thing that is. It would be a betrayal to incorporate it in existence by description, even by the most cautious description.[26]

Whereas these remarks do resonate with the two explanations of the *Bilderverbot*, explaining the *Utopieverbot* only with reference to Judaism remains deeply problematic, and for six reasons. First, Adorno was not a believing (nor a practising) Jew. Like many other members of the Institute in Frankfurt, like Horkheimer, Lowenthal and Pollock, Adorno was of Jewish background and grew up in a Jewish community.[27] In comparison with his colleagues, however, Adorno did not engage with Judaism and did not have a positive Jewish identity.[28] Whereas it is thus reasonable to acknowledge the ideas of Judaism as an influence on Adorno, it is questionable that he would have simply accepted them. Second, theological scholarship has raised substantial objections with respect to the validity of the view of God as an invisible or unknown being. In a high point of the history of salvation, namely the revelation of the Torah at Mount Sinai, God was held to have shown itself to Israelites: 'And Moses and Aaron, Nadav, Avihu and the seventy elders went up. And they saw the God of Israel [...]'[29] Third, as Fromm suggests, any argument for the *Bilderverbot* should be suspect because of the political role this prohibition is likely to have played in the spread of Judaism.[30] Fourth, as Albert Wellmer notes,

---

24   Adorno 1996 [1966], p. 22.
25   Adorno 1980 [1951], p. 287.
26   Adorno 1996 [1966], pp. 293–4.
27   See Jacobs 2015, p. 13.
28   See Jacobs 2015, p. 55.
29   Exodus 24. 7–11.
30   Fromm 1967, p. 42.

we will never be able to establish with certainty 'whether or not the Jewish taboo was actually causal or merely a *post facto* rationalisation' of the *Utopieverbot*. Fifth, as I demonstrated in the discussion above, the term *Bilderverbot* is merely a convenient epithet for an ambiguously interpretable web of assertions encoded in the Hebrew Bible, and a large degree of speculation is necessary to ascertain which reading the critical theorists followed. And, last, the spheres of the representation to which the respective prohibitions apply are distinct: whereas the *Utopieverbot* applies above all to the conceptual or discursive sphere, the *Bilderverbot* applies almost exclusively to visual arts. The *Utopieverbot* prohibits expressions of the perfected future society in the forms of concepts, discourse, or words. By contrast, the *Bilderverbot* prohibits the depiction of God in the form of icons, illustrations, sculptures or pictures. Apart from the prohibition imposed on pronouncing the name of God, which is not respected in the Hebrew Bible anyway – God is actually given a name, namely Yahweh or YHWH – it does not in any way outlaw worshipping God through conceptual representation. In fact, the critical theorists held an opposed view to the Bible about the ability of visual arts to portray the ideal. Relative to conceptual language, they perceived visual arts (together with music and architecture) to possess potentially more legitimate means to express a utopian society.

4   Marx's Influence on the *Utopieverbot*

In light of these issues, I contend that it is necessary to explicate the rationale of Adorno's *Utopieverbot* in other terms than by how it relates to the Jewish ban. And Adorno does indeed acknowledge an alternative set of ideas that have influenced him in this respect – those of Hegel and Marx. Here Adorno does not speak specifically of utopian thinking, but of positive thinking in general. However, since I am interested in utopian thinking as a type of positive thinking, these more general arguments are pertinent. Adorno claims that his aversion to positive thinking indeed stems from Marx and Hegel: 'If anything has penetrated my flesh and blood from Hegel and those who put him on his feet, it is the ascetic stance regarding the unmediated expression of the positive'.[31] Similarly, in his commentary on the poems of Friedrich Hölderlin, Adorno observes that the Romantic poet too is reluctant to positively describe the future, and further, that he shares this trait with Hegel and Marx:

---

31   Adorno 2002, p. 128.

Not forward: under the law of the present, which in Hölderlin is the law of poetry, with a taboo against abstract utopia, a taboo in which the theological ban on graven images, which Hölderlin shares with Hegel and Marx, lives on.[32]

Adorno, however, himself recognises that his *Utopieverbot* is not simply an extension of Marx's. In an address to the German sociologists' association in 1968, entitled 'Late capitalism or industrialised society?', Adorno highlights the inapplicability of one of Marx's objections to utopian thinking in the contemporary context:

> Ladies and gentlemen, let me say a few words about the category of utopia. It too is subject to a historical dynamic. For the moment, I will refrain from addressing the Marxian problem of the struggle against anarchist utopianism. But the productive forces, the material productive forces have developed today in such a way that if the society was rationally organised, material need would no longer be necessary. That such a state could be established on the whole earth, on a telluric scale, that would have been denounced in the nineteenth century as blatantly utopian [...] In that the objective possibilities have been so infinitely expanded, the kind of criticism of the concept of utopia that was aimed at perpetuating of the lack is no longer really relevant.[33]

Here Adorno observes that Marx's critique of utopian thinking was founded on the premise that, in the nineteenth century, the material conditions were not yet 'ripe' for a communist society: that is, the existing levels of economic production were yet too low to meet the basic needs of the entire population. This state of affairs, however, Adorno notes, no longer holds: the objective possibilities have been boundlessly extended, and material hardship is no longer necessary. In the radio conversation with Bloch, Adorno touches on the relation between the existing historical conditions and utopian thinking. He notes that the critical factor determining the possibility to envisage a utopian society lies in the existing 'proximity of utopia'.[34] This proximity is one reason why Adorno concludes the above address by declaring Marx's own critique of utopian thinking to be no longer relevant. Many ideals which were by Marx's time simply impossible could now have been realised. Critical theorists consider that, as

---

32   Adorno 1996 [1964], p. 483.
33   Adorno 1996 [1968], p. 585.
34   Adorno in Bloch 1977 [1969b], p. 353.

Raymond Geuss pointedly puts it, 'even if we do not (yet) have talking horses, we do have a socioeconomic formation that is sufficiently productive [...] not to require gross social inequality'.[35]

As demonstrated in the preceding chapter, Marx's critique of utopian thinking consists of more layers than Adorno seems to suggest above. It is thus unwarranted to understand Adorno to be on the whole dismissing the relevance of Marx's critique of utopian thinking for the world as it existed in the latter half of the twentieth century. Similarly, we should not understand Adorno to be dismissing any influence that Marx might have on his own arguments against utopian thinking. In fact, as I show below, Adorno's critique, just like Marx's, is grounded on the idea of the impossibility of utopian thinking. Furthermore, this aspect of Adorno's critique of utopian thinking, which is related to his understanding of positive thinking, was certainly strongly influenced by Marx, in particular by the arguments Marx engendered from his materialist standpoint.

Yet, in the quoted passage from his public address, Adorno clearly does dismiss one particular aspect of Marx's objection to utopian thinking. This dismissal, however, has not weakened Adorno's conviction in the ban on utopian thinking. Compared to Marx, Adorno was not only more general in his insistence on the *Utopieverbot* than Marx was, but also strictly adhered to it in practice. It is therefore plausible to think that Adorno's opposition to utopian thinking has sources other than in the Marxian legacy, sources that strengthened his opposition.

There are two other reasons which further reinforce the need to explicate Adorno's *Utopieverbot* in its own terms, and not only in relation to Marx's ideas. Adorno's dismissal of Marx's critique of utopian thinking is founded not only, as he explicitly posits above, on the changed historical circumstances, but also on his rejection of Marx's understanding of history as being primarily an objective process. Since the increased material wealth was not accompanied by the proletarian revolution that Marx predicted, the critical theorists in the 1920s deemed Marx's philosophy of history to be flawed. As I have alluded to in the Introduction, this rejection, which Adorno shared with other critical theorists of the time, was an important contributing factor to the emergence of a distinct strand of Marxism in the first place. In my Introduction, I argued that this rejection played a substantial role in making the question of utopian thinking more weighty for the critical theorists than for Marx himself. Here I highlight yet one more repercussion of Marx's objective conception of history and Adorno's

---

35   Geuss 2004, p. 132.

rejection of it. In that it was specifically this objective conception of history which served as an underlying rationale of Marx's critique of utopian thinking, we cannot simply perceive Adorno's *Utopieverbot* to be identical with, or an extension of, Marx's one.

As I have shown in the previous chapter, if we attempt to make sense of Marx's inconsistent opposition to utopian thinking, one possible approach is to distinguish between more and less detailed utopian thinking. We can then say that Marx's concerns lay primarily with the more detailed type, especially in the instances where, in Marx's estimation, the utopian outlines were not complemented adequately with a critique of the existing society. Adorno's *Utopie-verbot* is in comparison much more overarching – Adorno bans both more and less detailed kinds of utopian thinking. Adorno does distinguish Marx from those socialists and communists who were more in favour of utopian thinking – Adorno refers to this strand of utopian thinking as 'anarchistic utopianism' – and acknowledges Marx's reluctance to engage in such practice.[36] Adorno notes that Marx was sparing with words when describing a communist society.[37] Yet he also reprehends Marx for the descriptions of communism he includes in his writings, however sparing Marx might be with them. Adorno argues that Marx commits the very fallacy of which he accuses the authors of the 'Gotha Programme', namely of transferring the principles of the existing society into the tenets of the future one. In the 'Critique of the Gotha Programme' Marx notes that the alternative remuneration scheme proposed by the SAPD itself embodies the capitalist principles of commodity exchange and commodification of labour. In a similar vein, Adorno recognises that Marx's philosophy is premised on another capitalist tenet, that of 'the programme of absolute domination of nature'.[38] Adorno not only perceives the idea of the absolute control of nature to be constitutive of Marx's vision of communism, and moreover denounces Marx for it, but also identifies the source of the ability to construct such a fallacious statement. This is Adorno's idea of identity thinking, which he describes as 'the effort to take things unlike the subject and make them like the subject'.[39] I contend that this idea of identity thinking presents one important rationale of Adorno's *Utopieverbot*, which, even if not incongruent with Marx's materialist objection against utopian thinking, needs to be examined separately. Unlike materialism in the case of Marx, Adorno's argument about identity thinking is paralleled by the absence of positive think-

---

36   Adorno 1996 [1968], 585.
37   Adorno 1996 [1966], p. 192.
38   Adorno 1996 [1966], p. 242.
39   Adorno 1996 [1966], p. 242.

ing in his thought, and thus also of positive conceptualisations of utopia. This rationale is, as it is probably becoming evident, quite difficult to grasp, and prior to examining it further, I first outline two further ones, which I call 'Messianic future' and 'culture industry'.

5   The Removal of Utopia into the Messianic Future

The first rationale of Adorno's *Utopieverbot* I propose here is associated with Adorno's messianism, in particular with his conception of the future as messianic. To grasp this rationale it will be helpful to return to a few arguments elaborated in the previous chapter. Marx's philosophy of history renders utopian thinking unnecessary to the realisation of communism. Whereas Marx can be criticised for this point from an external perspective, it is consistent with the rest of his theoretical framework. Marx is, however, inconsistent with respect to the possibility of utopian thinking: on the one hand he contends that utopian societies cannot be envisaged prior to their realisation, and on the other, he himself envisions certain, economic dimensions of his kind of the communist society. Although this inconsistency cannot be fully resolved, one way to overcome it, at least partially, brings us back to his philosophy of history. According to this philosophy, history possesses a structure, goal and meaning. Even if one does not accept the strictly determinist reading of historical change, for Marx, this change can be divided into stages or phases which evolve from each other with some inevitability, and culminate in the final stage of communism. Marx's philosophy is bound up with notions of progress and teleology, as well as with a historiographical approach that Kant called universal history.[40] Universal history, for Kant, is historiography that, instead of accumulating and explaining facts about individual events, endeavours to discern their underlying trends.[41] It seems to me that this notion has substantial epistemological implications. If one contends that history possesses general trends, structures or even natural laws, then one at least in principle allows for the possibility of discerning or knowing these structures and laws. In Marx's view these laws exist at the economic level, and he was accordingly able to provide some substance to these laws. Adorno's view was very different. He dispensed with all generalised, abstract and universalising, as well as with all progressive and teleological, conceptions of history. I suggest that this rejection

---

40   Kant 1991 [1784], pp. 41–53.
41   Kant 1991 [1784], pp. 41–53.

further delimits, if not eliminates, the possibility to know the future, to foresee what a utopian society would look like.

The specific reason why Adorno finds universal histories problematic is their implicit search for meaning.[42] That is, in an attempt to interpret history as something more than merely sequences of unrelated and related events, universal histories posit all individual events as tightly linked to each other, and thus as forming a larger picture – the picture of meaning. This meaning takes the form of a purpose, an objective or a goal of history, which Marx perceived in the forthcoming communist society, and in the movement towards this goal. Adorno, however, turns against this approach, asserting that 'it is not enough for us to live in hope that the history of mankind will move towards a satisfactory state of affairs of its own accord'.[43]

Adorno argues that Marx's account of history, as one instance of the universal history, was discredited not only by the absent or failed proletarian revolutions but, furthermore, by the human atrocities which occurred before and during the Second World War: 'that very fact, the very assertion that, as people put it, the world has a meaning, can simply not be maintained in the light of all that we have experienced in our own epoch of history'.[44] Adorno often refers to these atrocities by using the term 'Auschwitz', contending that if there was any truth to these supposedly meaningful accounts of history, 'Auschwitz could not have happened'.[45] Adorno further contends that under no circumstances can Auschwitz be understood as progress, as contributing to it, directly or indirectly, but solely as regress, as relapse into barbarity and irrationality of the pre-modern epochs.[46] Even if the philosophy of history as a progressive process does not claim that each and every succeeding moment of history in itself, and thus every event that takes place in this moment, represents a step up in this progressive process, every moment is to be interpreted and thus tolerated as a constitutive part of this process. Adorno deems this to be unacceptable: whatever happens in the present can mean either progress or regress (or both), and judging which of the two it is must, in Adorno's view, be approached on its own terms, without consideration of what it could mean in the greater frame of history.

In countering this flaw in Marx's account of history, Adorno develops his own, which, however, is in turn heavily founded on Walter Benjamin's ideas.

---

42   Adorno 2001, p. 15.
43   Adorno 2003, p. 76.
44   Adorno 2003, p. 90.
45   Adorno 2001, p. 14.
46   Adorno 2001, p. 14.

The relevant question which Adorno poses to himself is 'whether we can construct history without committing the cardinal sin of insinuating meaning where none exists'.[47] That is, the account of history Adorno aims for is one which posits history not as meaningful but as meaningless. But what does it mean for history to be meaningless?

For Benjamin, meaningless history corresponds to a history devoid of an ultimate goal. Benjamin presents this idea most succinctly in his theses 'On the concept of history'.[48] Although Benjamin adopts Marx's vision of a society free of class division as the most desirable society, he rejects his conception of such society as a point at the end of time. Instead of as a goal of history, Benjamin conceptualises the communist utopia as its 'interruption'.[49] An interruption generally means an interference or a disturbance, an action on a certain state or process which is enacted from without, from a dimension external to it. In Benjamin's usage of the term, the dimension that is external to the process he is concerned with, namely history, is the dimension of 'messianic time'.[50] It is this messianic time, a domain interpreted by Werner Hamacher as being independent of our conventional time, of the 'past', 'present', and 'future', in which Benjamin situates the communist utopia.[51] This means that while utopia already exists in the present moment, it does so in the moment of a time which we cannot access. Irrespective of its inaccessibility, Benjamin sees this interruption as having 'frequently miscarried', meaning that so far history has already been interrupted, although not completely successfully: utopia has already burst from the messianic domain and showed up in ours, but not in its fullness.[52]

Benjamin's conception of utopia as existing in the domain of the messianic time accords neatly with Adorno's final aphorism in *Minima Moralia* in which he posits 'the standpoint of redemption' – by which he means the redeemed, that is, the utopian world – as being removed from the 'scope of existence'.[53] Adorno's own philosophy can thus also be interpreted as featuring this conception of utopia existing in the domain of messianic time, if

47   Adorno 2001, p. 16.
48   As it is well known, there exist different versions of this text. Benjamin revised his original manuscript numerously and added to it many notes. The quotations below are taken not from the most often published version of this text, but from one of the revised versions. See Benjamin 1977.
49   Benjamin 1977, p. 1231.
50   Benjamin 1977, p. 1231.
51   Hamacher 2014, pp. 221–34.
52   Benjamin 1977, p. 1231.
53   Adorno 1980 [1951], p. 281.

only implicitly. This interpretation helps us to see how Adorno strengthens Marx's view of the impossibility of conceiving of utopia in advance of its real- isation. Hypothetically speaking, we could foresee Marx's future by travelling forward in time, by fast forwarding the hands on the clock. But in order to arrive at Adorno's future, we would need a different method of time travel- ling altogether, a method that is difficult to conceive of. Adorno did not, of course, elaborate on the location of this future, nor on the means of how to reach it. Along the dimension of time Adorno completely erased any con- nection between the now and the future, thus preventing us from having any cognitive access to the latter. This connection is further dismantled by the absence of the figure of the messiah in Adorno's messianic philosophy. In Jewish messianism the messiah acts as mediator, as a carrier, thus linking the 'Kingdom of God' to the earthly one. Adorno, however, robs us of even this fictional construction which helps us to imagine or to think the con- tent of utopia, thereby making knowledge of it seem like a total impossibil- ity.

Messianic time can be understood not only as an alternative domain which already exists, although independently of us, as for example, in a parallel uni- verse; it can also be understood as a time which will only arrive with the emer- gence of utopia. For Hamacher sees 'the discourse of messianic time' as that of 'another time', as one 'which brings with it not merely another future but another futurity, not only another present but another presence, and which brings with it another time, another temporality – and perhaps, something other than temporality'.[54] Through this conception Hamacher proposes that time somehow runs differently in utopia. But the idea that time runs differ- ently somewhere else, that is, that the clocks located in utopia would record a different lapse of time than clocks in the existing world, is hard to grasp. Our experiences inform us of how time can run differently depending on what we do, and the science of how time can run differently depending on the location from where it is measured. However, the idea of objective time, of clocks tick- ing at the same rate always and everywhere, is one of those certainties we find difficult to relinquish, and which Marx did not let go of. Marx's utopia does differ from the present in terms of the relationships between people, of the individual to herself and to objects. The conception of time, however, remains that of the existing present. In Marx's utopia there might be another human being – the species-being – but there is no other time. In Adorno's future, by contrast, there is another time. Given that our understanding of time presents

---

54   Hamacher 2014, p. 223.

such a fundamental category of our relation to the world, how can we know, or even conceive of, our relation to the world which features this other time?

6   Culture Industry and Utopian Consciousness

The events in the first half of the twentieth century did not initiate only a revision of Marx's philosophy of history away from its progressivist tenets, but also of his version of materialism. More specifically, the failed and missed communist revolutions spurred doubts about the larger significance that Marx ascribed to the economic basis of a society relative to its ideological superstructure. The question that the critical theorists came to face in this respect was why the (unnecessary) material deprivations of the working class had not translated into revolutionary actions. Their answer, substantially influenced by Georg Lukács's *History and Class Consciousness*, was that Marx had neglected the superstructure, that is, consciousness, culture, and ideology as a potential arena of political struggle, and in turn, that the power of the ruling class resided not simply in their material wealth, their ownership of the means of production, but in their ability to control the worldviews, imagination and consciousness of workers. In Critical Theory, human consciousness is understood as a realm that is partially independent of the existing material conditions, possessing its own mechanisms, and initiating its own values and beliefs.

In that consciousness was a partially autonomous sphere for the critical theorists, in principle they opened up a possibility to conceive of ideas and values that would be incongruous with, opposed or subversive to the prevailing ones. In other words, they recognised the possibility of the emergence of new thoughts and beliefs prior to the manifestation of a different economic basis, or more generally a different material reality. In that utopian ideas are also supposed to be *new* ideas, we might say that the critical theorists allowed for the possibility of utopian thinking. However, for Adorno this is mainly a theoretical possibility. What might in the first instance seem to overturn Marx's materialist argument against the possibility of utopian thinking, on further investigation actually reinforces it. Under the conditions of an advanced, commercialised stage of capitalism, individuals are, in Adorno's view, basically unable to conceptualise these new ideas. The root of the cause lies in the increased material wealth of late capitalist societies and the new technologies responsible for this increase. Whereas Adorno, on the one hand, sees this technological progress as making the realisation of a utopian society possible, on the other hand he understands it as a factor preventing individuals from grasping this possibility in the first place. In his radio conversation with Bloch, Adorno

speaks of the 'proximity of utopia' as a cause for the 'shrinking of utopian consciousness' and for inhibiting 'the capacity to imagine the totality as something
that could be completely different'.[55] To better understand what, according to
Adorno, prevented individuals from conceptualising the new, I respectively discuss i) the sheer power and effectiveness of the propagation of the dominant
interests, ideas and beliefs, a late capitalist phenomenon for which Adorno and
Horkheimer coined the term 'culture industry'; and ii) identity thinking as the
prevailing mode of conceptual language.

'Culture industry', a title of one chapter in Adorno and Horkheimer's *Dialectics of Englightenment*, describes the culture which, in their view, characterises late capitalist society – the culture of mass-produced standardised films,
radio programmes and magazines. For Adorno and Horkheimer, the spread of
commodification from consumption goods into the sphere of culture occurred
only recently and is the most critical characteristic of late capitalist culture. For
the 'uniformity' of this late capitalist culture, Adorno and Horkheimer blame
technology and the embeddedness of its production in the capitalist system.[56]
Various practices halted the development and expression of creative opposi-
tional ideas. The homogeneity of ideas is ensured through 'social machinery'.[57]
Adorno and Horkheimer refer to 'the censors voluntarily maintained by the
film factories' and their 'counterparts in all other departments'.[58] For example,
in the case of the writing and publication of books, they present control and
censorship as absolutely effective:

> The process to which a literary text is subjected, if not in the automatic
> foresight of its producer then through the battery of readers, publishers,
> adapters, and ghost writers inside and outside the editorial office, outdoes
> any censor in its thoroughness. To render their function entirely superflu-
> ous appears, despite all the benevolent reforms, to be the ambition of the
> educational system.[59]

The central flaw of the culture industry lies not so much in the homogeneity of
the ideas, values and beliefs it propagates, but in its conformity with 'the economic system', and moreover in that it forces individuals to participate themselves in this control of their consciousness: 'Everyone must show that they

55   Adorno in Bloch 1977 [1969b], pp. 352–3.
56   Adorno and Horkheimer 1981 [1947], p. 141.
57   Adorno and Horkheimer 1981 [1947], pp. 12–13.
58   Adorno and Horkheimer 1981 [1947], pp. 12–13.
59   Adorno and Horkheimer 1981 [1947], p. 13.

identify wholeheartedly with the power which beats them'.[60] Herbert Marcuse clarifies further this thesis of the interpellation of individuals by the existing system, or, in the words of Adorno and Horkheimer themselves, of 'the cycle' formed between 'manipulation and retroactive need'.[61] In Marcuse's analysis of the capitalist society, *One Dimensional Man*, he posits that the system's control of the consciousness of individuals does not operate through ideas and beliefs alone, but also through the control of their needs or desires.[62] It is not only that the workers believe in the supposed freedoms and inevitabilities of certain social constructions, like the levels of material inequalities, but that they need, want and desire the commodities, and the type of entertainment and social interactions that capitalism provides for them. This means that the capitalist system is itself generative of these needs and desires, which in turn, through their expression and demand to be gratified, reproduce its normative tenets. In *An Essay on Liberation*, Marcuse writes of 'second nature' to describe the internalisation of social pressures and desires by individuals to such an extent that they will malfunction physically if these pressures and desires are not ful-filled.[63] This second nature is, in the view of critical theorists, the most powerful mechanism for conserving the existing normativity and for inhibiting its trans-formation. As Adorno and Horkheimer contend, in the system existing at the time, individuals:

> insist unwaveringly on the ideology by which they are enslaved. The per-nicious love of the common people for the harm done to them outstrips even the cunning of authorities.[64]

7   The Problem with Identity Thinking

In addition to the institutional mechanisms of cultural production and their internalisation by individuals, Adorno perceives the mode of nature of the pre-vailing conceptual thought itself hinders any articulation of a utopian society. That is, the obstacles to utopian thinking lie not only in practices external to, but also in those internal to, the conceptual language. He observes that:

---

60   Adorno and Horkheimer 1981 [1947], pp. 161; 176.
61   Adorno and Horkheimer 1981 [1947], p. 142.
62   Marcuse 1964, p. xv.
63   Marcuse 1969, pp. 10–11.
64   Adorno and Horkheimer 1981 [1947], p. 155.

even the most honourable reformer who recommends renewal in thread-bare language reinforces the existing order he seeks to break by taking over its worn-out categorical apparatus and the pernicious power-philosophy lying behind it.[65]

Under the phrase of the 'worn-out categorical apparatus and the pernicious power-philosophy lying behind it', Adorno subsumes a set of practices and premises associated with that which Adorno elsewhere calls identity thinking. Identity thinking is a term Adorno uses to describe positive or affirmative conceptual language which *identifies* or equates the subject of a sentence with its predicate or the object. I have, however, not yet sufficiently emphasised that for Adorno this form of language is fundamentally counterproductive when it comes to expressing utopian ideas. Adorno denounces identity thinking because it ensures that any attempt to conceptualise a properly different society is doomed: all that can be conceptualised are false utopias, copies of the existing society.

Adorno's opposition to identity thinking is partially derived from Hegel. Hegel rejects the view that formal definitions of concepts or terms in question are an overwhelmingly important philosophical virtue, and in fact he considers them impossible. This rejection is grounded in his idea that the essence of a term – as a timeless, historically invariant meaning – cannot be isolated from its contingent associations, superficial appearances and accidental accretions – meanings that ultimately depend on the existing historical context. For Hegel, the basic unit is not an individual term with a fixed meaning, but rather a larger unit, the argument. A philosophical argument is essentially one in which the meaning of the central terms in question shifts during the course of the discussion; a good argument is one in which the semantic content of the basic concept involved changes in a structured way. Eventually, a definition of the central terms is revealed in the course of the discussion: not as its final result or outcome, but in the course of its process as its pattern, the steps of argumentative progression. The definition of a concept as a process can, however, never be fully captured by a single linguistic formulation. The philosophical argument is what Hegel calls a totality, and although this totality is multifaceted, and formed of different elements, these facets or elements can never be isolated from it without their being transformed into something that they are not while still located within the totality.[66] Although Hegel's view applies

---

65   Adorno and Horkheimer 1981 [1947], p. 14.
66   See Geuss 2004, pp. 123–4.

primarily to philosophical language, and less to the more 'everyday' language employed in other areas of human life, what he says in his *Science of Logic* about 'a rose' nevertheless helpfully illuminates his argument:

> To say 'This rose is red' involves (in virtue of the copula 'is') the coincidence of the subject and predicate. The rose however is a concrete thing, and so not red only: it also has an odour, a specific form, and many other features not implied in the predicate red.[67]

Hegel's point is that by describing a rose as a red object one arbitrarily excludes other senses of what a rose is, and thus does not represent it truthfully. Adorno made a very similar observation with respect to the concept of utopia. To the interviewer's question of 'What is then the content of utopias?' Adorno responded with the following words:

> what is essential about the concept of utopia is that it does not consist of a certain, single selected category that changes itself and from which everything constitutes itself, for example, in that one assumes that the category of happiness alone is the key to utopia.[68]

That is, Adorno opposes not only explications of what could be plausibly thought as significant constituents of a utopian society, such as freedom or happiness. He objects to the very identification of these concepts, or, in fact, any other, as fundamental elements of a utopian society. He refuses to say what utopia *is* because that in itself would limit the utopian potential.

Adorno's rationale of this objection in part corresponds to Hegel's own concerns about identity thinking. Adorno, however, also strengthens this objection with two further considerations he adds to the Hegelian legacy outlined above. One is his diagnosis of the contemporary society, explicated most concisely in his *Minima Moralia* as a society that is profoundly and extensively wrong. He diagnoses the whole society as false, and subsequently each and every value, practice or idea manifested in this society: 'There is no right life in the wrong one'.[69] This means that Adorno preempts what, in Hegel, was a central impediment to identity thinking: namely a lack of criteria at hand to differentiate between what is essential and what is merely part of the immediate circumstances. For Adorno this impediment is of only secondary importance, since

---

67   Hegel 1975, p. 237.
68   Adorno in Bloch 1977 [1969b], pp. 353; 357.
69   Adorno 1980 [1951], p. 43.

society and its conceptual language are tainted in the first place by the currently prevailing irrationality, immorality, falsity, deception, illusion, etc.

The other consideration Adorno adds to Hegel is his own definition of identity thinking. While Adorno might not be saying anything substantially new in this formulation, it clarifies why, in his view, a utopian society cannot be articulated by means of this form of conceptual language. In the *Negative Dialectics*, Adorno draws a contrast between identity thinking and dialectics: whereas dialectics seek to say what something 'is', identity thinking says what something 'comes under, what it exemplifies or represents, and what, accordingly, is not itself'.[70] That is, in Adorno's reading, identity thinking functions on the basis of exemplification or representation, of representing a subject through its predicates. Since, for Adorno, all existing predicates are somehow false, or infected with falseness, then the resulting predicated subject will also be a false one.

For Adorno a *true* utopia simply cannot be envisioned, since all the material that is available for its construction is false, and thus any attempt to construct a positive conception of utopia will ensue in a *false* utopia. This view follows from each of the two strands of argumentation I have advanced above in terms of culture industry and identity thinking. I have, moreover, argued that Adorno's philosophy of history is incongruent with holding a positive notion of utopia in the present, and that any attempt to comprehend Adorno's reluctance towards utopian thinking needs to take this idea of messianic future into account, together with those of identity thinking and culture industry. Marx's own influence, as well as that of the *Bilderverbot*, does not suffice as an explanation for Adorno's reluctance. In this chapter I have not developed a systematic critique of Adorno's arguments of utopian thinking, but have instead simply elucidated some new understandings of these arguments and elaborated on those that the existing scholarship provides. My exposition of the arguments presented here is, however, yet to turn critical – by adopting Bloch's perspective, which I introduce in the final chapter. For Bloch, Adorno's concept of the culture industry was overly totalising, and he did not consider all ideas, desires, concepts, views, wishes and beliefs to be equally corrupted. Some of them embody *true* utopian content. As Francesca Vidal notes, 'Bloch sees the wishes of shop windows as still conditioned by the demands of the culture industry, but in stories and colportage he recognises these wishes as already oriented against the existing offers of happiness, and moreover, in theatre, most clearly by Brecht, as containing the will towards change'.[71] Bloch also has an alternative

70   Adorno 1996 [1966], p. 152.
71   Vidal 2012, p. 198.

conception of the future which allows for it to be substantiated. The exposition of these points is the objective of the final chapter. Prior to that, however, we need to examine and critically evaluate another very persistent view of the relation between Adorno's philosophy and utopian thinking, which, I argue, has contributed most to cutting it off from Critical Theory.

Negative Utopia?

In the face of Adorno's *Utopieverbot*, many scholars would dispute the claim that his philosophy is indeed devoid of utopian images: whereas Adorno might hesitate to describe these images positively, he does express them in a different way, in a different kind of language than the traditional terms of identity. Elizabeth Pritchard asserts that Adorno's philosophy 'does provide a glimpse of that which lies beyond the status quo'; similarly, Gerhard Schweppenhäuser contends that his writing 'points always in a single direction: imagining, through a specific negative insight, the overcoming of the prevailing negativity', while Andreas Bernardi sees it as engendering an 'imaginary refuge of the right life'.[1] These claims evoke what Axel Honneth once referred to as the 'disclosive power' of Adorno's texts, whereby the truth-content that his writing is supposed to disclose is not simply the world as it 'really' is (behind the veil of ideology) but the world that ought to be, that is, the right or the good world, the utopian one.[2] In short, the key claim of this strand of Adorno scholarship is that Adorno does provide a picture of utopia, albeit indirectly. The underlying argument is not an obvious one, for instance, that Adorno was inconsistent, that there is a mismatch between his theorising on what Critical Theory sought to become and his actual practice of it. These scholars are all united in suggesting that Adorno both instituted and respected the prohibition against conceptualising the idea of utopia which I called the *Utopieverbot*. They insist, however, on a more nuanced interpretation of Adorno's *Utopieverbot*: while Adorno did reject utopian thinking in its positive or identity form, he at the same time also replaced it with a new, alternative type of representation. In other words, the hitherto existing interpretation recognises the place of utopian thinking in Adorno's philosophy primarily as its preservation: in Adorno, utopian thinking is supposed to endure, albeit in a different, novel form.

One of Adorno's alternatives to identity utopian thinking is conceived as a residual or remainder of the positive utopia, as an exception to his general commitment to negativity or criticism. Given the very limited examples of this kind of utopian thinking that have been identified in Adorno's overall corpus, it has nevertheless been accorded substantial significance as an aspect of his philosophy. Rahel Jaeggi, for instance, emphasises 'the obvious presence of positive

---

1 Pritchard 2002, pp. 302–3; Schweppenhäuser 2009, p. 20; Bernard 2003, p. 17.
2 Honneth 2000.

images and motifs in *Minima Moralia* as in Adorno's work as a whole'.[3] These positive motifs have been cited again and again in the critical literature as if to prove the utopian dimension of Adorno's thinking. Among others, these utopian images have been identified by Raymond Geuss, who notes that for the critical theorists 'the only course is relentless criticism of the present', since 'any form of affirmation' was for them 'tantamount to complicity'.[4] Despite this attitude, Geuss continues, 'Adorno does occasionally give a glimpse of his view of what a good life in a fully emancipated society would comprise'.[5] In *Minima Moralia* Geuss points to three such glimpses of utopia:

> everyone should have enough to eat;[6]
> To be able to be different without anxiety;[7]
> *Rien faire comme une bête*,[8] lying on the water and looking peacefully
>   at the sky, 'being, nothing else, without further definition and fulfill-
>   ment'[9]

Whereas these allusions to a utopia are constituted of, loosely speaking, affirmative or positive statements, Geuss warns, they are not to be 'read affirmatively' but 'dialectically'.[10] By this he means they are not intended to form the constitutional principles of the new society but 'to *reject* any form of justification of high culture that depends on subjecting people to malnourishment, *Angst*, or forced labour'.[11] Thus, according to this reading, the affirmative character of these utopian images is merely superficial, and is in fact completely in accordance with Adorno's general negativistic approach. However, even if these specific utopian images are not seen as inconsistent with the others Adorno paints in *Minima Moralia*, or in his other texts, they are differentiated from them. That is, this kind of utopian thinking is presented as one dimension of Adorno that can, at least to a certain degree, be distinguished or separated from other, more strictly negative ones – those which constitute the majority of Adorno's writings.

However, these utopian statements do no tell the whole story of the supposed utopian thinking embodied in Adorno's philosophy. Authors such as

---

3   Jaeggi 2005, p. 127.
4   Geuss 2004, p. 135.
5   Geuss 2004, p. 135.
6   Adorno 1980 [1951], p. 176.
7   Adorno 1980 [1951], p. 176.
8   French for 'To do nothing at all like an animal'.
9   Adorno 1980 [1951], p. 177.
10 Geuss 2004, p. 135.
11 Geuss 2004, p. 135.

Pritchard see utopian thinking not merely as a dimension of Adorno's philosophy but as essentially constitutive of it. In this sense, utopian thinking is then not a residual but rather is central to Adorno. More specifically, it appears that Adorno's 'practice of determinate negation' is the aspect of his philosophy that provides the supposed vision of utopia. One can call determinate negation a methodological principle which Adorno appropriated from Hegel, but to do so would be problematic since it suggests the very separation of content and method that Adorno categorically rejected. As such, this principle will be explored further later in this chapter. For now, though, it should suffice to comprehend the act of determinately negating something, say utopia, first, as *negating* it, that is, positing what utopia 'is not', and second, as negating it *determinately*, that is, specifically: not making generalised but instead highly detailed and specific claims on what utopia is not. It is not, however, problematic to postulate determinate negation as Adorno's primary method: apart from his purely theoretical writings such as *Negative Dialectics* or *Aesthetic Theory*, which above all consist of reflections on theory itself (including, in *Negative Dialectics*, on the theory of determinate negation), determinate negation is the method of Adorno's writings; be it in those on music, literature or society more broadly. Drawing on, above all, two of Adorno's own statements, namely that 'utopia lies essentially in the determinate negation' and that 'the power of determinate' is 'the only allowed cipher of the other', this interpretation thus postulates determinate negation itself as a form of utopian thinking.[12] By 'das Andere' (the Other) Adorno means anything that is fundamentally different from the present, and as such also includes the utopian world. Therein this interpretation contends that determinate negation should not be read only as what utopian society 'is not' or what it 'does not comprise', but also as what it 'is' or what it 'comprises'. In short, Adorno supposedly provides us with glimpses of utopia *through*, *in*, or *by* detailed accounts of a non-utopia, negation of utopia, negative utopia. In this vein I call this kind of utopian thinking, identified by scholarship in Adorno's philosophy, 'negative utopian thinking'.

This negative utopian thinking could very plausibly be seen as a weakened version of its identity counterpart. After all, by positing, for example, that a utopian society is designated by the absence of commercialised free time, I merely exclude one of the many possible ways in which a society organises the time of its members. In contrast, by suggesting that in a utopian society individuals would spend at least a part of their days outdoors, I draw up a more specific vision of utopia. It seems more likely that the discrepancy between

---

12   Adorno in Bloch 1977 [1969b], p. 362; Adorno 1996 [1962], p. 341.

my image and the image others create upon reading mine will be smaller in the case of a positive image than in the negative one. Such a suggestion coincides with the distinction Kant draws between an 'infinite' and an 'affirmative' judgement.[13] For Kant, an infinite judgement – 'in a utopia free time is non-commercialised' – does not clarify the concept of free time or say anything contentful about it; it only takes away one possibility out of an infinite number of possibilities, thereby leaving an infinite number of possibilities as to what free time in utopia might consist of, or be like. In contrast, an affirmative judgement – 'in a utopia some free time is spent outdoors' – says something contentful about the concept of free time, by limiting it to one of the infinite possibilities it could take on. The existing interpretation of negative utopian thinking, however, does not adhere to this Kantian distinction, and hence does not conceive negative utopian thinking as an inferior variety relative to the identity thinking one. Adopting Adorno's own view, which he, in turn, adopted from Hegel, that (determinately) negative judgements supply no less content about reality than affirmative ones do, this scholarship sets the two kinds of utopian thinking side by side. In fact, negative utopian thinking is not conceived only as an equal but as a progressive alternative to the positive one.

In general, progress means an improvement from that which has been into that which is. The notion of progress moreover implies a certain mechanism of how this improvement is brought about: the new and the old are bound to each other, the new is not independent of the old but is supposed to be a certain, better reincarnation of the latter. When we talk of a progressive change, we do not think that the old was simply discarded on the whole and the new constructed out of nothing, but instead that only the bad or the false sides of the old were disposed of, while the new was devised from a combination of what was good or right in the old, augmented by something genuinely new. This is especially the case when progress is conceived as a dialectical process: Hegel saw each new phase in history as sublation or overcoming ('Aufhebung') of the old one, thereby explicitly emphasising that the former always contained something of the latter. To suggest that negative utopian thinking is a progressive alternative thus means it has supposedly preserved the valuable features of the earlier kinds of utopian thinking, discarded the bad, and added some new elements. What the new side of negative utopian thinking is is evident – its negativity. The form or the nature in which utopia is given to us is a negative one. What negative utopian thinking supposedly preserves is what we could call the very

---

13   Kant 1997 [1781].

essence of the previous kinds of utopianism, namely the vision, the picture, the image, the idea of utopia, the answer to the question of what utopia is, what it consists of.

The question that arises immediately, and which is the key question addressed in this chapter, is: how does Adorno preserve the image of 'what utopia *is*' in his images of 'what utopia *is not*'? How do non-utopias at the same time contain utopias? Although all the replies that the existing scholarship on Adorno offer are tightly intertwined with the concept of determinate negation, I suggest they can be placed in three distinct groups: first, positive utopia is always already included in the negative utopia in that the former represents the point of departure of the latter; second, positive utopia arises in the *process* of determinate negation itself; and third, positive utopia emerges out of a specific assembly of determinately negative statements, an assembly which Adorno came to call 'a constellation'.

1 Positive Utopia – a Point of Departure for Negative Thinking

The idea that a positive conception of utopia is contained in the portrayals of negative utopia as a point of departure, and as a precondition for the explication of the latter, has been advanced by Rahel Jaeggi, as part of her project of rehabilitating critique as a legitimate tool of Critical Theory. Jaeggi's project, which she set out in full in her habilitation published under the title *Critique of Forms of Life* (2014), can be interpreted as a response to Habermas's proceduralist turn.[14] In this intellectual development, Habermas, in the 1970s, displaced any normative theorising, including critique, with theorising that aims only at defining procedures or rules upon which norms can then later be established. Habermas found normative theorising problematic in that, in the course of it, a critical theorist herself presupposes certain norms without ascertaining why these norms should be respected by other members of the society as well. Even if these norms originate purely in a subject (in this case, a theorist), once incorporated into a theory they suddenly assume objective validity. The fear is that such theorising runs the risk of being paternalistic. Habermas thus maintains that both the questions of a utopian society as well of a non-utopian one ought to be refrained from, since these are both questions based on specific normative principles.[15] Opposing Habermas, Jaeggi insists that questions of

---

14   Jaeggi 2014.
15   See, e.g., Habermas 1985, pp. 344–89.

negative utopia, i.e. of social critique, can be justified, and thereby returns to Adorno's own position – one that Habermas in the first place sought to repudiate. In fact, Jaeggi argues not only that normative theorising can be justified, but that it is unavoidable. Invoking Hegel, Jaeggi contends that normativity is imputed in each aspect of the existing society, from the social relations, institutions, and practices to the attitudes and behaviours of individuals. That means that everything we say, do, know or think always already presupposes certain norms, certain ideas of what the good is, including what the good life is, either implicitly or explicitly.[16] Thus the neutral stance – the one Habermas seemed to have advocated – is in Jaeggi's view simply impossible: one is either for or against the existing society. However, that does not mean that for Jaeggi all kinds of objections to the existing society, that is, all kinds of social critique – in her phrasing, all kinds of 'critique of forms of life' – are equally good. She distinguishes between three different forms of critique: 'external', 'internal' and 'immanent'.[17] Whereas, in her view, the first form, just as with positive utopian thinking, runs the risk of being paternalistic or even violent, the last effectively overcomes this risk.[18]

Jaeggi sees this paradigmatic case of immanent critique in Adorno's *Minima Moralia*, which she discusses in detail in the article '"No Individual Can Resist": *Minima Moralia* as Critique of Forms of Life'.[19] According to Jaeggi, Adorno's immanent critique overcomes the risk of paternalism by criticising the existing social form from within; that is, according to its own standards. Since, as I have explained above, Jaeggi contends that each social form must always embody its own specific norms, these norms can then also be assumed by the critique of that social form. The norms underlying critique are thus not purely subjective, and merely imposed by a critical theorist, but are objective in the sense that they already possess a validity that extends beyond the subject, beyond the critical theorist herself. A function of critique in this case is to ascertain whether these norms are in fact attested to, that is, whether they are actually realised in a social form, as opposed to existing purely in an ideal form.[20] As an illustration of this function Jaeggi cites Adorno's discussion of the bourgeois virtues. In Adorno's view, the virtues of 'independence, perseverance, forethought, circumspection' have, in capitalist society, been preserved merely as ideals – that is, individuals still strive to perform them, but cannot

---

16   Jaeggi 2014, pp. 288–9.
17   Jaeggi 2014, pp. 261–320.
18   Jaeggi 2014, p. 269.
19   Jaeggi 2005.
20   Jaeggi, 2014 pp. 297–8.

actually do so.[21] In Adorno's analysis this is because the economic conditions of these virtues have fallen away.[22] How am I to act independently if I am, in my economic, that is my material existence, always dependent on participating in the labour market, and selling my labour?

But immanent critique does not criticise the existing society simply on the latter's own terms – this form of critique Jaeggi calls internal, and whereas she sees it as non-paternalistic, she contends it runs another kind of risk, that of conservatism.[23] By relying entirely on the established norms, that is, by treating them as absolute and, as such, as fixed standards, internal critique ultimately contributes also to conservation of the existing society. Immanent critique is, however, for Jaeggi, not only non-paternalistic but the opposite of conservative – it is 'transformative'.[24] This is because immanent critique is based not only on the prevailing norms as they *are*, in their existing form, but also on their possible future form, on what they would *become*. In this vein, Jaeggi draws a comparison between the norms of internal critique as static and of imman-ent ones as dynamic. In Adorno's model of immanent critique, one could say that Jaeggi refers to these dynamic norms as an idea of the right society that is constantly renewing itself.[25] This idea is a very compressed expression of an argument that Jaeggi devises in relation to Hegel's dialectical understand-ing of history, whereby the new or the renewed continuously emerge from the contradictions inherent in the old. Another way in which Jaeggi invokes the dynamic character of norms in the case of Adorno's immanent critique is more pertinent to our immediate purposes. This is the notion which she refers to as 'a positive idea of a good universal'.[26] This positive idea of a good univer-sal is not 'a finished picture of the good, right, or successful life'.[27] However, it does contain a notion of 'what utopia is' – even if it is a highly vague one. On Jaeggi's account, this corresponds to 'a way of living together', that is, 'freed from the yoke of necessity and the coldness of instrumental relations, as the unforced unity of differences'.[28] Whereas this other, better social form is one that Adorno's analysis ultimately aims at, Jaeggi claims, it is also what his ana-lysis starts with.[29] That is, Jaeggi appears to argue that a certain affirmative

21   Adorno 1980 [1951], p. 37.
22   Adorno 1980 [1951], p. 37.
23   Jaeggi 2014, pp. 272–4.
24   Jaeggi 2014, pp. 302–4.
25   Jaeggi 2005, p. 136.
26   Jaeggi 2005, p. 131.
27   Jaeggi 2005, p. 133.
28   Jaeggi 2005, p. 132.
29   Jaeggi 2004, p. 131.

conception of utopia is present in Adorno's negativism from the very start, as its precondition or point of departure. In this sense, the positive and the negative are never to be perceived as independent of each other – their relationship is rather one of reciprocity. Thereby Jaeggi supplies one explanation of how the positive can be contained in the negative – the central claim we investigate here.

Jaeggi's argument, that the criticism of the existing society presupposes a certain positive image of utopia, is reminiscent of the scholarship that has identified Adorno's philosophy as 'inverse theology'.[30] The term 'inverse' applies to the object of concern of this theology: instead of the world of the divine, that is, the good, inverse theology investigates its opposite, its inverse, that is, the false and wrong existing world. What instead distinguishes the inverse theology scholarship is the argument it makes in relation to *how* this falseness or wrongness can be identified, that is, to how certain features of the existing society can actually be determined as false: not from within the existing world, but from its outside, and more specifically from the outside as the utopian world. This argument is derived from one specific maxim of Adorno's found within the concluding aphorism of *Minima Moralia*:

> Perspectives must be fashioned that displace and estrange the world, reveal it to be, with its rifts and crevices, as indigent and distorted as it will appear one day in the messianic light.[31]

The term 'messianic light' is here interpreted as 'utopian perspective', and the 'rifts and crevices' as the falseness. The aphorism can thus be read that in order to see the falseness one needs to look at the existing world from the utopian perspective – the view one has when residing in utopia. But since, of course, as also Adorno observes, this perspective is out of our reach – 'it is the utterly impossible' – one needs instead to feign it, and pretend that one is already in the utopia that has not yet materialised.[32] This can conceivably be done by possessing a certain idea of what this utopian society is. What this scholarship thus contends with respect to the place of utopia in Adorno's philosophy is similar to

---

30 See Brittain 2010, pp. 83–113; Pritchard 2002. Adorno himself also uses this term, e.g., in one of his letters to Benjamin in which he refers to his and Benjamin's work as instances of inverse theology (Adorno 1995, pp. 90–1). In addition to 'inverse theology' also the concept of 'negative theology' is sometimes used to describe Adorno's philosophy. See Finlayson 2012.

31 Adorno 1980 [1951], p. 37.

32 Adorno 1980 [1951], p. 37.

Jaeggi's argument, in that a positive conception of utopia is present in Adorno's philosophy as a prerequisite for exercising the critique of the existing society.

This reciprocity between the positive and the negative was also acknowledged by Adorno himself. In *Negative Dialectics*, Adorno notes that greyness could not fill us with despair unless we maintained a concept of a different colour.[33] In other words: whatever despairing assertions we make about the existing social world, they will always presuppose some kind of a conception of how a better one might look. In this sense, Jaeggi's argument could be considered only as a restatement of Adorno's own view. Adorno, however, did not uphold this position on the whole: sometimes he sees the negative conception as strictly preceding the positive one. For instance, in the radio conversation with Bloch, Adorno contends that the negative is possible to know exactly, whereas the same cannot be said for the positive image.[34] Similarly, in his lectures on moral philosophy, Adorno states that we cannot know the absolute good or the absolute norm, and also not what the human, humane and humanity are, but that we can know exactly what the inhumane is.[35] Jaeggi does not concede with Adorno to this complete separation of the negative and the positive, and in this respect her view cannot be seen simply as a restatement of Adorno's own. Furthermore, she describes her position in greater detail than Adorno ever does. In particular, Jaeggi elaborates on the source of the positivity, that is, on how we are in the first place to arrive at a conception of a good life, irrespective of the unrefined or unelaborated nature of this conception.

While Jaeggi recognises the positive and the negative sides to utopian thinking as not existing independently of each other, in that one is always already contained in the other, she does not see them as one another's sole origins. That is, while she recognises the image of utopia as coexisting with the image of the false world, she does not see the latter as the only source of the former. Instead, she sees the positive conception of utopia developing from 'the inner normativity of historical reality itself'.[36] That is, even if Jaeggi insists that Adorno's positive universal does not exist 'in a glass jar' – existing as an already worked out formulation which only needs to become accessible – her argument does assume it as being inherent in reality.[37] Even if in a very weak sense, this argument does appeal to a certain teleological conception of history, and could as

---

33   Adorno 1996 [1966], p. 370.
34   Adorno in Bloch 1977 [1969b], p. 362.
35   Adorno 1996, p. 261.
36   Jaeggi 2004, p. 135. This view is directly disputed by Martin Seel, who argues that Adorno's point of departure are his experiences from childhood. See Seel 2004.
37   Jaeggi 2004, p. 126.

such be challenged further. What is, however, more relevant to our concerns here is that Jaeggi's explanation of where the positive conception of utopia emerges from is not entirely complete.

This becomes clear if we differentiate between two kinds of positive conceptions of utopia, a distinction that Jaeggi herself implicitly draws. One is the positive image as the starting point of critique, a starting point that is also coexistent with the negative image. Jaeggi describes this kind of positive images as a 'preconception' that is anticipated, and moreover as 'positive counter-images' that are 'necessarily indeterminate and vague'.[38] The other kind is the positive image that ensues from, is consequent to, the negative images. This is the positive to which Jaeggi refers as 'the positive' which is 'conveyed only through the views of that which should not be' and similarly, as the one which 'is concretised only via the negative'.[39] The central difference between the two kinds of positivity lies in the degree of their determinateness: the former is a vague, unspecific, general conception of a good society – a preconception rather than a conception; the latter is its specific, that is, its determinate, conception. The same distinction cannot be drawn between the negative images. Whereas it might be the case that in each step of the dialectical process each ensuing negative image is more determinate than the previous one, already the negative image entailed in the very first step is supposed to be determinate as such – a critical theorist is supposed to be able to diagnose the wrongness and falseness of existing society in a very determinate way from the very start. That means that the relationship between the positive and the negative is, in Jaeggi's framework, an asymmetrical one – despite their relation of reciprocity, as she herself acknowledges. Moreover, this means that her explanation does not account fully for the claim that 'what utopia is' is always contained in 'what utopia is not'. Jaeggi clarifies this claim only for the initial step of critique, for what I called a positive preconception of utopia. In Jaeggi's view this positive preconception is universal, which must mean that it is inherent in the historical reality. It could be said that the relationship between this positive *preconception* and the negative is thus 'perfectly' reciprocal: each constitutes and is constituted by the other. The same cannot be said for the positive as a *determinate conception*. This positive determinate conception is only constituted by the negative side. On its own its constitution, vis-à-vis both constitution and 'constituentness' of the positive preconception, is not problematic. The remaining question, however, is the following: how is this constitution of the positive through the negative to func-

---

38   Jaeggi 2004, pp. 133–4.
39   Jaeggi 2004, p. 134. See also Wenzel 1992, p. 358.

tion? Only then might we be able to ascertain the given claim that utopia is indeed contained in the non-utopia.

The answer seems to lie in the practice of determinate negation. This contention, that the more concrete positive conception is constituted through determinate negation, that is, through a disavowal of that which is false or wrong in the existing society, has been most clearly articulated by Elizabeth Pritchard in the following passage:

> Adorno argues that the practice of determinate negation which focuses attention on the precise contours of damaged life, actually does provide a glimpse of that which lies beyond the status quo [...] determinate negation is indicative of the character of the absolute. This negation forms a script of the absolute; it does not actually accomplish the transformation of society from damaged life to reconciliation [...] What Adorno is suggesting is that this script, composed from the ruins of damaged life, contains a code of the absolute.[40]

What needs to be noted in this passage is that determinate negation is bestowed with a certain active or constructive power. Whereas determinate negation might indeed not be able to *realise* a utopian society ('actually accomplish the transformation of society from damaged life to reconciliation'), Pritchard sees it can *form* or *provide* a conception of this society ('negation forms a script of the absolute', 'provide a glimpse of that which lies beyond the status quo'). This claim points to the fact that the kind of positive image of utopia which Pritchard appeals to is not merely that which is always already contained in the world as it exists, but one which arises or ensues from determinately negating this world. It seems as if there was something innate to the very process of determinate negation that would transform or amplify the vague preconception of utopia into a determinate conception of it. But, is there? Does determinate negation in fact enhance the determinate negativity into determinate positivity?

2   Does Determinate Negation Make Sense?

The concept of determinate negation was originally devised by Hegel. Hegel defines determinate negation in opposition to abstract negation, which he

---

40   Pritchard 2002, pp. 302–3.

articulates as the negation of everything: in the course of the negation the object that is negated is completely annihilated, obliterated on the whole. As Michael Rosen puts it, one can think of abstract negation as 'wiping clean of a blackboard'.[41] The act of abstract negation is independent of the content or form, or any other quality of the writings on the blackboard; irrespective of these qualities, abstract negation rubs off what was on the blackboard. The result of abstract negation is what Hegel calls nothingness as well as inde-terminacy, or an indeterminate being. In contrast, by determinate negation Hegel refers to the negation of merely one aspect, or one feature of the neg-ated object. Accordingly, the result of determinate negation is also different to that of abstract negation. Hegel gives the following account of the result of determinate negation:

> the cognition of the logical proposition that the negative is equally posit-ive, or that that which contradicts itself does not dissolve into Zero [Null] but essentially only into the negation of its particular content, or that such a negation is not all negation but the negation of the determinate subject-matter [Sache] which dissolves and is thus determinate negation, so that that from which it results is essentially contained in the result – which actually is a tautology, for otherwise it would be something immediate and not a result.[42]

In this passage Hegel defines determinate negation as 'the negation of the determinate subject-matter', which means, as I have already pointed out above, negation of one particular aspect of the negated object. Further on, by stat-ing that 'that from which it results is essentially contained in the result' Hegel explicates another defining feature of determinate negation – one that is of particular interest to us.

To comprehend what Hegel means by this, it helps to think of the *result* and the *act* of determinate negation as one and the same. To determinately negate an object is to assert that a particular aspect of the object 'is not'. This asser-tion, this *act* of asserting, that the object 'is not', is at the same time also the *result* of determinate negation. In that the assertion that the object 'is not' is the result of determinate negation, this result is, of course, negative. Yet, this is not everything that the result is. Hegel renders that 'the negative is equally pos-itive', implying that the result of determinate negation is not only negative but

---

41   Rosen 1982, p. 32.
42   See Rosen 1982, p. 31.

also positive. In other words, the assertion that a particular aspect of the object 'is not' entails an additional assertion, namely that another particular aspect of the object 'is'. This idea is certainly not intelligible simply in its own terms, which actually is not problematic in itself. The real issue lies in that Hegel does not seem to explain it elsewhere either. As Rosen observes, while 'this thesis about the nature of [determinate negation] – that it leads to a positive result – is fundamental to Hegel's understanding of the nature of his enterprise', Hegel does not really guide us through how he reaches this conclusion.[43] With respect to this conclusion, Rosen further inquires:

> how is it to be established? Does it, perhaps, even need establishment? Hegel had, indeed, claimed that it is 'actually a tautology' that to negate is to produce a negated something, not nothing. Yet very little examination shows the doctrine of determinate negation to be in fact anything but a tautology in the sense of being trivially true.[44]

Here, Rosen highlights very clearly that Hegel makes an unjustified causal link between the two defining characteristics of determinate negation, namely between 'the negation of the determinate subject-matter [Sache] which dissolves and is thus determinate negation' and 'that from which it results is essentially contained in the result' with a conjunctive 'so that'. Rosen moreover shows that for Hegel the causality of this link does not require a justification because he sees this link as a tautology: that the result of determinate negation is at the same time a determinate positive is simply true by itself.

If something is true by itself, then, of course, it does not need to be further explicated. We can, however, challenge Hegel's claim that the identity between the positive and the negative is a tautology and look for possible justification elsewhere than Hegel's own perspective. An established justification is associated with the understanding of Hegel's philosophical system as a teleological one. This justification is also shared by Adorno, who articulated it in his lectures on negative dialectics. In his third lecture Adorno states that 'in Hegel the positivity of dialectic is at the same time its premise (i.e. the subject, the spirit) and its telos, it carries the system'.[45] In one way, Adorno's point here appears especially illuminating regarding the issue I have been trying to grasp, of this apparently perplexing point about the relationship between the positive and the negative. Adorno's simple answer is that Hegel's alleged imbrication of the

---

43   Rosen 1982, p. 31.
44   Rosen 1982, p. 31.
45   Adorno 2003, p. 40.

two presents a premise or a presupposition of his philosophical system: the positive outcome or result of determinate negation is assumed to be there from the very beginning.

Adorno's view of the procedure of determinate negation, however, does not strictly coincide with Hegel's. In the lecture cited above Adorno argues that in contrast to Hegel, his own conception of determinate negation does not possess its own positive aspect.[46] According to Adorno, this absence of positivity results from the suspension of the teleological dimension that Adorno identified in Hegel's dialectics – which he too, alongside his reconfiguration of determinate negation, came to modify. In contrast to Hegel's dialectics, which, according to Adorno, leads to synthesis – a positive result – his own, negative, dialectics brings about what he called 'the non-identical'.[47] Whereas a synthesis amounts to an *identity* between thesis (identity) and anti-thesis (non-identity), Adorno's non-identical amounts to a *non-identity* between the two – a negative result. As I pointed out above, Adorno contends that in the framework of his thought determinate negation is free from not only a synthesis but also from possessing a telos – two concepts which are for Adorno closely intertwined with that of positivity. We might thus expect that Adorno disposes with positivity as such too. This, however, is not the case. Whereas he does indeed contend that determinate negation does not possess its own positive aspect, he nevertheless recognises positivity and locates it as lying in the negative.[48] That is, in Adorno's conception, determinate negation retains a certain positivity, yet it appears as if this positivity is weakened or toned down, robbed of its own self – it does not exist as its 'own aspect' but only in the intertwinement with its more prominent counterpart of negativity.

In that Adorno's notion of positivity is always already contained in the negative, it corresponds only to one of Jaeggi's kinds of positivity, namely that of the positive good universal. However, elsewhere in Adorno's writings we can identify also the other kind of positivity Jaeggi distinguishes, the more concrete positive, the positive that results from the process of determinate negation. Above all I have in mind one particular statement that Adorno makes in *Minima Moralia* – 'the consummate negativity, once squarely faced, explodes into the mirror-image of its opposite'.[49] Here Adorno does hint at some form of positivity that is not merely always already there, but is instead created or pro-

---

46   Adorno 2003, p. 40.
47   Adorno uses this term very frequently in *Negative Dialectics* as well as some of his other works, see, e.g., Adorno 1996 [1966], pp. 125–8.
48   Adorno 2003, p. 40.
49   Adorno 1980 [1951], p. 281.

duced. Adorno suggests that only once reality is articulated fully in its detail is its utopian opposite delineated or created. To be more precise, Adorno does not say it is created but that it *explodes*. The distinction between the two is crucial in that the explosion has an even greater connotation of a transformation, production or creation than emergence does. But where does this transformative or creative power of negation come from? In that this negation is 'consummate'? And can this transformative power even be ascribed to negation?

Precisely this ascription of transformative power to negation is a point which Bloch openly disputed. It is worthwhile to quote Bloch's objection at length:

> In the negative of objective dialectics (sickness, crisis, imminent decline into barbarism) there is doubtless some association of annihilation, thus not only of the Not, as the active motive force, but also of nothingness, as merely effacing negation, which of itself by no means automatically has the negation of its negation within itself. It is consequently an action which, of itself without the intervention of the subjectively active contradiction, leads rather to the development of an In Vain than to the All. Indeed, a subjectively active counter-move against annihilation can be necessary, in order that the latter can be used for annihilation of what is worth annihilating and, by this means, for the opening-up of new life. An automatism of objective dialectics towards the good, with the comforting motto: Through the night to the light, simply does not exist. Rather, only a co-move and – in times of catastrophe – a counter-move of the subjective factor can make negativity in the objective dialectics completely the servant of a possible success. While negativity of itself – as in the Thirty Years' War, the Peloponnesian War, and all complete downfalls whatsoever – bears no fruit historically, that is, the negation of the negation is by no means capable of developing itself from its own objectivity alone.[50]

The key claim Bloch makes in this passage that is of interest to us at this point is that Adorno's idea of the transformative power of negation and its corresponding production of the positive presumes 'an automatism'. He illustrates this automatism through the analogy he draws between the relationship between the positive and the negative, and that between day and night. As long as the Earth circles the sun, the sunlight will always appear following the night. This is not the case with the emergence of utopia. Even if the negative aspects of the existing society are identified – such as 'sickness, crisis, imminent decline into

50   Bloch 1977 [1962], pp. 515–16.

barbarism' – Bloch contends there is simply no equivalent law which would guarantee their transformation into the positive, and moreover into the positive that could be designated as a utopian society.

3   The Emergence of the Positive in Constellations

A third possible reply to the question of how a positive utopia can be preserved in its negative is contained in the notion of constellation. Presumably, Adorno himself first encountered the relevant usages of this word when he read Benjamin's *The Origin of German Tragic Drama* in the late 1920s.[51] However, the word recurs in Adorno's work throughout his career, from his inaugural lecture as 'Privatdozent' in 1931 on 'The Actuality of Philosophy' to the late pieces collected in *Interventions: Nine Critical Models* (1963), in the course of which it obtains its own distinct meaning. Put simply, a constellation is a distinct rhetorical figure that Adorno both advanced theoretically and employed in his writings. In terms of some better known rhetorical figures, constellations resemble allegories, aphorisms or tropes, that is, concise metaphorical expressions of a certain higher meaning relating to reality.[52] In the words of Susan Buck-Morss, constellations constitute a 'method in action', which in turn Max Pensky sees as 'somehow Adorno's most influential and enduring intellectual legacy'.[53] Adorno himself attributed significant weight to constellations. In the inaugural lecture mentioned above he postulated that bringing concepts into constellations amounts to the most important task of philosophy.[54]

That constellations could intimate positive utopias has been hinted at by Jaeggi herself. Although it is not completely clear whether she employs this concept in the specific Adornian sense, she highlights clearly the link between constellations and positive utopias: 'not infrequently the positive content of such negative models lies solely in very specific constellations, in balancing acts between the wrong possibilities which Adorno retraces in a dizzying manner'.[55] A number of other scholars share this view, and have in fact advanced it further. For example, Gerhard Richter has made the argument in terms almost identical

---

51   For a historical evolution of this concept by Adorno, especially in relation to Benjamin's work see Buck-Morss 1977, pp. 96–109.

52   In his book *Marxism and Form* Fredric Jameson dubs Adorno's constellations 'historical tropes.' See Jameson, 1974, pp. 3–59.

53   Buck-Morss 1977, p. 98; Pensky 1997, p. 4.

54   Adorno 1973 [1931], p. 335.

55   Jaeggi 2004, p. 135.

to Jaeggi's. Richter observes that this distinctiveness of Adorno's rhetorical figure – for which instead of a constellation Richter uses a closely related term
of 'thought-image' ('Denkbild') devised originally by Benjamin – lies in their
distinct negativity, 'a negativity that in its relentlessness also activates a sense
of the futurity of the positive'.[56] In other words, Richter seems to concur with
Jaeggi that constellations are not purely negative constructions, portraying the
present solely as ill and wrong, but rather are constructions which alongside the
falseness of the present engender the goodness of the future. Similarly, in his
study of Adorno's constellations, David Kaufmann has argued that this notion
can be best understood as an 'image of a whole that is the truth', and furthermore as 'the outline of Redemption, of differences conjoined without domination'.[57] The meanings of the two central concepts of 'truth' and 'Redemption',
which Kaufmann uses in the senses peculiar to Adorno, both converge with
that of a positive conception of utopia. Kaufmann himself sees 'Utopia' as nothing but the 'political name' for 'redemption.'[58]

What, however, is this rhetorical figure of constellation more specifically?
What does it look like? And, more critically, how could it engender a positive
image of utopia? Given that Adorno regards concepts themselves as an inherently unsuitable vehicle for conveying the content of a utopian society, how
are then constellations supposed to accomplish this task? After all, the building blocks of a constellation are concepts as well. Or, to appropriate a remark
made by Richter, how are constellations supposed 'to say in words that which
cannot be said in words?'[59]

I suggest that constellations can be better understood through their relation to determinate negation. The two methods are in fact not as distinct as
they might initially seem, in that one has to do with logic and the other with
rhetoric. Constellations could in fact be seen as a more complex product of
determinate negation compared to the product of one determinately negated
statement. In one determinately negated statement, one feature or one object
of the existing society is identified as false and thus as non-utopian. A constellation brings together a multiplicity of these statements, thereby simultaneously
criticising multiple aspects of society. Constellations could thus be considered

---

56   Richter 2007, p. 14.
57   Kaufmann 2000, p. 77.
58   Although the terms 'utopia' and 'Redemption' might not be exactly synonymous in Ador-
      no's own writings, the meaning of the concept of utopia I have set out in the beginning
      does substantially overlap with Adorno's usage of 'Redemption'. See, e.g., Adorno's final
      aphorism in Adorno 1980 [1951], p. 281.
59   Richter 2007, p. 13.

to present a specific assembly of disparate, determinately negated statements. As I will elaborate further below, a key for an explanation of how a positive utopia might arise from initially purely negative ones could lie precisely in this step of bringing together several of the latter. This question of *how* a positive utopia might arise at this rhetorical level in fact presupposes another key premise of the concept of the constellation that is shared also by that of determinate negation. This is the premise that what a utopian society comprises has, to a certain extent, already been determined, that its actual content, its apparent features and underlying norms are somehow, to some extent, inherent in the world as it exists now. This premise does not at all correspond to universalism in its strongest sense, namely that there is one correct form of how one should live one's life. In a way, Adorno's conception of utopia could be understood as the exact opposite of this view. As Adorno phrased it in one of what I have called his residual positive utopian images, he emphasised the value of the difference among individuals, positing a desirable society as one in which 'one can be different without fear'.[60] However, in the face of this pluralist conception of utopia, Adorno does admit to the existence of certain universally valid norms. These norms are entailed in what Jaeggi, in the context of determinate negation, refers to as the positive good universal, and what Benjamin, in the context of constellations, calls 'truth'.[61]

The nature of Benjamin's concept of truth is completely unrelated to the one which we are likely to be more familiar with, one that sees truth as a correct correspondence between the objects of material reality and empirical facts. For this conception of truth, according to which a certain idea or a theory counts as true depends on whether it accords with our experiences of reality, Benjamin used the term 'scientific knowledge' ('Wissenschaft').[62] To this concept of knowledge Benjamin contrasted that of truth, which instead of being concerned with correspondence is concerned with the *meaning* of reality. Eli Friedlander has framed Benjamin's distinction between the two most succinctly: 'For Benjamin, knowledge is the correctness of our way of looking at the world, but truth is a unity of being recognized in reality *itself*'.[63] This formulation of the notion of truth might indeed resemble Plato's concept of the Idea. The Platonic Ideas, however, presuppose a dualism which Benjamin rejected, namely between, on the one hand, the realm of language, concepts, meaning, truth, ideas and, on the other hand, the realm of matter, material objects of

60   Adorno 1980 [1951], p. 176.
61   Benjamin 1977 [1928], pp. 207–37.
62   Benjamin 1977 [1928], pp. 207–37.
63   Friedlander 2012, p. 12.

reality. For Benjamin, truth too is primarily an aspect of material reality – it is inherent in the objects which are the building blocks constituting this realm of the reality. This, however, does not mean that Benjamin saw truth as unrelated to ideas, language and concepts: even if truth resides in matter, it only becomes accessible once we recover it from the medium of matter into that of concepts.[64]

Adorno appropriated Benjamin's concept of truth, but, under the influence of a Marxist worldview, Adorno was less concerned with the truth of material reality in its most general sense, that is, of any material object as such, but more so with that of the social or political world. That is, the objects of material reality Adorno was concerned with above all were the social ones, such as social relations or social institutions. In this sense Adorno recognised the existence of what could be called a 'social truth'. That this social truth in fact overlaps with Jaeggi's notion of the positive good universal is evident in David Kaufmann's discussion of it. Kaufmann points out that, for Adorno, the 'truth of an object' was not limited to 'what it has become' but also 'to what it should be'.[65] Social truth is thus not only what a specific society has become, but also what it should be, that is, it corresponds to a set of universally valid principles defining certain aspects of a good, utopian society.

Adorno's thinking furthermore accords with Benjamin's contention that such a truth could in principle be expressed by the means of conceptual language, but not by one in a positive or identity form. Benjamin regarded translation, quotation and naming as the conceptual practices which could convey truth. For example, naming – giving names to objects – accomplishes this because a name, for Benjamin, as opposed to a concept, does not abstract from the object it refers to – it does not emphasise certain characteristic of an object at the expense of others. A name, in Benjamin's view, captures all of one object's particularities, and also its wholeness – the being as such – its truth. Naming, however, has also an evident defect – it lacks a cognitive function. This has been noted not only by Benjamin but also explicitly by Adorno. Referring to positive thinking he noted that:

> How to think otherwise than [through identity thinking] has its distant and hazy archetype in the names, which do not categorically spin over the thing, admittedly at the price of their cognitive function.[66]

---

64   Friedlander 2012, p. 16.
65   Kaufmann 2000, p. 73.
66   Adorno 1996 [1966], p. 61.

By this Adorno means that naming cannot realistically be employed as a means of communication, since 'talking in names' would correspond to each of us speaking our own individual language, thus failing to understand each other on the whole. Thus, for Benjamin, expressing truth is what naming can only wish, or hope for, and not actually accomplish. Other conceptual practices, such as translation or quotation, must instead take over this function. In Adorno's case, this task of expressing truth has been passed onto the construction of constellations. Adorno's view is reflected in the already mentioned remark in which Adorno defines constellations as the objective of philosophy:

> philosophy has to bring its elements, which it receives from sciences, into changing constellations, or, to say it with less astrological and scientific-ally more current expression, into changing trial combinations, until they fall into a figure which can be read as an answer, while the question disappears.[67]

In this passage Adorno does indeed not call truth by its name. However, its constituting phrase – 'the figure that can be read as an answer, while the question disappears' – can be construed as a cipher of truth. Adorno posits that an answer is what can be read, that is, what can be gathered or inferred from constellations. That this answer does not simply present a reply to a pre-formulated question, but instead to something more general, Adorno indicates by stating that its recognition has a certain consequence – the disappearance of the question. This means that the answer annihilates or overcomes the originally posed question, thereby conveying a certain content which reaches beyond the answer which this question has sought, something contained in the reality beyond its existing form. It does seem that Adorno in general refrained from calling truth by its name, at least in the context of his deliberations on constellations. Another of his remarks is similarly concealing of what Adorno regarded as that which constellations are meant to express:

> Only concepts can fulfill what the concept hinders [...] The determinate failure of all concepts necessitates the citation of others; therein originate those constellations, into which alone something of the hope of the Name has passed.[68]

---

67   Adorno 1973 [1931], p. 335.
68   Adorno 1996 [1966], p. 62.

Instead of using a determinate form of the noun indicating what concepts (in the plural) can accomplish, which is at the same time what a concept (in the singular) prevents, Adorno uses the indeterminate form of 'what'. This practice he repeats often, also in the following claim: 'Constellations alone represent from the outside that what the concept has cut away from the inside'.[69] Again, in this sentence Adorno does not specify what it is that the concept has cut away from the inside and leaves the reader with the indeterminate 'what'. Returning to the previous quotations, we are, however, given another cue that this indeterminate 'what' could stand for truth. The cue lies in the very last part of the sentence: something that is passed over from the hope of the name. As I have explained above, although naming cannot in practice express truth, this function of expressing truth is what defines it most befittingly, even if only in its potential and not as it actually exists. This potential of naming, or, in Adorno's words, what the name hopes for, has, however, been passed onto other conceptual practices, including in this case onto the construction of constellations.

As I have shown, the notion of constellation, just as that of determinate negation, presupposes the existence of a certain 'universal' delimiting reality as it ought to be, that is, some norms that are supposed to remain valid irrespective of the specific form this reality takes at any particular point of time. In the context of social reality specifically, this universal corresponds to a set of principles affirming what a society ought to become, in other words, what a utopian society is – its positive image. However, in sharing this premise, determinate negation and constellations are set apart by one significant difference. The act of articulation of this positive good universal, that of recovering it from material reality, is much more prominent in the case of constellations. Whereas determinate negation too is bound to concepts – it is, after all, a method of theory and as such must necessarily proceed via concepts – it does not appear that the conceptualisation it entails is by itself somehow productive. This is different in the case of constellations. Therein the act of fabricating them, that is, of assembling concepts in a specific structure or configuration, is considered as essential to recuperating the positive universal from its materiality. Adorno attests to this idea in a remark quoted above: in citing concepts alongside each other, a constellations arises. That is, it is only in the very undertaking of organising concepts into a specific figure, image, form or structure that a constellation emerges and together with it the positive universal. What this means is that the figure into which concepts (or more precisely, into which determin-

---

69   Adorno 1996 [1966], p. 164.

ately negated statements) are assembled is precisely that which might allow negative utopias to be developed into a positive one. Here also the initial reference to constellations as *rhetorical* figures becomes clearer: that which this conceptual practice is supposed to convey is not limited strictly to the content of its building blocks, of the determinately negated statements, but to the specificity of the *manner* in which these building blocks are employed or manipulated. Just as when looking into the night sky, we are likely to spot not only individual stars, but also 'Orion' or the 'Little Bear' (two better known astronomical constellations), we are, by reading Adorno's *Minima Moralia*, supposed to comprehend not only the individual wrongs and ills of the existing society, but also the whole of the good and the right. But does this positive image of utopia in fact emerge in constellations to its readers? Is the positivity sufficiently distinct and resolute to shine through the underlying negativity?

4   Something Is Missing

As I have illustrated above, many of Adorno's commentators endeavour to interpret his decisive insistence on negativity not as pure negativity but also as positivity; not as negativity that comes to a halt with the acts of denial, criticism and rejection of the wrongness of the existing social world but as negativity that reaches beyond the negative as such, into the spheres of the positive, the spheres of affirmation and avowal of the rightness of an alternative social world. However, paralleling this tendency to emphasise the existence of positivity in Adorno's thought is a certain awareness that this positivity does not quite compensate for the positive utopian thinking Adorno aimed to supersede in the first place. Does the image of the right society really materialise from an image of the wrong society? Adorno's scholars have thought of creative ways as to how Adorno's thought might be imbued with alternative kinds of positivity, but perhaps we should, nevertheless, question whether these alternative interpretations do deserve to be perceived as positivity.

Among others, Adorno's contemporary and friend Thomas Mann could not discern from *Minima Moralia* Adorno's conception of a better society. In a letter he wrote to Adorno in October 1952 recounting his opinion of the book published in a previous year, Mann craves for something positive in Adorno's constellations:

> If there were only a positive word from you, my revered one, that would permit as much as a glimpse of the true society to be postulated! Your

reflections from damaged life too were lacking in this, and only in this. What is, what would be, the right thing?[70]

Whereas on the one hand Mann concurs with the commonplace reading of Adorno in that he sees his writings as lacking 'a positive word', on the other hand, he also opposes it. In contrast to the efforts of some of Adorno's later commentators Mann finds that Adorno's constellations do not warrant any insight into his conception of a utopian society. Mann contends that Adorno's reflections from damaged life don't permit even a glimpse of a true society. Mann is not simply making the obvious claim that *Minima Moralia* does not amount to a detailed and expansive exposition of a utopian society in any pro-grammatic form. This view is incontestable. Mann is making a more nuanced claim that *Minima Moralia* contains no explication of a utopian society, of any form or kind: that this text does not provide us even a slightest insight into such a society.

Even if we accept that positive images of a utopian society do underlie and/or coexist with the negative ones of the existing society, it is undeniable that the former are buried deep down beneath the latter and thus are hardly accessible to the reader, if at all. The positive images are secondary to Adorno's text, whereas the negative ones constitute its primary layer. The most common account of *Minima Moralia* represents it as an assembly of critical and detailed reflections on certain wrong beliefs, habits, values, qualities and practices that in Adorno's view characterise the society of his time. In one of the many stud-ies of this text, Andreas Bernard describes it as 'Adorno's attempt to spell out the alienation of the individual into its minutest ramifications in everyday life and to think the decline into barbarism from the invention of doorknobs, gift articles, and room service'.[71] 'Genuineness', is for example one of these every-day ramifications.[72] Adorno condemns this moral trait to be an illusion in the existing bourgeois society: the impulses which we believe are genuine are in fact not, since, as Adorno sees it, they always contain 'an element of imitation, play, wanting to be different'.[73] Each of the in total 153 aphorisms articulates a concrete manifestation of what Marx, as well as his later followers, such as Lukács, diagnosed as the main ills of the capitalist society – that is, the phe-nomena of alienation, commodification, fetishisation, exploitation, reification and others. The first aphorism shows how specialisation and division of labour,

---

70   Mann 2002, p. 122.
71   Bernard 2003, p. 8.
72   Adorno 1980 [1951], p. 171.
73   Adorno 1980 [1951], p. 172.

the practices introduced by the Industrial Revolution initially in the production of material goods, have now also penetrated the domain of knowledge production: 'The occupation with things of mind has by now itself become "practical", a business with strict division of labour, departments and restricted entry'.[74] The second aphorism laments a disintegration of social relations, specifically those within a nuclear family. Within this sphere the estrangement of an individual from their community has, in Adorno's view, reached the extreme of a complete disintegration of a family.[75] The third aphorism attests to the instrumentalisation and marketisation of the activities people engage in during their 'free' time, time outside their jobs. Adorno argues that in the modern society all activities are instrumentalised, that is, are in need of a goal or purpose: 'Today it is seen as arrogant, alien and improper to engage in private activity without any evident ulterior motive'; and moreover, that these activities are now being exchanged on the market, that is, bought and sold, produced and consumed: 'the entire private domain is being engulfed by a mysterious activity that bears all the feature of commercial life without there being actually any business to transact'.[76] The fourth aphorism corroborates the absence of any authentic emotions, either of affection or dislike, and so does the fifth. Adorno presents the modern society as profoundly damaged, deeply, at its core, though these damages and wrongs are often disguised – on the outside they appear as their opposites, as the good and the right. The rightness of the existing society is thus for Adorno always only a 'pseudo' rightness. *Minima Moralia* contains no single mention of a 'properly' good or right habit, aspect, belief or practice existent in the modern society. This uncompromisingly negative attitude towards the object of Adorno's study is augmented stylistically by the dark and sarcastic tone of the language, reflected in the ubiquity of unappealing verbs and adjectives and lamenting metaphors. Already in the very first paragraph, the paragraph which ends in one of the better known, utterly cynical decrees, that 'there is life no longer', the reader is overwhelmed by this negativity implied by the choice of language.[77] Today's 'passions' and 'individuals' Adorno respectively compares to 'cheap jewellery' and 'components of machines'.[78] The alleged positivity of this text is submerged even more by the density of diverse, often seemingly unrelated motives. In the aphorisms, which on average scarcely amount to more than a page, such as for example the one entitled 'Always speak of it, never

---

74   Adorno 1980 [1951], p. 21.
75   Adorno 1980 [1951], p. 23.
76   Adorno 1980 [1951], pp. 22–3.
77   Adorno 1980 [1951], p. 4.
78   Adorno 1980 [1951], p. 13.

think of it', Adorno deplores mass culture, psychoanalysis, identity thinking, standardisation of individual lifestyles, the loss of the 'self', as well as positivism and the Enlightenment's belief in reason.[79] Amidst this richness of negative motives, the three aforementioned explicitly positive references to a good society easily escape the reader, and furthermore, rather than (as the defenders of Adorno's utopianism contest) 'activating the positive' through the mechanism of constellations, they also work directly against it.

A more adequate way of framing how a positive utopia is entailed in Adorno's writings in terms of the existence of a *possibility* of a utopian society. Here I take a cue from one of Adorno's own remarks, namely that 'there is no longer beauty or consolation except in the gaze falling on horror, withstanding it, and in unalleviated consciousness of negativity holding fast to the possibility of what is better'.[80] Assuming that Adorno's writings really do reveal the existing world as it truly is, and that this revelation depends on adopting a utopian standpoint, then determinate negation or constellations offer a way of thinking how the existence a utopia as a possibility might be affirmed. However, the affirmation of the mere possibility should be distinguished from positing the content of this possibility. Adorno's negative utopia does not say anything *about* the utopia.

This, however, has not been a view so far embraced by the scholarship, which has basically equated Adorno's negative utopianism with a positive one, albeit cured of the issues which positive thinking generates. By drawing this identity between positive and negative utopian thinking, more weight has been placed on what there is (left) of utopia in its negative form, as opposed to what is lost, or more precisely what dimensions, functions, parts and effects of utopian thinking have been lost in its reconfiguration by Adorno. That something has indeed been lost in this reconfiguration – from envisioning a utopia in an open and explicit way to a more concealed and complex one – and moreover that this something is valuable, was acknowledged by Adorno himself: he told Bloch in the already referred to radio conversation that something terrible has occurred in this reconfiguration.[81] That what has been lost is indeed desirable is visible even more clearly in how Mann framed his remark about the absence of positive images of the good society in *Minima Moralia*. Mann did not make this remark in a neutral manner, simply stating that these images are lacking. Instead, in exclaiming to Adorno, 'if only your texts included a positive word

---

79   Adorno 1980 [1951], pp. 71–2.
80   Adorno 1980 [1951], p. 26.
81   Adorno in Bloch 1977 [1969b], p. 363.

[...] What is, what would be the right?',[82] Mann is longing, wishing and craving for these images. As such, even the efforts of those scholars of Adorno to recover in his writing a positive notion of a utopia testify to the value and desirability of positivity.

For his part, Adorno only hints at what this valuable something might be. He implicitly acknowledges that an explicit positive explication of a utopian society is valuable in that it reinforces utopian consciousness and thereby also the will for things, for the world, to be different.[83] In what way, however, are these kinds of utopian images supposed to reinforce the utopian consciousness? An even more elemental question concerns the utopian consciousness itself – what does Adorno mean by it? And how it is related to the will to live in a different society?

---

82   Mann 2002, p. 122.
83   Adorno in Bloch 1977 [1969b], p. 363.

CHAPTER 4

Bloch's Rejection of the *Utopieverbot*

1   Bloch's Life and Times

Ernst Bloch (1885–1977), a Marxist philosopher of hope, utopia and the future, in many respects presents an anomaly among critical theorists.[1] A contemporary of Adorno and other members of the Institute for Social Research in Frankfurt, his work is non-contemporaneous, substantially removed from the kind of thinking and writing involved not only at the Institute but more broadly in his times. Born into a family of assimilated, working-class Jews, Bloch's interest for intellectual matters dominated his life from an early age onwards – from as early as his teenage years, Bloch spent considerable amounts of time reflecting on abstract philosophical issues and discussing these in the correspondence he had with some of the major contemporary thinkers in Germany, Ernst Mach, Theodor Lipps, Eduard von Hartmann, among others. Many of his most important ideas were formulated in this early formative period between 1902 and 1918, the year in which he published his first manuscript, *The Spirit of Utopia*. His career as an academic philosopher followed a different track, however. He only obtained his first academic post, a professorship at the University of Leipzig, at the age of 64. Bloch and his wife Karola settled in Leipzig in 1949, upon their return from exile, the last nine years of which they spent in the United States. There Bloch led an isolated life, never learning English, and maintaining barely any contact with other expatriated critical theorists. By 1950s Bloch was an established Marxian theorist in East Germany. His own variety of Marxism, however, was then seen as (and still remains) highly idiosyncratic. What marks it off from those advanced by other critical theorists is its style, its uncommon intellectual heritage – chiliasm, mysticism, gnosticism, German Expressionism and Kabbalistic Romanticism, to mention a few of his subjectivist and idealist influences – and its explicit dealing with ontological questions of being, becoming and existence. Throughout his life Bloch worked on developing a new, processual type of ontology, which he formulated with the help of many mind-boggling neologisms. Although his ontology is implicit in all his writings, it only received its most complete, systematic explication in his final

---

1   This section draws on Hudson 1982, pp. 1–21. For a more extended account of Bloch biography see Münster 2012, and Zudeick 1987.

manuscript, *Experimentum Mundi*. This work was published in 1975 in West Germany, where Bloch spent roughly the last two decades of his life, after the East German regime reached its final verdict on Bloch's philosophical, as well as political, outlooks – in short, that he was too heretical. He was consequently granted political asylum by West Germany in 1961. Bloch, however, continued to believe in socialist principles and supported other socialist-inspired movements, including the 1968 student protests. Neither did his disillusionment with the Soviet experiment lead to a reverse in his philosophical outlook. As he explained in his inaugural lecture on being appointed professor in Tübingen, disappointment is inherent in hope.

Bloch introduced many new concepts and ideas into the world of Critical Theory, and philosophy more broadly. The crucial ones are those that relate to utopia, educated hope, matter, upright gait, and pre-appearance of objectively-real possibilities. Bloch also revised some of the traditional dualisms, including those of subjectivity and objectivity, and religion and atheism. Underlying all these reconceptualisations, inventions and revisions, however, is his term 'Not-Yet'. In this and the subsequent chapter I attempt to provide an intelligible if not comprehensive overview Bloch's philosophy. The focus, however, remains the ends of utopian thinking in Critical Theory, this time, of course, from a Blochian perspective.

2   Utopia as the 'Not-Yet'

Bloch has a very broad conception of utopia and utopian thinking. In contrast to the sense I examine in this book, as a discursive practice confined to philosophy with a commitment to radical social change, Bloch's initial contention about utopian thinking is that it permeates almost every human engagement: most of what we say, do or make is to be interpreted also as an expression of a utopia. Thereby Bloch augments the definition of utopian thinking to an even greater extent than his fellow critical theorists. Indeed, Adorno, as well as Horkheimer and Marcuse, partially shared Bloch's understanding of utopian thinking as ideas that reach beyond their individual articulation, into the social or collective consciousness. As Lucien Hölscher observes more generally in relation to post-First World War Western European thought, the concern with utopian thinking shifted from an individual literary work or project of social reform to the state of collective consciousness which had generated them.[2]

2   Hölscher 1996, p. 48.

Besides Bloch, it was Karl Mannheim who, in his juxtaposition of utopia to ideology, contributed to this more general refocusing of utopian thinking as 'utopian consciousness'.[3] In light of this shift, Adorno's concern with utopian thinking remains rather restricted. In his view it was above all the great works of art that effectively apprehended and seized this utopian consciousness. Bloch was by comparison much more generous in his appraisal of the utopian element in human practices. For Bloch, the question of which human practices most adequately capture the utopian element was secondary to his contention that utopian element was always already inherent in these practices.

Bloch's claim about the ubiquity of utopian thinking is not simply an a priori one, but is at least in part founded empirically. His three-volume magnum opus, *Principle of Hope* (1954, 1955, 1959), which Bloch wrote in the course of his exile in the United States between 1938 and 1949, attempts to establish this claim about the ubiquity of utopian thinking as a historical fact. Francesca Vidal sees *The Principle of Hope* not as a list of images of hope, but as a working out of a proof that it is innate to humans always to exceed the given.[4] In particular, the last three of the five parts of this thousand-page-plus manuscript can be read as a documentation of the presence of utopian thinking in human history. Therein Bloch posits and examines the claim that cultural artefacts such as fairytales, films, everyday thinking, sea voyages of medieval Irish monks, folk songs and dances, alchemists' attempts to synthesise gold, theatre performances, myths, travellers' tales, paintings, architectural plans, and furthermore all the fields of religion, medicine and technology are manifestations of utopian thinking. Bloch observes that for a long time utopian thinking was recognised exclusively in the form of social utopias, among which he counts the classics of literary utopias such as More's *Utopia*, Campanella's *City of the Sun*, and Bacon's *New Atlantis*, but that these were historically preceded by fairy tales, like the *Arabian Nights*, which, Bloch suggests, can be read as 'a compendium of innovations'.[5] The oldest form of utopian thinking, however, Bloch locates in religion. For Bloch, ideas propagated by religious movements are not merely the means by which the ruling class managed to keep other classes down, but are ways in which these oppressed classes express their utopian longings. Although Bloch certainly advances and revises this understanding of religion as a positive tendency, he claims that its roots lie in Marx's own thought: Bloch is eager to point out that in a well-known passage from Marx's introduction of his *Critique of Hegel's Philosophy of Right*, Marx designates religion not only as 'the *opium* of

---

3 Mannheim 1952, pp. 169–225.
4 Vidal 2012, p. 198.
5 Bloch 1977 [1969b], pp. 352–4.

the people' but also as 'the *expression* of real suffering and a *protest* against real suffering'.[6] A significant part of Bloch's corpus, besides the few chapters in *The Principle of Hope*, are dedicated to further analysis of how religious ideas can be understood as revolutionary material, not least the two books Bloch dedicates to exactly this topic, namely *Thomas Münzer* (1921) and *Atheism and Christianity* (1968).

In more general terms we could say that Bloch considers the wishes, dreams and ideas produced by our imaginations as utopian thinking. On this point Bloch's view conflicts with that of Marx. In the first chapter I suggested that Marx adheres to a dichotomous distinction between rational and imaginary knowledge, which roughly corresponds to the realms of the objective and the subjective. In fact, the ideas that Marx held to be produced by the cognitive faculty of imagination could not, in his view, in any way be considered as knowledge, but instead are to be understood as wishful images, conceptual material that is wholly irrelevant to objective reality. To these products of the imagination, Marx and Engels juxtapose their own theories of communism, which are supposedly scientific and objectively valid. Bloch almost completely annihilates this dichotomous relation between wishing and knowing. For while Bloch too ascribes a superior value to Marx's writings, one of the reasons he does so lies precisely in his view of Marx's thought as effectively fusing the subjectively desirable ('subjektiv Wünschbare') with the objectively inevitable ('objektiv Unvermeidbare').[7] Bloch exalts the *Manifesto* as the epitome of writing that possesses qualities of both realms, specifically a passage in which Marx and Engels declare that the decisive, pre-revolutionary moments are characterised also by the joining of one particular section of the ruling class, the 'intelligentsia' to the revolutionary class. In Bloch's view this passage exemplifies:

> the *collaboration* of feeling, conscience, and above all knowledge, in order to present a socialist consciousness in opposition to one's own past social being, with the significant and contrasting result that one's consciousness can no longer be permitted to correspond to the social nature one had possessed for so long, so that then gradually the state arises, as described by the *Communist Manifesto*.[8]

---

6   Marx 1981 [1844], p. 378. Bloch quotes Marx in his *Atheism in Christianity*. See Bloch 1977 [1968], p. 91.

7   Bloch 1977 [1954/55/50], p. 1604.

8   Bloch 1977 [1954/55/50], p. 1604.

To return to Bloch's conception of utopian thinking: dreams of a better life are what in his view bind together various utterances, and spiritual and somatic acts as forms of utopian thinking. This does not mean that Bloch denies anything other than utopian meanings and functions to these human practices, but only that this utopian function, which Bloch refers to as a cultural surplus ('kultureller Überschuß') presents a very significant one.[9] In the *Tübingen Introduction to Philosophy* (1963), which presents Bloch's attempt to systematise his philosophical framework, cultural surplus is:

> something that moves above and beyond the ideology of a particular age. Only this 'cultural surplus' persists through ages, once the basis and ideology of an epoch have decayed; and there remains as the substratum that will bear fruit and be a heritage for other times. This substrate is of utopian Nature.[10]

In this passage Bloch speaks of cultural surplus in relation to the two traditional Marxian categories of (economic) basis and ideology, or, more generally, the superstructure. For Marx, a certain society can be understood adequately in terms of these two categories. Adorno retains them, although revises their relation to each other, by giving more prominence to the superstructure. For Bloch, however, these need to be complemented by the third category of cultural surplus. Cultural surplus amounts to those social features or practices that are captured neither by the concepts of economic basis or ideology. What Bloch furthermore points out is that, unlike economic basis or ideology, which over time decay, cultural surplus persists, that is, remains unchanged. In this sense, as something that remains constant, and thus common to various different societies, this surplus is posited as somehow universal, fundamental or essential to humanity itself.

What immediately arises is a massive common sense reproach. How can this fundamentality or essentiality hold for surplus itself? Is not a surplus defined by its superfluity, its non-essentiality, as that which is superfluous, in excess of an essence? This common understanding of the concepts of surplus and essence are, however, not applicable to Bloch's philosophy. In this case, one is not to think of essence as something that *really* is there, as completed and developed, full and fixed, but rather as something that is not yet fully worked out.

In a review of an earlier book by Bloch, *Traces* (1930), Adorno criticises precisely this essential dimension to Bloch's utopian thinking, arguing that it is

9   Bloch 1977 [1954/55/50], p. 170.
10   Bloch 1977 [1963/64], p. 101.

too encompassing, too general, and thus bereft of any use or meaning. Roughly speaking, 'trace' ('Spur') is Bloch's word for indications or manifestations of the cultural surplus, as well our experiences in which we become aware of something utopian. From a philosophical point of view, Adorno considered this concept to be effectively useless:

> For just as there is nothing between heaven and earth that cannot be taken over by the psychoanalysts and given a sexual interpretation, so too there is nothing which cannot be regarded as a Blochian trace, and this indiscriminate use of everything comes close to meaning nothing.[11]

Adorno's indictment, however, conceals a very important sense of Bloch's concept of utopia and, correspondingly, of Bloch's conception of utopian thinking. As Adorno himself was well aware, Bloch revises the concept of utopia as an ontological category, a category he calls the 'Not-Yet' ('das Noch-Nicht'). Cat Moir highlights this central operator of Bloch's as 'a drive or tendency within the fabric of reality itself', and furthermore as 'a tendency' which aims 'towards the achievement of ultimate perfection'.[12] For Bloch, reality as such is utopian in the sense of being literally not yet 'there'. If utopia as this Not-Yet is constitutive of our reality at the ontological, most fundamental level, it is then by no means surprising that Bloch sees it manifested in all human practices.

Bloch's insistence on the ubiquitous presence of utopian thinking across a diverse set of human practices does not, however, preclude a conception of utopian thinking specifically as a philosophical practice, that is the activity of utopian thinking in which philosophers, more precisely Marxist philosophers or critical theorists, are to engage. In fact, the core of Bloch's interest lies in Marxist philosophy, and it is clear that one of Bloch's ultimate goals was to revise it by enriching and strengthening its utopian current. This implies that Bloch must have been interested in what utopian thinking as a philosophical practice could look like. To see what Bloch's idea of this might have been, I look first, as I have done with Adorno and Marx, at his own pursuits in imagining a utopian society.[13] Subsequent to Bloch's practice of utopian thinking, I then turn to his theoretical reflections in this pursuit.[14]

---

11   Adorno 1996 [1960], p. 244.
12   Moir 2018.
13   Here I apply an already defined notion of utopian practice to Bloch's philosophy. This approach could be considered problematic, as it is likely to significantly narrow down the utopian practices that could be identified in Bloch's philosophy in the first place.
14   Here I sharply distinguish between theory and practice of utopian thinking, which might

3   The Warm and Cold Streams of Marxism

Given the reputation of Bloch as both a Marxist and an advocate of utopian thinking, his readers might expect to find in his writings an advance on Marx's vision of the communist society, that is, a more developed or a more complete specification of its structure and function. What Bloch called Marxism presented the core of his interests. Like many of his contemporaries with similar political views, Bloch considered that Marxism needed to regain its progress-facilitating momentum. In the decade before the First World War, Georges Sorel construed the problem of orthodox Marxism in terms of its insufficient emphasis on the redemptive, captivating and irrational forces, as opposed to the scientific and objective ones. Famously, the concept of myth was the one through which Sorel posited his solution for a more effective Marxism.[15] Similarly to Sorel, Bloch highlighted the lack of utopian thinking as the key flaw of Marxism that needs to be attended to. Whereas his very first philosophical work, *The Spirit of Utopia*, which was first published in 1918, frames utopia as the central concept, it was his later writings which integrated it with Marxist theory. Like Benjamin, Bloch in his youth was not yet familiar with the works of Marx.[16] In the 1920s Bloch begins to investigate Marxism itself, adopting its terminology and point of view. In *The Heritage of Our Times* (1935), a book which, *prima facie*, reads as a contemporary analysis of the rise of National Socialism, Bloch asserts his Marxist perspective: in its preface Bloch notes that 'the tenor of this pages, the position from which things are examined, is specifically Marxist'.[17] In this explicit embrace of the Marxist perspective, he is, however, at the same time critical of it. In the same preface Bloch identifies 'a particular Marxist problem'.[18] He contends that Marxism has overlooked 'an element of an older, romantic contradiction to capitalism, which misses things in present-day life and longs for something vaguely different', a utopian element to which Bloch here refers as 'Irratio', and which overlaps significantly with his later concept of cultural surplus.[19] Instead of cordoning off this surplus, Bloch suggests, Marx-

---

seem unjustified given that the context in consideration is Critical Theory, an intellectual tradition which is distinctively defined by the softening of this dualism. This, however, does not mean that all theory is equally practical and all practice equally theoretical. The writings by critical theorists can still be differentiated as being more theoretical or more practical.

15   Sorel 1999 [1908].
16   Hudson 1982, p. 7.
17   Bloch 1977 [1935], p. 15.
18   Bloch 1977 [1935], p. 16.
19   Bloch 1977 [1935], p. 16.

ism must examine its particular contradictions from case to case and occupy their territory.[20] This criticism of the lack of utopianism in Marxism is most clearly formulated in an interview Bloch gave in 1965 upon receiving a cultural prize from the German Trade Union Federation:

> This is about perspectives that go beyond next five-year plan, about 'Where to?' and 'What for?' of the whole freedom movement. This is insufficiently elaborated in Marxism. Marx was justifiably horrified of utopian depictions of the future. He did not want to create social-fiction. As a result, he had only one private expression: classless society.[21]

In this reply Bloch points to the deficiency of Marxism – it insufficiently develops the long-term goals of where and towards what the socialist society is headed. However, in this instance Bloch discusses not only Marxism, as an intellectual tradition that draws on Marx's own ideas, but refers explicitly to Marx's own thought. Whereas this passage should not be taken to represent fully the complex view Bloch held with respect to the place of utopia in Marx, it does clearly indicate one important side to this view, corresponding to the general scholarly consensus I outlined in the first chapter, that Marx provided no comprehensive account of his ideal society. And although Bloch observes that Marx's hostility to offer such an account was justified, it does, in his view, clearly present a shortcoming in Marx's thinking.

Comments such as these might lead us to expect that Bloch would mitigate this shortcoming by supplying an account of the communist society. This, however, is not the case. As Wayne Hudson notes: 'Bloch was not a social utopian of any standard sort. He devised no ideal society'.[22] In fact, just like Marx, Bloch never drafted a systematic, structured or detailed outline of his utopia.

Bloch's – as well as Marx's – indications of how utopian society will look are rather limited in length, and they are scattered throughout his corpus. At the same time there are, however, many marked differences between Marx's and Bloch's remarks on the content of the utopian society: first, Bloch's elucidations of a utopian society are 'warmer' than Marx's, to use a Blochian term derived from the distinction he drew between cold and warm streams of Marxism.[23] Although Bloch most often discusses this pair of concepts of the cold and

---

20   Bloch 1977 [1935], p. 16.
21   Bloch 1977 [1965a], p. 202.
22   Hudson 2013, p. 24.
23   Bloch first introduced these concepts in *The Heritage of Our Times*. He advances them later in *The Principle of Hope* (see especially Bloch 1977 [1954/55/50], pp. 235–42) and in *Experimentum Mundi*.

warm streams in the context of Marxism, they take on a more general meaning in his philosophy: as anthropological categories, as two attitudes, perhaps best thought as two distinct stances, that humans can adopt in their relation to the world.[24] At the most basic level, the cold and warm streams correspond to the rational and affective sides of our relation to the world. In her account of the cold and warm streams in their specific relation to Marxism, Silvia Mazzini highlights the tools of 'ideology critique, precise analysis of the economic and historical conditions, detection of false consciousness' as characteristic of the cold stream and 'enthusiasm, moral determination, and the work of objective imagination' as the features distinctive of the warm Marxism.[25] Importantly, this distinction should not be understood normatively, in the sense that Bloch considered one to be superior to the other. For Bloch, both streams are 'equally important', and effective only when working 'together, in union'.[26] Bloch's ideal form of Marxism is just as cold as it is warm. Bloch never explicitly described Marx's own writings in terms of this distinction. To the extent, however, that Marx and Engels espoused their studies and analysis of the past and present socio-economic conditions in the form of scientific models, and to the extent that they considered an objective application of our rational faculties to be the only viable way of obtaining knowledge, we can perceive their writings as dominated by the cold stream. Yet, the warm stream is in Marx not undetectable in, for instance, the *Manifesto*. This text does have a specific intensity and emotional appeal, and illustrates the idea of communism 'through imagery, through tempo, through expressions', which Bloch perceived as typical of the warm stream.[27] Moreover, Bloch recognises the concept of the realm of freedom as highly significant for Marx.[28] This concept Bloch perceived not only as another label for the communist society but for the ultimate communist society, the most distant conception of it. This distance or the long-term perspective is another characteristic of the warm stream. In a section in *The Principle of Hope* in which Bloch elaborates this distinction, he writes the following of warm Marxism:

> But the prospect-exploration of What-Is-in-possibility goes towards the horizon, in the sense of *unobstructed, unmeasured expanse*, in the sense of the Possible which is still unexhausted and unrealized. Only then of

24   Bloch 1977 [1972], p. 372.
25   Mazzini 2012, p. 224.
26   Bloch 1977 [1972], p. 372.
27   Bloch 1975, p. 222.
28   Bloch 1977 [1954/55/50], p. 149.

course does prospect in the authentic sense result, that is, prospect of the authentic, of the Totum of what is occurring and what is to be pursued, of a not only respectively prevailing, but overall historical, utopian Totum.[29]

Whatever the relative significance of this long-distant horizon in Marx according to Bloch was, it is clear that he perceived it as diminished in the later developments of Marxism, especially the Soviet one. In particular, in *The Heritage of Our Times*, a text in which Bloch for the first time introduced the distinction of warm and cold streams, Bloch perceived Soviet Marxism as being monopolised by the cold stream, giving as reasons its emphasis on short-termism and with it on quantitative planning and policy as well as, more generally, its emphasis on the economic and the mechanistic interpretation of history. In contrast, Bloch's own variety of Marxism appears to be dominated by the warm stream: it is centred not on the objective world but on the living and feeling individual, its content is arrived at not through the means of reason but through hopes, wishes and dreams, and its language is expressionist and poetic rather than theoretical and analytical. It belongs to the realm of the 'human-qualitative' rather than the 'economic-quantitative'.[30] It is almost as if Bloch's Marxism is too warm according to his own standards – effective Marxism was supposed to combine the two streams – but perhaps his overemphasised warmth was intentional, in that he attempted to illustrate positively the faults he found with Soviet, and to some degree with Marx's own, Marxism.

The government officials in the German Democratic Republic (GDR) where Bloch moved in 1949 to take up a professorship and the directorship of the 'Institut für Philosophie' in Leipzig certainly considered Bloch's Marxism too removed from its official interpretation. Bloch was the only one among the critical theorists who, upon their interwar exile, first in Europe and than the United States, returned to the Eastern Bloc of their native land. Bloch was unique in his belief that the Soviet Union even at that time still presented a viable socialist alternative to the then existing capitalism. Other critical theorists denounced the Soviet Union already in the 1930s after the Moscow show trials.[31] Bloch, however, considered that one's hope always requires an outlet, that it needs to be invested in a certain political alternative. Whatever reservations he might have held towards the Soviet Union were overridden by the need to endorse and defend its supposedly genuine commitment to the principles of socialism. In his lecture upon assuming his (first) academic post, Bloch observed

---

29   Bloch 1977 [1954/55/50], p. 240.
30   Bloch 1977 [1972], p. 374.
31   Jay 1973, p. 20.

that those who want to follow truth must travel with Marx into the realm he opened, and that there is no other truth that remains.[32] Of course, besides this theoretical principle, Bloch's decision to move to the GDR was founded on some more pragmatic considerations, and not least by publishing opportunities.[33] Although Bloch's version of Marxism was highly idiosyncratic from its conception, and never fully aligned with the Soviet version, the discrepancies between the two gained significance only once Bloch started publicly expressing his criticism of the regime in the mid-1950s. Following Khrushchev's acknowledgement of the Stalinist purges during the twentieth Party Congress in February 1956, Bloch became more open about his concerns regarding really existing socialism, namely its restrictions on individual freedom and its dogmatism.[34] After this, leading Party officials came to see Bloch's philosophy as revisionist, even as non-Marxist.[35] The core flaw that the Party found with Bloch was his emphasis on the individual, as opposed to the collective, that is, the Party, and the role that the individual plays in effecting historical change, as opposed to it being already determined by objective conditions. This subjectivism is another aspect of the warm strand of Marxism, and one that the Party eventually deemed unacceptable; as a result, in 1957 they not only discharged Bloch from his academic post, but almost completely blocked his research, writing and publishing.[36]

How Bloch's and Marx's references to utopian society fit into Bloch's schema of cold versus warm kinds of Marxism presents one major difference between them. The second difference regards the scope of their references to the utopian society: which of the authors' utterances attempt to reveal something substantial about the nature or the form of a utopian society? Which of their remarks should we consider in our reconstruction of their ideas of a utopian society? As I have established in the first chapter, in the case of Marx, scholars are relatively united in how his idea of utopia is to be reconstructed from his writings: above all this consists of assembling the positive references Marx makes in relation to communism in the *Manifesto* and the 'Critique of the Gotha Program'. Scholars of the Young Marx, including Daniel Brudney and David Leopold, emphasise in addition to these texts Marx's philosophical anthropology, arguing that this is an essential ingredient of his utopian thinking. In the case of Bloch, no such consensus has yet been established. I thus

32   Bloch 1977 [1969a], p. 276.
33   Zudeick 1987, pp. 184–5.
34   Amberger 2013, p. 565.
35   See Münster 2012, p. 282; Markun 1977, pp. 95–6.
36   See Münster 2012, pp. 275–302.

adopt below a similar approach to the one that has been taken with Marx, and reconstruct the content of Bloch's utopia via what I call a key signifier of their utopias, in Marx's case the concept of communism and in Bloch's the one of 'Heimat'.[37]

4   Bloch's Utopian Society: *'Heimat'*

It should be noted that this approach is likely to imply a restricted understanding of Bloch's vision of the utopian society. As I have pointed out, a large proportion of *The Principle of Hope* amounts to an assembly of utopian wishes that have already been articulated by others in the past. A function of this assembly is to make evident the ubiquity of utopian thinking in human lives. But perhaps all these utopian wishes could also be considered as representing or pointing to Bloch's own utopia? As Gerd Koch observes, Bloch's *Principle of Hope* depicts the already known wishful images, and, moreover, revises and sketches them anew.[38] Where, however, does the line lie? How can we distinguish between those images that are already known and exist, that is, the utopian ideas which Bloch duplicates, includes them in his assembly in a more or less unmodified way, and those images that he revises and modifies? Of course, no line neatly divides these different types of utopian wishes, but they could nevertheless be loosely distinguished. To do so, however, given the volume of these images, much philological research would have to be conducted. I thus focus only on those images which can plausibly be related directly to the concept of *Heimat*.

Heimat certainly presents a variation on Marx's idea of communism. For example, Bloch describes the desired future as 'another world beyond hardship', as one 'without expropriation and alienation, in real democracy'.[39] This phrase of real democracy is also a political one, as the democracy that exists in the 'the really existing socialism' ('Realsozialismus') within the Eastern Bloc countries and the Soviet Union, as opposed to that prevailing in the Western ones. Another, less well-known metaphor of Marx's demarcating the commun-

---

37   The German word 'Heimat' is most often translated into English as 'home' and 'homeland'. Neither of these translations, however, captures adequately the meaning of 'Heimat', which is why I stick to using the German term. Another term that Bloch appears to use synonymously with that of Heimat is 'Zuhause' (Koch 2012, p. 178). For a discussion of difficulties of translating *The Principle of Hope*, including the concept of Heimat, see Wuilmart 1985, p. 217. Although Wuilmart discusses the translation of Bloch specifically into French, his ideas have a wider relevance.

38   Koch 2012, p. 174.

39   Bloch 1977 [1954/55/50], pp. 310; 1628.

ist society, is present in Bloch's work to an even greater extent than those of non-alienation, non-exploitation and democracy. Marx's metaphor too originates in his 'Economic-philosophical manuscripts', more precisely, in the phrase of 'the perfect essential unity of man with nature, the true resurrection of nature, the accomplished naturalism of man and the accomplished humanism of nature'.[40] Bloch develops this idea of 'the naturalization of man, humanization of nature' into his key motif of *Heimat*, positing it as 'the goal', and, further as 'the content of the realm of freedom'.[41] Although the concept of *Heimat* was made infamous by National Socialism, its roots lie earlier in history, in the Romanticism of writers such as Novalis, Hölderlin, Schelling and Herder. In this epoch *Heimat* unites multiple dissatisfactions with the onset of modernisation, industrialisation, rationalisation and urbanisation and in turn aims at reestablishing an idealised, local-based, rural, simple, pre-modern order.[42] *Heimat* presented for Bloch the epitome of the remnants of the past that need to be salvaged for present political purposes, which, in his view, meant assimilating this concept into the Marxist register. As the very final word of *The Principle of Hope, Heimat* is Bloch's answer to the opening lines of this work – 'Who are we? Where do we come from? Where are we going? What are we waiting for? What awaits us?'[43] *Heimat* can thus be taken as Bloch's name for his utopian society. Later in the introduction of *The Principle of Hope* Bloch refers to *Heimat* as 'positive Utopikum' and as 'the All' ('das Alles').[44] The key idiosyncrasy of *Heimat* as Bloch's utopia is the already mentioned idea of 'socialized humanity, allied with a nature that is mediated with it'.[45] For Bloch the figure of *Heimat* stands for the state 'of fulfilled human beings themselves and their environment fully mediated with these images'.[46] Bloch further describes the relationship between nature and humanity in *Heimat* as one of 'co-productivity'.[47] Bloch does contend that the creation of such a relationship between nature and humanity would require a new kind of technology, one which we would probably today call 'green technology', and which Bloch once refers to as the 'the bosom of a friend'.[48]

---

40   Marx 1968 [1932], 538.
41   Bloch 1977 [1954/55/50], p. 241.
42   See Blicke 2002.
43   Bloch 1977 [1954/55/50], p. 1.
44   Bloch 1977 [1954/55/50], p. 11.
45   Bloch 1977 [1954/55/50], p. 334.
46   Bloch 1977 [1954/55/50], p. 15.
47   Bloch 1977 [1954/55/50], p. 802.
48   Bloch 1977 [1954/55/50], p. 782.

Apart from some short references to technology Bloch does not offer other details on the content of this reconciled humanity with nature. Gerhard Koch subscribes to this view by observing that *The Principle of Hope* does not make evident what the content of *Heimat* is.[49] Yet, Bloch does indeed substantiate the concept of *Heimat* even if not by describing its aspects and characteristics concretely. 'Something which shines into the childhood of all and in which no one has yet been', is the most concise Bloch's formulation of this substantiation of *Heimat*.[50] By examining closely two fragments of this contention, which too features in the final passage of *The Principle of Hope*, we can grasp what Bloch could have meant by it. The first fragment corresponds to the second half of the sentence, namely 'where no one has yet been'. Although Bloch uses a location-relative pronoun 'where', *Heimat* is here not a spatial term. Somewhat analogous to the temporalisation of the concept of utopia in the nineteenth century, Bloch sees *Heimat* as a place that exists in time but not in space. The spatial dimension of *Heimat* is one that is present in the colloquial usage of the term today, as well as in one that was not only present but crucial to how it was used by the National Socialists, where it was synonymous with 'Deutschland', the territory of the German nation-state.[51] In Bloch's view, however, as Francesca Vidal notes, 'Heimat is not a place'.[52] The analogy to the modification undergone by the concept of utopia is, however, a slight simplification of Bloch's revision of the concept of *Heimat*. An important difference regards Bloch's idiosyncratic conception of time according to which the past, present and the future are not simply phases which consecutively displace one another. Bloch's temporalisation of the concept of *Heimat* is not a transfer from a place we cannot reach (a distant island) into a time we cannot access (the future). Instead it is a transfer into the time that cannot (yet) be fully accessed. That means that while *Heimat* is already partially here in the now – we had some sort of experience of it in the childhood – it is also partially not here – no one has actually been there.

The second fragment of the contention under concern is the word 'all'. *Heimat* is for Bloch something that has appeared to all, that is, to all human beings. What Bloch is saying here is that our ideas of what utopia is, of the better world we wish to see realised, are shared, at least to a certain extent. In other words, Bloch professes a certain universality or transcendence of norms of what the right and the good society is. We could perhaps say that

---

49   Koch 2012, p. 174.
50   Bloch 1977 [1954/55/50], p. 1628.
51   Blicke 2002, p. 47.
52   Vidal 2000, p. 45.

Bloch's *Heimat* presents some kind of universal core of utopian ideas expressed throughout history. Bloch contends that this idea of *Heimat* was something that Marx himself touched on, even if he did not develop it fully. In *The Principle of Hope* Bloch quotes a line that Marx included in a letter he wrote to Arnold Ruge:

> the world has long since dreamt of a thing which it must simply become conscious of in order to possess it in reality. Then we will also see that there is no great conceptual break between past and future but rather the *completion* of the dreams of the past.[53]

The concept of *Heimat* is also not antithetical to the tradition of Critical Theory itself. More specifically, the contention of the existence of a transcendental conception of the good, and moreover, as I explained in the previous paragraph, as a conception that is at every point in time in some form entailed in individuals' expressions, is constitutive of Benjamin's thought. It is precisely this idea which is implicit in one of this tradition's paradigmatic passages, an excerpt of Benjamin's 'On the concept of history':

> The past carries with it a secret index by which it is referred to redemption [...] There is a secret agreement between past generations and the present one. Our coming was expected on earth. Like every generation that preceded us, we have been endowed with a weak Messianic power, a power to which the past has its claim.[54]

In this passage Benjamin contends that 'redemption', that is, the current redemptive, revolutionary act, the transformation of the existing society into the utopian one is only a continuation of the already attempted past revolutions. The attempts at transforming a society into a better one all have something in common, they are joined by carrying what Benjamin termed 'the secret index', and what Bloch referred to as 'the invariant of direction' ('Invarianz der Richtung').[55]

In fact, Benjamin's conception of utopian thinking had much in common with Bloch's. For Benjamin, everyday life serves as the material for utopia, and no preconceived plan or set of universal concepts can suffice for its determina-

53   Bloch 1977 [1954/55/50], p. 1613.
54   Benjamin, 'Über den Begriff der Geschichte', in *Walter Benjamin Gesammelte Schriften*, Vol. 1, pp. 691–706 (pp. 693–4).
55   Bloch 1977 [1954/55/50], pp. 355; 1565.

tion. More specifically, utopia derives from what Benjamin called 'the debris of history' – the look of a forgotten boulevard, postage stamps, children's literature, eating, collecting books, the euphoria of hashish, memories of revolutionaries shooting at the clocks.[56] As Peter Thompson notes, Bloch and Benjamin took 'from the Lurianic Kabbalah the idea of the daily manifestations of hope as surplus "shards of light", left over from the creation of the word as negativity'.[57] There is, however, an important distinction between Benjamin's and Bloch's understandings of these 'surplus shards of light'. Whereas for Benjamin they manifested themselves in the forgotten, repressed and the neglected histories of the world, for Bloch their presence was, corresponding to his view of the ubiquity of utopian thinking, not limited to these supposedly more marginal histories. It is also important to mention that while Bloch's early writings resemble those of Benjamin in their expressionistic style and unwillingness to substantiate new ideas with a new conceptual framework, Bloch does later provide them with an ontological basis, something that Benjamin never managed or attempted to do.

5   The Utopian Core: 'Invariant of Direction'

Bloch's notion of invariant of direction appears in *The Principle of Hope* also in the form of the phrases 'Invarianz', 'Invarianzinhalt', 'Invariante', and finally as 'Unum necessarium' (the one necessary).[58] For Bloch this invariant is founded on something that has been 'constantly intended', corresponding to 'an always identically disposed element of the utopian final state'.[59] It is not unlike Benjamin's 'secret index' which the past carries with it and which signifies the world to arrive after its 'redemption'. The closest Bloch comes to a definition of this concept is in the following passage of *The Principle of Hope*:

> The invariant of this direction leads in the end [...] to the only archetype which has nothing archaic about it. That is: to the *purely utopian archetype, which lives in the evidence of nearness, to that of the still unknown, all-surpassing Summum bonum.* The archetype: highest good is the invariance-content of the most felicitous astonishment, its possession would be

---

56   Benjamin 1977 [1942], p. 697.
57   Thompson 2013, p. 84.
58   Bloch 1977 [1954/55/50], pp. 557; 355; 921; 255; 336.
59   Bloch 1977 [1954/55/50], p. 336.

that which transforms in the moment and in fact as this moment, into its completely resolved That.[60]

It should have by now become evident that the invariant of direction is closely tied to the utopian, the highest good ('*Summum bonum*'). This passage, however, additionally touches on another aspect of the invariant of direction that I have not discussed so far, namely the knowability of its content, or better, its unknowability: Bloch plainly asserts that this content is not yet known. That is, we do not know what the universal norms and values of a good society are, those universal aspects of it that we all share. The underlying reason Bloch gives us is also rather that we do not know what this utopian society is because it has not yet been realised: 'the final state' has not yet been realised, 'neither as the negative of pessimism and its Nothing, nor as the positive of optimism and its All'.[61] This reason conforms with the basic materialistic contention, the very contention to which both Marx and Adorno subscribed: as material beings, humans are embedded and thus conditioned by their material circumstances which cannot be cut loose, the mind cannot pretend it can assume a position outside this material world in which it would be free to work out, or find an already developed conception of what the truly good society is. Similarly to Marx and Adorno, Bloch denounces the idealist contention that concepts, ideas and thought are self-determining entities carrying meanings that remain unconnected to the existing material reality. Bloch's materialist stance explains why his figure of *Heimat* remains uninhabited by specific features characterising this society.

As we see now, Bloch concurs with Adorno that we cannot know in the present how the utopian society of the future looks. However, at least two significant differences can and should be identified between their understandings of this assertion. The first difference is that, unlike in Adorno, in Bloch the idea that we cannot know the future utopian society does not result in the *Utopie-verbot*. On the contrary – for Bloch it is not the case that we *should not* be envisaging the future, it is rather the opposite: this is what we *should* be doing. In their radio conversation Adorno contended that one may not cast a picture of utopia. Bloch, by distinction, insisted on the *need* to cast a picture of it.

For now, I leave this view on the side; I will come back to it in the final chapter. I first elaborate on the second difference between Adorno's and Bloch's positions on the impossibility of utopian thinking, namely that Bloch does

---

60   Bloch 1977 [1954/55/50], p. 355.
61   Bloch 1977 [1954/55/50], pp. 354–5.

not render this impossibility as absolute. That is, in Bloch's view, it is not the case that nothing at all can be known about the utopian society of the future: while he maintains that its fundamental tenets (e.g. the harmonious relation between humanity and its environment) or its core values (e.g. freedom) cannot be determined, and elaborated on in any extended way, some aspects, elements or features of the utopian society can be known. We can grasp or comprehend some aspects of the invariant of direction, of the absolute utopia itself, through our most inner experiences of the world that we can gain by adopting a specific attitude towards it. This attitude Bloch refers to as wonder ('Staunen'). These experiences are consciously articulated in different ways, in the wide range of expressions and practices that Bloch counts under his category of utopian thinking, extending from dreams and wishes to paintings and poems. Bloch's own attempt to capture the content of this wondering is a particular literary form, some type of a short narrative of events, which just like the experience of the utopian moment itself carries the name of 'traces'.

6   Traces – Experiences and Expressions of Utopia

The most accessible account of both of these two meanings of traces Bloch offers in *The Principle of Hope*:

> The briefest *symbol-intentions of an Absolute* have always been experienced in this keeping still, subjective at first, in fact appearing to be lyrical and yet arch-philosophically founded in the matter itself, namely in a flash of a utopian final state. Such experiences of a utopian final state certainly do not determine it, otherwise they would not be experiences of mere *symbol-intention* and not utopian experiences, let alone central utopian ones. But they actually touch upon the *core of latency*, and in fact as final question, echoing within themselves. This question cannot be construed towards any readily available answer, or referred to any material already settled anywhere in the available world. Examples of this are given in the book 'Traces'.[62]

The basic idea behind traces as *experiences* of utopia is one which Bloch shares with some non-occidental philosophical systems, like Buddhism of the Sankya school, namely that other-worldliness exists in this world and that we

---

62   Bloch 1977 [1954/55/50], p. 337.

have access to it. In Bloch's own system this is related to the 'the darkness of the lived moment'. In the above passage Bloch contends that these lived moments are pervaded with the 'utopian final state', which become accessible or visible to us as 'the symbol-intentions of one possibility'. Although these indications of utopia do not determine or fix the utopian society that might actually arise in the future, they do capture something substantial about it. Such experiences of utopia are purely subjective in the very moment they are experienced. They are the very first experience of utopia a subject can have, and are thus tied to the subject. It is therefore also not a coincidence that Bloch chose his book *Traces* to feature as the first volume in his collected works. However, once these experiences are reflected on, elaborated, shared with others, some aspects of them do start gaining objective validity. Although I do not elaborate on this contention in this project, this idea of the process through which some at first purely subjective contents are worked through to become something more objective – from these premonitions, to dreams, wishes and then knowledge – is one of Bloch's important contributions.

Insofar as these experiences of utopia capture it only in bits and pieces, they also need to be expressed in a partial, fragmented form. These *articulations* of the experiences of utopia is the second meaning of Bloch's concept of traces. As he notes in the above passage, he provided the examples of what he means by these moments in his book *Traces*. The specific writing style, which merges the poetical with the philosophical, was already explored by Bloch in his earliest publications, including *Through the Desert (Durch die Wüste)* (1923) and *The Spirit of Utopia* (1918). Bloch objected to philosophical thinking in the form of abstract concepts put together in structured theories. In his view, such a way of thinking had too much in common with doctrines and dogmas which have historically been an important means of manipulating the masses. In many of his early writings his preferred way of conveying his ideas, which nevertheless remained profoundly philosophical, was thus the alternative of narratives, stories, images, anecdotes, jokes and reflections. Traces as a literary figure bring these forms together. Another defining aspect of this literary figure is, as Laura Boella observes, its briefness or shortness.[63] According to Bloch, one is in one's experiences of reality most susceptible and open to the 'little things'.[64] For Bloch these little things capture some little fragments of the utopia, which he then in turn also himself represents as short fragments. In their brief exposi-

---

63   Boella 2012, p. 512.
64   Bloch 1977 [1930], p. 16.

tion, and in the sense that traces are also intended to convey a certain deeper meaning, they resemble both aphorisms as well as Adorno's constellations and Benjamin's thought-images.

In Bloch's view the content of utopia can be expressed in another, less literary way than via traces, which is related more closely with my project. This concerns utopian thinking that retains some of the qualities of philosophy – qualities that are not immanently interchangeable with artistic ones. Although traces point to many reasons for why the line between philosophy and art can be completely permeable, especially when it comes to ultimate questions like that of utopia, the objective of my project remains the exploration of articulations of utopian society that are less metaphorical, more analytical, less ambivalent, and more easily comprehensible, and to consider the subject of a utopian society more explicitly. The other form of Blochian utopian thinking I investigate here in more detail is more closely related to my interest. This form of utopian thinking is grounded in Bloch's concept of 'concrete utopia'.[65] Concrete utopias are images of an ideal society contained in the answers to the question of the 'here' and 'now', that is, to the existing economic, political and social issues. This concept of concrete utopia needs to be distinguished from the invariant of direction, the absolute utopia, the final form of our societies, the *Heimat*. Concrete utopias can perhaps be best comprehended as various pre-forms of *Heimat*, and in that respect are also formative of what *Heimat* will eventually become. Thus Bloch's view that, on the one hand (and as I discussed above in relation to the emptiness of Bloch's *Heimat*), we cannot conceptualise the utopian society in any particular way, and on the other, as I claim now, that in fact we can, is not contradictory, as long as we keep the categories of concrete utopia and *Heimat* somewhat separate.

Bloch himself never actually talked explicitly of 'concrete utopian thinking' – this is a term I introduce here to describe the form of utopian thinking that can be derived from his concept of concrete utopia. In the very first instance, concrete utopian thinking can be thought of as a fusion of one's premonitions, the glimpses of utopias that arise in one's most inner experiences, wishes and longings with the existing historical situation and its problems. In the following section I proceed by first untangling the concept of concrete utopia and then consider what concrete utopian thinking could look like more specifically.

---

65   This phrase appears on numerous occasions in *The Principle of Hope*. See, e.g., Bloch 1977 [1954/55/50], p. 180.

7   Concrete Utopian Thinking

By the concept of concrete utopia Bloch does not mean an actual utopia, in the material sense, as a perceptible community that would actually exist in our reality. The applicable antonym of concrete utopia in this sense would be 'abstract utopia', a merely conceptual representation of a good society. This dualism between the realms of concepts and matter is in general not applicable to Bloch's philosophical system. Therefore it cannot be applied also to this specific distinction between abstract and concrete utopias. Instead, as Peter Thompson argues, Bloch's usage of the term concrete should be understood in its Hegelian sense.[66] Hegel adopted the terms 'the concrete' and 'concrete' from the Latin verb *concrescere*, meaning to 'grow together, condense', and contrasted it to *abstrahere*, 'to draw away, remove (something from something else)'.[67] For Hegel, then, the concrete presents a point, material and conceptual at the same time, which emerges out of the given reality and embodies it in its totality, effectively bringing together the various strands of that reality. The abstract, on the other hand, entails merely one strand of this reality, and moreover, it embodies it by drawing one specific strand or feature away from it, by removing this strand from the totality. Once this strand is abstracted from the totality, it can appear as something existing independently, while in truth it cannot really exist as such.

Keeping in mind these Hegelian meanings of the concrete and the abstract will help us later on to make sense of concrete and abstract utopian thinking, practices which, as I have mentioned, Bloch does not define explicitly. Nonetheless, in relation to the concepts of concrete and abstract utopia, Bloch regularly employs the same set of motives, metaphors and analogies. The motives consonant with abstract utopia are those of dreaminess, clouds and immaturity, whereas those of erudition, advancement, forward motion and maturity appear symbolic of concrete utopia. The following excerpt from *The Principle of Hope* brings together these various motives most succinctly:

> Thus the only seemingly paradoxical concept of a concrete utopia would be appropriate here, that is of an anticipatory kind which by no means coincides with abstract Utopian dreaminess, nor is directed by the immaturity of merely abstract Utopian socialism. The very power and truth of Marxism consists in the fact that it has driven the cloud in our dreams fur-

---

66   Thompson 2021, p. 34.
67   Inwood 1999, p. 29.

ther forward, but has not extinguished the pillar of fire in those dreams, and rather strengthened it with concreteness.[68]

What this passage immediately makes evident is that the distinction between abstract and concrete utopia presents, for Bloch, a certain dichotomy. Bloch states that the concept of concrete utopia by no means coincides with those of 'abstract-utopian dreams' and 'abstract-utopian socialism'. Bloch contrasts the latter with Marxism, which can be taken as overlapping with concrete utopia.[69] In the passage it further becomes apparent that despite the dichotomous relation between abstract and concrete utopia, Bloch perceives the latter as related, or more specifically as developing out of the former. Bloch's dichotomy of abstract and concrete utopia thus needs to be understood as a dialectical relationship. It seems as if the content of abstract utopias is taken as the initial basis for the advancement of a concrete utopia. What concrete utopia preserves is 'pillar of fires' ('die Feuersäule'), something that dreams manage to capture. This basis is, then, strengthened and becomes more powerful in the concept of concrete utopia. As Bloch posits, the key of this strength and power lies in concreteness, or perhaps – and this might be a more intelligible way of putting it – in the process of concretisation. This passage, however, is silent on the question of what this concreteness might be, what the process of concretisation entails, in other words – how is an abstract utopia transformed into a concrete one?

One of the very first further explications of what this concreteness might entail is provided by Bloch in *The Principle of Hope*. It concerns a well-known passage written by a nineteenth-century Russian writer, Dmitry Pisarev, in which different kinds of dreams are discussed.[70] This passage was popularised by Lenin, who quoted it at length in his pamphlet *What is to be Done?* Whereas Pisarev rendered dreams as a highly significant stimulus which would 'induce man to undertake and complete extensive and strenuous work', he recognised that only a specific kind of dreams has this purely positive effect.[71] Pisarev recognised that some dreams can also have negative repercussions, namely, that they may 'distort or paralyze labour power'.[72] The purely beneficial dreams, however, cause no harm, and their distinguishing characteristics,

---

68   Bloch 1977 [1954/55/50], pp. 165–6.
69   As Ruth Levitas notes, Bloch's distinction can be interpreted as an advance on Marx and Engels' own differentiation between their version of socialism and that supplied by Saint-Simon, Fourier and Owen. See Levitas 1990, p. 16.
70   Bloch quotes Pisarev in *The Principle of Hope* (Bloch 1977 [1954/55/50], p. 9.).
71   Bloch 1977 [1954/55/50], p. 9.
72   Bloch 1977 [1954/55/50], p. 9.

Pisarev writes, is that 'the person dreaming believes seriously in his dream', 'attentively observes life', 'compares his observations with his castles in the air' and 'works conscientiously for the achievement of his fantasies'.[73] In the case of these dreams, Pisarev continues, there is still a 'rift' separating them from 'reality', but he does not recognise this rift as problematic. The key question to be answered here is how these two kinds of rifts differ from each other. It seems that the rift devoid of danger is narrower than the other one, in the sense that life and dreams are brought closer to each other. The good kind of dreams are arrived at by fusing them with our experiences of our reality, or, as Pisarev writes, with our observations of life. Later on in *The Principle of Hope*, in an explicit elucidation of the difference, this time explicitly in terms of the difference between concrete and abstract utopias, Bloch himself uses very similar terminology, contending that it is 'the point of contact between dreams and life' which furnishes dreams as a concrete utopia.[74] Without this point of contact, dreams yield only abstract utopia.[75]

Bloch makes a similar remark in his inaugural lecture upon assuming his second professorship, this time in West Germany, in Tübingen. From 1956 onwards, the year in which Bloch's never perfectly loyal allegiance to the Communist Party took on a new character – as he pleaded publicly for a more humanist and democratic alternative to the Soviet model of socialism, denouncing its dogmatic, dictatorial and violent character – the Party increasingly came to censor his work and placed other restrictions on his activities. When an opportunity arose to leave the GDR, Bloch took it, and was subsequently, in 1961, granted political asylum in West Germany. In the same year he obtained a professorial post in Tübingen, where he delivered his famous inaugural lecture on the disappointment of hope. This lecture illuminates how it was that Bloch's political outlooks had not been reversed by his disillusionment with the Soviet experiment. Once in the West, Bloch continued to believe in socialist principles and support other socialist inspired movements, including the 1968 student protests.[76] As he explained in this lecture, disappointment is inherent to hope – 'hope must be unconditionally disappointable' – and disappointment is in fact necessary for the eventual fulfillment of the content of hope, in Bloch's case of socialism.[77] If what we hope for was always to be fulfilled, then it would not be the affect of hoping but something else that we are engaged in; this alternat-

---

73   Bloch 1977 [1954/55/50], p. 9.
74   Bloch 1977 [1954/55/50], p. 165.
75   Bloch 1977 [1954/55/50], p. 165.
76   Hudson 1982, p. 17.
77   Bloch 1977 [1965b].

ive affect, Bloch suggests, would be 'confidence'.[78] Because hope is 'open in the forward direction', and committed to change, rather than repetition, it must 'contain in itself also an element of chance'.[79] This element of chance then in turn means there is no certainty that the content of hope will actually be realised.

The other feature of hope that Bloch addresses in this lecture is related to concrete utopian thinking. He warns that when 'even serious expressions of faith' is brought to bear 'on the course of real events *abstractly* and without constant *control*', it is liable to lead 'to their opposite'.[80] In place of this kind of utopian thinking, Bloch calls for 'well-founded hope, mediated, guiding hope' which contains a 'timetable' and 'appropriate skepticism'.[81]

Taking these cues, and further pursuing meanings of concrete and abstract utopia, I suggest that concrete utopian thinking can be thought of as conceptual representations of a utopian society that are differentiated, detailed, comprehensive and particular. This is in accordance with for example Bloch's account of concrete utopia as 'the most powerful telescope of the polished utopian consciousness'.[82] The emphasis on particularity and specification, in opposition to vagueness and generality, is however not the only feature of concrete utopian thinking. A conception of utopia that is full of specific details could still in fact be classified as abstract utopian thinking. In fact, utopian fiction, which, among others, Ruth Levitas reads as an instance of what Bloch meant by abstract utopianism, is often highly detailed. The key of concrete utopian thinking is that its details are arrived at through a process of close scrutiny of the existing reality. It is not sufficient to be more specific, that is, to construct new categories, classes and concepts; one must argue through them, establish why they are plausible, realistic and possible.

In this vein one not only needs to square dreams with reality by empirically comparing the two, but by making use of reason. While Pisarev might not have referred to reason and rationality, Bloch does. I suggest that the process to which Pisarev refers as connection between dreams and life, is advanced further by Bloch under the name of *docta spes*, which is a Latin phrase for educated, rationally informed hope.[83] My point here is that this education of hope in turn stands for what I above called the process of concretisation, the

---

78   Bloch 1977 [1965b], p. 387.
79   Bloch 1977 [1965b], p. 387.
80   Bloch 1977 [1965b], p. 386.
81   Bloch 1977 [1965b], p. 386.
82   Bloch 1977 [1954/55/50], p. 11.
83   'Doctus' is the Latin for 'having been taught, instructed', and 'spes' for 'hope.'

transformation of abstract into concrete. It is the fusion of the rational and the emotional, more specifically of the hopeful content of our emotions which for Bloch defines the idea of *docta spes:*

> The docta spes-combine operates on this knowledge [contained in past utopian ideas] as expectant emotion in the Ratio, as Ratio in the expectant emotion. And predominant in this combine is no longer contemplation, which for centuries has only been related to What Has Become, but the participating, co-operative process-attitude, to which consequently, since Marx, the open becoming is no longer sealed methodically and the Novum no longer alien in material terms.[84]

Here Bloch contends that the vision of utopia constituted through this process of the education of hope is no longer alien to material and methodically sealed. By this I understand that this vision, while holding fast to something that seems essential to hope, the optimist attitude perhaps, or as Bloch calls it elsewhere, 'the upright gait' ('aufrechter Gang'), at the same time converts it into an actually possible future. The key here is that the possible nature of this future results not simply from our hope, but is in turn backed by rational, objective reasons.

Conceiving how concrete utopian thinking would actually look is incredibly difficult, in part also because Bloch's concept of concrete utopia is, as is his philosophy in general, open, thus allowing for many different possible conceptions. This inherent openness could be a reason why Bloch scholarship has not properly pursued this idea so far. Within the Bloch scholarship the only example I have identified of what concrete utopian thinking might correspond to in more practical or pragmatic terms has been given by Rainer E. Zimmerman. Zimmerman defines concrete utopian thinking as 'creating scenarios according to theoretical principles and drawing conclusions about their feasibility in practice'.[85] However the openness of Bloch's thought is of course not indefinite, which instigates us to further pursue the concretisation of Bloch's concrete utopia. Above I have already suggested 'particularity' and 'specificity' as defining features of concrete utopian thinking. Below I suggest further that expressions of concrete utopias are, at least to some degree, positive, that is, that the content of a utopia is formulated positively, in terms of what utopia is and what it looks like.

---

84   Bloch 1977 [1954/55/50], p. 166.
85   Zimmerman 2013, p. 256.

This might indeed appear to be a far-fetched claim. Bloch was by no means an uncritical advocate of conceptual representations of utopias, which for most of the history were in fact formulated positively. His intervention into the discussion of the value and function of utopian thinking was original: he did not simply claim that all conceptual utopias produced so far have been misread on the whole and supply a different reading and valuation of them. His intervention was creative in the sense that he developed a hierarchy of different forms of utopian thinking, or at least provided some material for such a hierarchy. This observation is often made in the field of Bloch scholarship. What, however, I find has been missed in the discussion of Bloch's re-evaluation of utopian thinking is his view of positive thinking. That this aspect of Bloch has been neglected is not surprising, given that he never directly criticises nor advocates the positivity of utopian thinking per se.[86] But once we look at the examples of utopian thinking Bloch supplies, it is indisputable that positive thinking is in some sense fundamental to them. For example, towards the end of *The Principle of Hope* Bloch considers the desirable form of a working day. In principle he identifies two possible forms for it: 'that of action' (*vita activa*) and 'that of contemplative stillness' (*vita contemplativa*).[87] Bloch further observes that the most desirable form is likely to consist in some combination of the two: one where 'the two forms may alternate directly with one another' (as in the sequence workday-Sunday), or where 'they may permeate one another' (which will only be possible after the abolition of forced labour).[88] Bloch also notes that even if the utopian workday entails both of these activities, he is interested in the question 'which wishful image predominates, even in the possible permeation, which more evidently contains that which is man's'.[89] Bloch finds that the question of 'action or contemplation, primacy of the will or of the intellect', was first posited in the Bible, framed as what he calls 'the Martha-Mary problem'. Martha was supposed to symbolise active life, and Mary the intellectual one. To address this problem Bloch first considers the relevant biblical interpretations offered by thinkers including Thomas Aquinas, Dante and Meister Eckhart, who valued intellect more highly. Later on Bloch explores how these

---

86 The only explicit reference to the positivity of Bloch's utopian thinking I have been able to identify is the following contention by Thompson: 'What appear to be negative manifestations of the void in traditional Kabbalistic thought thus become in Bloch, through this negation of the negation, positive indications of the latent possibilities in the content of the Real' (Thompson 2013, p. 85).

87 Bloch 1977 [1954/55/50], p. 1119.

88 Bloch 1977 [1954/55/50], p. 1119.

89 Bloch 1977 [1954/55/50], p. 1119.

ideas were reversed in protestant ethics and capitalist logic.[90] Although Bloch
recognises that different religious movements and intellectual traditions ten-
ded to prioritise one side of the intellect-contemplation pair, he emphasises
that this establishment of hierarchy always remained open to doubt and ambivalence. This ambivalence culminated in Marxism, specifically in its idea of
'revolutionary praxis', which is defined essentially by the fact that it contains
both the elements of contemplation and action.[91] Bloch concludes this section
on the form and content of the utopian working day by suggesting that the
contemplation-action dualism is not only complicated or ambivalent, but that
it is 'ultimately groundless'.[92] Bloch also offers his own suggestion on how this
dualism could be resolved:

> The good part, ultimately, is chosen neither by Martha nor Mary, it is the
> authentic element which shows *activity its centre of rest* from which it
> comes, to which it moves. Thus in the Greek legend the men of action
> Achilles, Asclepius, Hercules and Jason at least had as their tutor the cen-
> taur Chiron, the allegory of wisdom and action in one.[93]

My contention has been that, while Bloch directly investigates the concept
of concrete utopia from which an idea of concrete utopian thinking can be
derived, he does not himself engage in the practice of concrete utopian thinking. The above example of Bloch's deliberations on the ideal working day thus
serves to illustrate not concrete utopian thinking per se but more generally the
positivity of Bloch's notion of utopian thinking as the Not-Yet. Bloch talks about
the 'the good part' of life in its own terms, and not in terms of its wrong part.[94]
He elaborates on the historical understandings of this good part, in terms of
what this good part *is*, or in what it consists of, and not in terms of what it *is
not*, or what is does not consist in. And although his own concluding proposal
on the content of an ideal working day is highly dialectical in the way it formulates the relationship between the stillness and activity, rest and movement, it
does state what this content *is*.

To establish more firmly the overlap between Bloch's overall notion of utopian thinking grounded in the Not-Yetness of his utopia and positive thinking would require further work. I have, however, provided enough evidence to

---

90   Bloch 1977 [1954/55/50], p. 1120.
91   Bloch 1977 [1954/55/50], p. 1123.
92   Bloch 1977 [1954/55/50], p. 1124.
93   Bloch 1977 [1954/55/50], p. 1124.
94   Bloch 1977 [1954/55/50], p. 1124.

establish that this overlap is a plausible one. Unlike Adorno's portrayals of a utopian society which source their material from the ills and the wrongs of the existing society, Bloch's images are derived from the already existing conceptions of the good and the right. Given that concrete utopian thinking presents one form of Bloch's overall notion of utopian thinking, I therefore argue that it too must formulate utopia at least partially positively. Concrete utopian thinking cannot be reduced to negation or negative thinking.

This claim brings this chapter to its end. In this chapter I have shown that Bloch calls for an integration of utopian thinking into Critical Theory, or, to put it in his own terms, for an intensification of the warm stream of Marxism. That Bloch's demand indeed amounts to a rejection of Adorno's *Utopieverbot* I have made evident by exploring what Bloch means by this warm stream of Marxism, and I have suggested that concrete utopian thinking is one of its possible varieties. Through the consideration of Bloch's concept of *Heimat* and the invariant of direction I have emphasised that Bloch's overturning of the *Utopieverbot* does not imply a complete reversal of Adorno's position; that is, Bloch's advocacy of utopian thinking is not uncritical or dogmatic. It is, however, grounded on the contrasting view regarding the possibility of utopian thinking, and moreover, it does imply that utopian thinking in the sense I use in this book, namely as a form of positive thinking, is a necessary element of Critical Theory. In the next chapter I provide justification of Bloch's view; that is, the reasons why, according to Bloch, utopian thinking is possible and necessary. By considering these reasons I open the ontological basis of his philosophy, which in turn offers some material to further concretise my thoughts on how utopian thinking as a critical-theoretical practice would actually look. Above, I have attempted to do so by substantiating the concept of concrete utopian thinking; at the end of the next chapter I do so by considering what we might understand by what I call 'processual utopian thinking'.

CHAPTER 5

An Ontology of Processual Utopia

In contrast to Adorno, Bloch believes that we are able to envisage utopia: we have been able to do so historically, and we are able to do so now, under the conditions of late capitalism. This does not mean that we can foresee or know exactly the utopian society that might one day arise in the future. Bloch refers to this society with the term *Heimat*; Adorno, meanwhile, terms it 'the Other' ('das Andere'). It has many other possible names. For example, the contemporary French philosopher Quentin Meillassoux, who, like Bloch, belongs to the tradition of speculative materialism, usefully calls it by the name of 'the Fourth World'.[1] As explained in my previous chapter, in Bloch's view, *Heimat* cannot be known and thus articulated comprehensively and systematically, but can only be vaguely intimated. Bloch, however, holds that *concrete utopias* can be conceptualised. One way to paraphrase this view is to say that while we cannot know the actual utopian society of the future, we can *anticipate* it: our conceptualisations of the utopian society do not correspond to its actual manifestation in the future, but instead present its possibilities or potentials. This idea of utopian visions as potentialities of the ultimate, actual utopia is closely related to Bloch's conception of utopia as the Not-Yet being. For Bloch, *Heimat*, the fully completed utopia, just as any other being, has historical prefigurations, beings which entail the actual content of *Heimat*, even if in an undeveloped or incomplete version. The operator of the Not-Yet in Bloch substitutes for the identity which seems implicit in both Marx and Adorno, and which, at least in part, led them to reject the possibility of utopian thinking. Unlike Marx and Adorno, Bloch is not making a claim to an identification between our visions of utopia and utopia itself. Why Marx and Adorno deemed utopian conceptualisations impossible was dependent also on the fact that the object of these conceptualisations was limited to the actual utopian society of the future. For Bloch, by contrast, utopian thinking is an attempt to envisage the potentials of this utopian society, to articulate outlines that may nonetheless only approach, resemble or approximate it. This difference in what the exact object of utopian thinking is partly explains the contrast between Adorno's and Bloch's views regarding the question of the possibility of utopian thinking. What, however,

---

1 This phrase appears in Meillassoux's unpublished manuscript *L'Inexistence Divine*. See Harman 2011, pp. 99–100.

remains unexplained so far is why Bloch believes that conceptualisations of these potentialities of the utopian society are possible. How does Bloch justify the idea that what we currently take the utopian society to be does, in fact, somehow resemble it? Why does Bloch not see, as Adorno did, all conceptual articulations of the utopian world to be merely rearticulations of the present one?

The answer to this question is not simple, and depends on the perspective of Bloch's philosophy from which we attempt to formulate it. The first two sections of this chapter provide two answers based on Bloch's conceptions of human mind and matter. An exploration of these ontological aspects of Bloch's philosophy will in turn enable us to consider the question of the necessity of utopian thinking, that is, why, in Bloch's view, utopian thinking presents a necessary ingredient of Critical Theory. In the penultimate section I return to the question of the possibility of utopian thinking, and approach it negatively – why is it that the actual utopian society *cannot* be known? The key lies in Bloch's philosophy of history, my investigation of which will help to transform the idea of concrete utopian thinking into a practice I call 'processual utopian thinking'.

1   The Prefigurations of Utopia in the 'Not-Yet-Conscious'

In the radio conversation with Bloch, Adorno mentions the phrase 'utopian consciousness'. I have suggested that this phrase points to Adorno's belief that, in principle, human beings are able to engender visions of utopia. I have further elaborated on how this consciousness, in Adorno's own view, is coopted by the oppressive and controlling mechanisms of the capitalist ideology which in turn hinder its functioning. I have also explained that although this idea of utopian consciousness is detectable in Adorno, it is left underdeveloped. The situation is very different with Bloch. Bloch has a highly developed conception of utopian consciousness for which he uses the term 'the Not-Yet-Conscious' ('das Noch-Nicht-Bewußte'). The most significant difference between Adorno's utopian consciousness and Bloch's Not-Yet-Conscious is, however, not in how far these concepts are advanced philosophically. Instead, this difference regards their nature as such: Bloch's Not-Yet-Conscious is an *essential* part of the human psyche. Although its content does depend on existing historical conditions, it will always retain some independence from these conditions and produce what is truly its own utopian content. Bloch sees this Not-Yet-Conscious as 'the mental representation of what is coming up', 'the actual space of receptivity of the New and production of the New' and as 'the preconsciousness of that which is coming up, the birthplace of the New'.[2] Wishing, desiring, hoping, and imagining are the cognitive processes that occur within this part of the human psyche, and the contents of these processes, that is, our wishes, desires and hopes, are prefigurations or adumbrations of the utopian society.

Bloch contends that the Not-Yet-Conscious has so far remained 'disregarded' and 'unnoticed'.[3] This disregard has, in Bloch's view, resulted in a multilayered misunderstanding of the meaning, nature and functions of the human mind. He posits that, for a long time in the intellectual history of the human mind, it was believed that human beings are generally aware of their inner mental life. A breakthrough was achieved when it was discovered that this is not the case, that 'mental life does not coincide with consciousness'.[4] This breakthrough in turn led to the discovery of the unconscious, that is, those mental activities which we are not aware of. And in this identification Bloch determined a mistake: namely that the unconscious was understood to be completely subordinated to the conscious. In his own words, the unconscious is recognised as something that 'lies beneath consciousness and has dropped out of it'.[5] Instead, Bloch suggests, the correct understanding of the unconscious holds that it has two sides: one that is subordinated to the conscious – Bloch calls this side 'the No-Longer-Conscious' ('Nicht-Mehr-Bewußte') – and the other side that is supraordinated to the conscious.[6] The Not-Yet-Conscious is this second side of the unconscious.

The way Bloch talks about this disregard and misinterpretation of the human psyche is exemplary of his understanding of the advancement of our knowledge more generally. He certainly considers this advancement to be progressive, but in a very peculiar way. His notion of progress entails a temporal structure of a continuously delayed development. As the advancement of a certain idea progresses, it never arrives as a fully formed insight, but always lacks something of that which it strives for. At first, all our inner life was conceived of as conscious, then also as unconscious, and now with Bloch this unconscious is further differentiated into the No-Longer-Conscious and the Not-Yet-Conscious. Each of these categories, however, anticipates the forthcoming ones: that of consciousness anticipates that of unconsciousness, and that of unconsciousness those of the No-Longer-Conscious and the Not-Yet-Conscious. As Wayne Hudson notes, this temporal structure even applies to

2 Bloch 1977 [1954/55/50], pp. 157; 131.
3 Bloch 1977 [1954/55/50], pp. 150; 131.
4 Bloch 1977 [1954/55/50], p. 130.
5 Bloch 1977 [1954/55/50], p. 130.
6 Bloch 1977 [1954/55/50], p. 130.

Bloch's own thought and writing.[7] Bloch, in fact, never fully answers the questions at the point when he poses them.

It is thus more accurate to claim not that Bloch argues that the existence of the Not-Yet-Conscious has been disregarded, that is, left out entirely from the previous understandings of human minds; but rather that it has been misunderstood. In the following I explain what exactly this misunderstanding of the Not-Yet-Conscious amounts to. I suggest that there are two aspects to this misunderstanding: first, in viewing the Not-Yet-Conscious as a purely subjective sphere, and second, in seeing it as being interconnected only with the past. Further on, I show that Bloch objects to these two ideas, and in turn perceives the Not-Yet-Conscious not only as a subjective but also as an objective phenomenon, and as one interconnected not only with the past but also with the future.

Bloch argues that the Not-Yet-Conscious has been interpreted as a purely subjective phenomenon, as originating, advancing and terminating in the subject. The misinterpretation Bloch highlights is the mere subjective relevance of the cognitive material produced by this Not-Yet-Conscious, the idea that our wishes and dreams pertain only to ourselves and have no wider significance, neither for individuals around us, nor for humanity as such, nor indeed for the world at large. One intellectual source of this misinterpretation identified by Bloch is Freud's theory of dreams.[8]

According to Bloch, Freud sees the main function of dreaming to be the provision of a space in which the subject expresses and provisionally gratifies essentially unrealistic wishes or fantasies. Here, this provisional gratification is perceived as an aspect of expression: by dreaming that I live by the ocean, my dreams not only reveal to me that living by the ocean is my wish, but also fulfil this wish – since in my dreams I am living by the ocean and am, thereby, 'realising' my wish.[9] There is, of course, a difference between realising this wish

---

7　Hudson 2012, p. 23.

8　Besides his motives of the drive and the unconscious, Freud's theory of dreams is the key idea that Bloch critically adopted from Freud. For an account of the influence of Freud on the genesis of Bloch's philosophy, see Schiller 2017, pp. 27–86.

9　Freud, however, considered that, most often, dreams do not represent our wishes as openly as in this example. According to Freud, dreams are a disguise of wishes, and their manifest content does not directly reveal these wishes. Suppose I have murderous feelings towards my boss because he or she frustrates me. I probably would not act out the wish of killing them in my dream, but I might dream of something else that disguises or displaces that wish. I might dream that I kill myself, or die, and that everyone grieves over me. In order to understand what the underlying wish of this dream is, what this dream is actually trying to accomplish, the dream needs to be analysed. In particular, what would need to be subjected to analysis

in my life materially and realising it through dreaming. Bloch thus talks about
this gratification as 'hallucinated wish-fulfillments'.[10] In order for these wishes
to be fulfilled, even in this twisted, immaterial way, the space in which dreaming takes place – namely the unconscious – must be completely removed from
reality. Only then can our minds feel secure enough to express these wishes,
which are deemed to be incompatible with reality.

Although Bloch does not object to Freud's reading of nocturnal dreaming,
he criticises him for not adequately distinguishing nocturnal dreaming from
daytime dreaming, for seeing the latter as a subcategory of the former.[11] Bloch
argues instead that daytime dreams are not merely a 'stepping stone' to the
nocturnal ones, and that they should be examined and analysed separately.[12]
The initial distinction Bloch identifies between nocturnal and daytime dreams
is between the backward or past remembering of nocturnal dreams, and the
forward or future anticipation of daydreams. Whereas 'night-dreams mostly
cannibalise the former life of the drives, they feed on past if not archaic image-
material, and nothing new happens under their bare moon'; daydreams are
'forerunners and anticipation'.[13] I return to this distinction below. The other
distinction Bloch indicates relates to the creative or productive potential of
daydreams:

> In contrast to the nocturnal dream, that of the daytime sketches freely
> chosen and repeatable figures in the air, it can rant and rave, but also
> brood and plan. It gives free play to its thoughts in an indolent fashion [...]
> political, artistic, scientific thoughts. The daydream can furnish inspira-
> tions which do not require interpreting, but working out, it builds castles
> in the air as blueprints too, and not always just fictitious ones.[14]

Here, Bloch notes that the material engendered by our daydreaming is not
merely fictitious or unrealistic. Precisely because daydreaming does not occur
in the realm of the unconscious but in the conscious one, a link with external

---

are what Freud called 'the dream-work', namely, the processes by which the wish disguised
itself in a dream. See, Freud 1989 [1899], pp. 129–41.

10   Bloch 1977 [1954/55/50], p. 87.

11   Bloch seems to exaggerate the degree to which Freud neglects the category of day-
dreaming. In some of his writings Freud clearly distinguish daydreams from the night
ones. See, e.g., his lecture from 1908, 'Creative Writing and Day-Dreaming', in Freud 1989
[1908].

12   Bloch 1977 [1954/55/50], p. 96.

13   Bloch 1977 [1954/55/50], p. 96.

14   Bloch 1977 [1954/55/50], p. 96.

reality is maintained. Because during daydreaming 'the relationship to the outside world is in no way screened out', as it is in the night-dream, Bloch continues, this type of dreaming produces wishes which are relevant for reality, are
realistic, able to be fulfilled in the future – they are objective.[15] Or, in Bloch's
own words: 'what is essential to the daydream' is the seriousness of the pre-
appearance of the possibly Real ('Vor-Schein von möglich Wirklichem').[16] This
category of 'the possibly Real' is one of Bloch's phrases for the objective or realistic ideas we have about the future. The reason why the products of daydreams
indicate objective possibilities lies for Bloch not only in the fact that they main-
tain this relationship with external reality in the course of their production, but
also in that they are extroverted, that is, oriented towards external reality, the
reality outside the subject itself. That is, while nocturnal dreams are oriented
towards themselves, in that they can find their fulfillment in themselves, this
is different for daytime dreams. Bloch writes that the fulfillment of daydreams
proceeds via their effects on our actions, which then in turn affect the external
reality: 'more than one daydream before now has, with sufficient vigour and
experience, *remodelled* reality to make it give this consent'.[17] Whereas the night
dream is supposedly idle, the day dream contains a self-innervation, a tire-
less incentive towards the actual attainment of what it visualises.[18] That is, the
daydream is not fulfilled through its mere articulation, but through its actual
fulfillment, that is, once reality is modified in accordance with the content of
these dreams.

The other way in which Bloch sees the Not-Yet-Conscious as having been
misunderstood, besides in this objective-subjective relation, is that it has been
seen as being tied only to the past. By being tied to the past, Bloch means that
the Not-Yet-Conscious is comprehended simply as a manifestation of what has
already happened, of what has always been. In other words, Bloch contends
that others have perceived the Not-Yet-Conscious to function as some sort of a
collection device or repository of experiences of already undergone and completed events, as a passive storage device for these events and experiences.

Bloch traces these ideas back to the early nineteenth century, in the intellec-
tual-artistic movement of Romanticism. The Romantics – Bloch singles out
Byron, Shelley and Pushkin, as well as the pre-Romantics of *Sturm und Drang* –
were, however, for Bloch, still ambivalent with regard to the relation of their
ideas to time. For Bloch, it often appears as if these artists and writers were

---

15   Bloch 1977 [1954/55/50], p. 102.
16   Bloch 1977 [1954/55/50], p. 109.
17   Bloch 1977 [1954/55/50], p. 98.
18   Bloch 1977 [1954/55/50], p. 98.

simultaneously glorifying both the past and the future, looking both backwards and forwards, seeing the golden age they were describing as an age that has already passed, and as one that is yet to arise. It was only the theory of psychoanalysis, which started to emerge at the turn of the twentieth century, that supposedly cemented the content of the Not-Yet-Conscious as content purely of the past. Yet Bloch does find in the writings of German Romantics, such as Joseph Görres, some real precursors to Freud's and especially to Carl Jung's psychoanalytic work. Bloch asserts that, for all the ambiguities and complexities of Romanticism, its progressive character and revolutionary strands, it was primarily rooted in and to the past: 'in a way which can hardly be recaptured any more, the Romantic was enslaved by the past' and 'preferred to raise nothing but knights' castles in the magic moonlit night'.[19]

In Romantic literature and music, Bloch identifies images of the good and the new, such as for example the knights' castles ('Ritterburgen'). Bloch does not condemn these images themselves. In fact, he sees them as constitutive of genuinely utopian material, providing visions of something that is better. That is, Romanticism possesses its own ideas of what a better world could be. The issue Bloch sees is that 'the Romantic does not understand utopia, not even his own'.[20] More precisely, Bloch argues that the Romantics misperceived the location of utopias they were envisaging. In Romanticism, utopia is viewed as belonging to the past, as a world that did exist but that has passed and is now gone. Bloch makes this point clearly by differentiating between the acts of production and of reflection, the former corresponding to the creation of an artwork, and the latter to the interpretation of the artwork once it has been conceived. He illustrates this difference by commenting on the German Romantic novelist Jean Paul: 'even Jean Paul, the creator of the most beautiful wishful landscapes shimmering ahead, finally sought the light, as soon as he was not creating but rather reflecting on it, only in the past, not in the future'.[21] Bloch considers Jean Paul the creator of 'the most beautiful wishful landscapes', and does not dispute the aesthetics or desirability of the content of his writings. Instead, Bloch criticises Jean Paul's own view of what writing about and describing these landscapes entailed. According to Bloch, for Jean Paul writing entailed *representing* the past, as opposed to *creating* or *producing* the future. Bloch sees the landscapes Jean Paul described as objects of thought, as ideas created by the author, ideas that do not possess a corresponding material counterpart: these landscapes existed for the time being only in Jean Paul's mind

---

19   Bloch 1977 [1954/55/50], p. 152.
20   Bloch 1977 [1954/55/50], p. 160.
21   Bloch 1977 [1954/55/50], p. 154.

and on the paper. One could say that, for Bloch, the Romantics were too modest with respect to their own artistic or creative potential: where they were in fact producing something new, they thought they were only reproducing the old. They wrongly perceived themselves as epigones, as merely following or imitating past practitioners. This is what Bloch means when he writes that: 'All productivity, especially the expectation which paradoxically characterizes so much of Romanticism, lost itself here in antiquarian images, in the past, in the immemorial, in myth'.[22] The new ideas the Romantics created were deprived of their own newness because they were deemed as having been sourced from the past. In that their productivity of the Not-Yet-Conscious part of the human mind was not actually comprehended as productivity, but instead as reproduction, or as epigonism, something valuable was lost.[23]

Bloch argues that the correct interpretation of the Not-Yet-Conscious is to view it as being tied not only to the past but also to the future, and thus to recognise its productive, creative and dynamic capacities. For Bloch the Not-Yet-Conscious does not merely collect events and experiences that have already happened but engenders events that could happen in the future.

One reason why Bloch sees the content of the Not-Yet-Conscious as something that could yet happen, as anticipating the future, is because he does not regard the past and its events as completed, as having occurred fully or entirely, as being realised to their full possibility. This idea is entailed in one of the better known of Bloch's dictums – that the 'S is not yet P'.[24] One way to interpret this claim is to say that 'P' represents the entirety, or the full extent of possibilities of an event or an object; and 'S' the event or the object as it actually existed, that is, those possibilities of P that were in fact already realised. The valuable function of the Not-Yet-Conscious lies for Bloch precisely in the fact that it does not store these events merely as 'S' but that it can capture them also as 'P'. In the act of capturing 'P' resides the productiveness or the creativeness of the Not-Yet-Conscious – it does not *articulate* events as they were but *rearticulates* them as they could have been. Bloch perceives the gap between what they were and what they could have been as their unrealised possibilities or as their future content. One could say that the Not-Yet-Conscious somehow *misremembers* past events by endowing them with something more that they actually were.

---

22   Bloch 1977 [1954/55/50], p. 153.
23   Bloch 1977 [1954/55/50], p. 141.
24   Bloch 1977 [1975], p. 42.

2   Incompleteness of the World as the 'Not-Yet-Become'

Via this revision of Freud's interpretation of dreams, we can now see more specifically how Bloch modified Marx's dismissal of our wishes and desires as a valuable tool of achieving social transformation. Unlike Bloch, Marx did not discuss the value of dreams and dreaming. He did, however, touch on a related cognitive capacity he referred to as imagination or fantasy, as outlined in my first chapter. For Marx, fantasising was synonymous with producing ideas of a good society that cannot possibly be realised, and the reason he offered to support this contention was that fantasying is not influenced at all by external, objective reality – it takes place within the subject itself, removed from non-subjective conditions. As I elaborated further in that chapter, this view of Marx is paradoxical: whereas in his general materialist orientation he considers the whole of reality, including the subjects and their consciousness, to be conditioned by matter, his comments on fantasising have a heavily idealistic overtone. While still residing in consciousness, fantasising is supposed to be wholly autonomous, and not at all affected by the objective conditions, as if the engendered ideas were to emerge from themselves.

Bloch's own variety of materialist philosophy is free of this paradox.[25] Although Marx does not frame the relation between the objective and the subjective, or between matter and consciousness, in a strictly deterministic fashion, he does not recognise these categories in a fully dialectical sense. For Marx, there is always some separation maintained between the object and the subject. Whereas consciousness is heavily conditioned by material reality, and in turn, also influences the latter realm, it nevertheless exists, in Marx's system, as something separate from matter. The situation is very different for Bloch. For Bloch, as Hans Heinz Holz puts it, all 'layers of the living, the spiritual and the psychological' are grasped 'as manifestations of material nature', and moreover, the consciousness itself is 'a kind of material being'.[26] This means that mind and consciousness are themselves part of material reality, are partially objective themselves. Thus, for Bloch, any product of consciousness, including wishes, dreams and imaginary ideas, is not a purely subjective but also an objective phenomenon. Bloch's term 'objective imagination' ('objektive Phantasie') is a perfect example of the operation of his dialectical analysis of the rela-

---

25   Different names were used by Bloch himself and later by his scholars to designate his kind of materialism, including 'speculative materialism' and 'ontology of the Not-Yet,' and 'philosophy of the unfinished world'. For Bloch's use of the term 'speculative materialism', see Moir 2016, pp. 329–30.

26   Holz 2012, p. 485.

tionship between the subject and the object, or consciousness and matter. In this relationship, fantasy, hope, dreams and possibility are predicated on what is objectively possible. But at the same time, what is objectively possible is changed by the way in which dreams, hopes, and fantasy are expressed and mobilised.

A helpful term to conceive of Bloch's consciousness-matter relation is in terms of *articulation* or *manifestation*: ideas, wishes, hopes and dreams are one possible manifestation of the material reality. This relation, however, does not apply only to ideas, etc. but to consciousness as such. In Bloch's ontology, each individual dimension of consciousness should itself be understood as a manifestation of a certain dimension of matter, including the Not-Yet-Conscious. Its corresponding material dimension is 'the Not-Yet-Become' ('das Noch-Nicht-Gewordenes'). Bloch defines this category as the correlate of the Not-Yet-Conscious.[27] The importance of the Not-Yet-Conscious lies in how it gives us access to the Not-Yet-Become, which is not, on its own, directly comprehensible or accessible to human beings. However, what Bloch actually means by his idea of the Not-Yet-Become is far from obvious. The concept implies that something that is material – in the sense of being tangible, physical, and as such already existent – at the same time, in virtue of its belonging to the Not-Yet, also does not exist. But how can this ontological non-existence hold for matter itself? Is not matter defined by its ontological existence or presence? If matter is that which really exists out there, does it simply have to exist and be present?

The answer lies in Bloch's distinct view of what matter is. In his *Tübingen Introduction to Philosophy*, he formulates this view in the following words: 'the world-substance, mundane matter itself, is not yet finished and complete, but persists in a utopian-open state, i.e. a state in which its self-identity is not yet manifest'.[28] Bloch's materialism is more complex than the basic contention that matter is the only thing there is, that there is nothing that is not material. With this contention Bloch combines a view of matter as a process, as an essentially dynamic entity, which he calls 'creative matter' or *natura naturans*.[29] Bloch objects to the conception of matter as 'Klotz,' as a lump of dead and inert stuff.[30] He refashions this view of matter by adopting ideas which he refers to as Left-Aristotelian ideas. More specifically, Bloch's category of the Not-Yet-Become can be understood as a certain reconceptualisation of the Aris-

---

27   Bloch 1977 [1954/55/50], p. 160.
28   Bloch 1977 [1963/64], p. 102.
29   Geoghegan 2013, p. 45.
30   Bloch 1977 [1963/64], p. 1371.

totelian categories of the *dynámei on* (that which might become possible) and *kata to dynaton* (that which is possible). Whereas these Aristotelian categories themselves are difficult to grasp, and furthermore it remains unclear how exactly Bloch converts them into his Not-Yet-Become, the key idea to understand here is that the actual and potential forms of the existence of matter are both seen as essential to matter. That a form which has not yet actualised is in fact present in matter is thus no oxymoron: it is simply a different initial presumption about what matter is from what we see to be the common sense one.

3   The Necessity of Utopian Thinking

Bloch's Not-Yet-Conscious is not a repository of past objects or events as they happen, but instead a method that produces or creates possibilities not yet attained in reality. Prima facie, Bloch's criticism of Freud can be read simply as Freud's failure to recognise a side of the human psyche, or as a misinterpretation of the psyche. As Thompson puts it, Bloch's objection to:

> the Freudian *Urtrauma* and psychologization of the political and philosophical debate was that the Socratic idea that all thought is simply anamnesis, that is, constant remembering and repetition of past events, does not take into account the fact that most people actually spend most of their time projecting forward.[31]

That is, Bloch is claiming that for a large part, human thought has to do with the future, of what we will do, could do, with projecting, planning, anticipating, living in the future, and that Freud failed to notice this. He disputes the mere existence of anamnetic repetition as a defining anthropological feature.

This, however, is only the most basic layer of Bloch's objection to Freud. It is rather an explicit one, and in principal it amounts to an empirical objection. Beyond this, I find there is another, less straightforward critique, yet a more significant one. It is evident that for Bloch this misinterpretation is deeply problematic, that the subordination of the Not-Yet-Conscious to a past world has detrimental implications. What is not so evident is why this misinterpretation is problematic, why it is detrimental to conceive of the Not-Yet-Conscious as merely an archive of the past and not also of the possibil-

---

31   Thompson 2013, pp. 86–7.

ities of the future. What is the point, in Thompson's words, of Bloch's 'accus-ation of anamnetic circularity?'[32] Why is it important, as Žižek puts it, 'not to adopt toward the present the "point of view of finality", viewing it as if it were already past', but instead 'to reintroduce the openness of future into the past, to grasp that-what-was in its process of becoming, to see the contingent process that generated existing necessity'?[33] The closest that Bloch comes to an answer is in the following assertion: 'the vision of the utopian conditions, the yield of its content, thus encountered the most powerful block [...] in anamnesis, a re-remembering'.[34] By the 'yield' of a utopian vision, Bloch refers to an actually existing utopian society. What anamnesis obstructs is the realisa-tion of a utopian society, its actualisation. In another instance in *The Principle of Hope* Bloch makes a basically identical remark – he describes anamnesis as a 'block against the being sui generis', that is, as the obstruction *sui gen-eris*, obstruction as such, that which is the block itself in being.[35] What Freud lacks in Bloch's view is thus not simply the mere faculty of looking forward but the transformative or productive power that this faculty has in relation to our reality. That anticipation plays a constructive role in facilitating pro-gressive social transformation is a contention many scholars ascribe to Bloch. Among others, Ruth Levitas posits that, in Bloch's view, utopian thinking plays the function of a 'catalyst of a better future', that it not only anticipates this future but 'helps to effect' this future.[36] Similarly, Douglas Keller asserts that 'it is his [Bloch's] conviction that only when we project our future in the light of what is, what has been, and what could be can we engage in the creat-ive practice that will produce the world we all want and realize humanity's deepest hopes and dreams', and moreover points to the 'unrealised potenti-alities' as that which 'propel us to change and self-realization'.[37] Yet another question remains to be answered, namely: what is this productive function of our anticipation, how does it work, and why, on the other hand, does re-remembering not possess it? As I have argued above, the object of dispute is the interpretation or recognition of a specific wish or desire, and not the con-tent of this desire or wish itself. The same wish can be comprehended either as a forgone moment in the past, or as one that might yet come. Why and how does this twist matter? Why is the former 'enshrined feeling, this inces-

---

32   Thompson 2012, p. 42.
33   Žižek 2013, p. xviii.
34   Bloch 1977 [1954/55/50], p. 154.
35   Bloch 1977 [1954/55/50], p. 158.
36   Levitas 1990, p. 14.
37   Kellner and O'Hara 1976, p. 26.

tuous phenomenon of the desire to return to the womb of the night and the past', a block to the realisation of a utopian society, and the latter conducive to it?[38]

Bloch does not explain why utopian thinking plays a productive role in the realisation of the future. It is not even the case that he intends, but then fails, to give any kind of answer. He does not posit this question since the claim that utopian thinking creates the future is the very starting point of his philosophy. To be more precise, Bloch does not make this claim with respect to utopian thinking itself, but to a closely related, more general act of hoping. Evidently, or perhaps not so evidently, this claim is enclosed in the phrase 'Prinzip Hoffnung', which suggests above all that hope is a 'principle'. Here Bloch uses the concept 'principle' as a fundamental element or determinant of reality. Put more simply, Bloch understands hoping as something that *is*, as an activity in which humans engage, an activity that is essentially constitutive of humans, as an anthropological fact.

A starting point of Bloch's philosophy is a specific anthropological view, according to which human beings are controlled strongly by their drives or impulses ('Triebe'). But whereas Freud postulates libido as the most important of these drives, Bloch argues that there exists a more general drive, of which libido is merely one manifestation. In accordance with another starting point of Bloch's philosophy, namely the 'not-yetness', the incompleteness of reality, human beings too are incomplete. As the opening heading of the first chapter in *The Principle of Hope* tells us: 'WE START OUT EMPTY'.[39] This emptiness or incompleteness of human beings is analogous, for Bloch, to our lack of self-possession, self-awareness or self-recognition. This idea permeates Bloch's writings and is often articulated aphoristically right at their beginnings. For example, in the *Tübingen Introduction to Philosophy*, Bloch contends: 'I am. But I do not possess myself'.[40] According to Bloch, the most fundamental anthropological drive is thus the drive towards completion, towards exceeding what we already are, but at the same time towards merely recognising what we already are. As he explains in the same text, for the subject to see itself, 'it must grow out of itself. It must grow out of itself, if it is to see anything at all'.[41] And furthermore: 'The mere am of I am, only to achieve self-awareness, must take to itself a something from without'.[42] The critical point to understand here is that for

---

38   Bloch 1977 [1954/55/50], p. 153.
39   Bloch 1977 [1954/55/50], p. 21.
40   Bloch 1977 [1963/64], p. 13.
41   Bloch 1977 [1963/64], p. 13.
42   Bloch 1977 [1963/64], p. 13.

Bloch the acts of recognising and exceeding ourselves are inseparable. Bloch names 'the inside' ('das Innen') that what we already are – 'The "is" is inside' – and 'the outside' ('das Außen') that which we are not yet.[43] The anthropological constant of the drive towards exceeding ourselves can thus be reformulated as the drive towards the outside.

One idea of Bloch, however, may provide the grounds from which a more nuanced, worked out answer can be developed. This idea is the distinction Bloch draws between anamnetic and anticipatory thinking. This idea is, of course, one of the essential building blocks of Bloch's philosophy and Bloch is at pains to emphasise just how fundamentally, and in how many different ways, these two sorts of thinking differ. The particular difference that I consider relevant to the above question is the difference between memory as being finished, closed, completed, and anticipation as being unfinished, open, incomplete. Bloch describes memory as 'a finished simultaneity' ('fertiges Zugleichsein'), as the flash where the closedness of what is opening up has long since been decided.[44]

The distinction has the following significant implication: if a certain idea is in fact yet to be realised, if there exists a gap between our conception of it and its actual material existence, then there exists scope for us to influence and to help with this realisation. If ideas are mobilised in the service of the future, only then can they become productive for the realisation of the desirable future, and for the transformation of the undesirable present. On the other hand, if something has already been realised then there is nothing more that can be done, and in this sense memory as such does not provide any incentive for us to act or to change our behaviour.

4   Processual Utopia and Processual Utopian Thinking

Bloch's position on the possibility of utopian thinking as I have outlined it so far can be summarised as follows: whereas the content of the absolute utopian society, that is, of the one specific better society that might in fact come into being in the future and that would exist materially, cannot be known in the present, the multiplicity of potential utopian societies can be known. Bloch maintains that we are able to plan for the unforeseen and to map out what we think this unknown might possibly hold for us. His conceptions of human con-

---

43   Bloch 1977 [1963/64], p. 13.
44   Bloch 1977 [1954/55/50], p. 158.

sciousness and of matter as containing the Not-Yet serve as justification of this position, in particular of its positive dimension, that we *can* know; or, to use a more appropriate term, that we can *anticipate* the future. These conceptions, however, do not fully account for the other, negative side of Bloch's position, namely, for why we *cannot* know the one actual utopian society. The answer to this question lies in Bloch's idea of history as an open process, instead of as a predetermined path; and correspondingly in his idea of utopia as an outcome of this process, instead of as a telos of the path.

History, for Bloch, is an open process in that each event is an outcome of existing conditions – it is contingent on these contingencies. In this vein, Peter Thompson has termed Bloch's conception of history as being underpinned by the 'metaphysics of contingency'.[45] This emphasis on contingency does not, however, imply that these events are completely arbitrary, as if emerging from nowhere. No: for Bloch, as Thompson holds, each event is determined by everything else that preceded it.[46] This means that each event is, besides being contingent, also necessary, in the sense of being the unique outcome of all the events that have happened before it.

As any other event, the really existing utopian society of the future should also be understood as the outcome of everything that has happened up until its emergence. This idea of utopia is implied in Bloch's probably most often-quoted fragment, the final passage of *The Principle of Hope*:

> man everywhere is living still in prehistory. Indeed all and everything still stands before the creation of a right and proper world. *True genesis is not at the beginning but at the end* and it starts to begin only when society and existence become radical, i.e. grasp their roots. But the root of history is the labouring, creating human being who reshapes and overhauls the given. Once he has grasped himself and established what is his, without expropriation and alienation, based in real democracy, there will arise in the world something which shines into the childhood of all and in which no one has yet been: Home.[47]

The reputation of this passage does not necessarily facilitate our grasp either of the passage as a whole, or of the paradoxical claim that lies at its heart, namely: '*The true genesis is not at the beginning, but at the end*'. Here Bloch rewrites the meaning of genesis, disentangling it from its Biblical meaning. In the biblical

---

45   Thompson 2016; 2013; 2012.
46   Thompson 2016, p. 443.
47   Bloch 1977 [1954/55/50], p. 1628.

context, the term genesis coincides with God's creation of the human world, and thus implies simply a fulfillment of God's creativity. In contrast, in Bloch's sense, genesis is only present at the end and as a result of the process of becoming. But how can something that is by definition supposed to present the start, the onset or the commencement, be present also at the end, as the conclusion or termination? To answer this question, Thompson helpfully employs the obstetric metaphor, otherwise a commonplace in philosophies of historical change. Thompson contends that 'after all, birth comes at the end of a pregnancy, not at the beginning, even though from the first day we anticipate what the birth and the life of the new New will be like'.[48] Adopting this analogy, it becomes clearer how the true utopian society of the future, the 'new New', can be present both at the beginning and at the end at the same time: as the last phase of pregnancy, it presents the end, and as the start of the life of a new human being, or at least the more independent kind of life, it presents the beginning. The essential point to understand here is that even if the essence of the true utopian society lies in its radical difference from the whole of history that preceded it, or as Bloch, in following Marx, calls this era, 'prehistory' ('Vorgeschichte'), the true utopian society cannot be thought of as something separate or independent of it. The true utopian society comes into being only as the outcome of this process of prehistory.

The nature of this concept of utopia, to which Thompson has referred as 'processual utopia', comes out most clearly when contrasted to teleological utopia.[49] The notion of the teleological utopia predicates that utopia simply needs to be realised or implemented in practice, and must thus already exist as such, completed and perfected, even if not in material form. In Christian thought, for example, the counterpart of this utopia is the Kingdom of God. All that needs to happen is for this world to be transferred onto the earth. The coming about of the earthly kingdom must happen by some miracle or apocalypse from outside the material world and without active human intervention. This is not the case for the processual utopia. This utopia indeed also already exists now, but only as a potentiality, and is thus not fully but instead only partially prefigured. It will become fully formed only once it starts to be realised, which in turn demands human action. Furthermore, it does not exist in some separate domain of reality but is constituent of reality itself.

---

48   Thompson 2012, p. 45.
49   This phrase of 'processual utopia' ('prozeßhaft gehende Utopie') appears also in Bloch's own writings, including in his lecture on the disappointment of hope. See Bloch 1977 [1965b], p. 388.

Bloch's exposition of the concept of utopia does not have nihilistic epistemological implications; that is, it does not imply that *nothing at all* can be known,
said or foreseen about this ensuing outcome. As explained earlier, because
Bloch conceives the existing reality as being penetrated by possibilities which
we can access through our Not-Yet-Conscious, we do know something about
the utopian future. The crucial thing, however, is not to claim that a vision of
utopian society that we posit in the present moment *is*, in the sense that this
vision is identical to, or that it corresponds perfectly or exactly with, the society of the future. To reiterate this point, to make it perfectly clear: the utopian
society that we can conceptualise does not coincide perfectly with the society
that might in fact be realised in the future. The existing conceptualisation of
this society might perhaps best be thought of as one constitutive step in the
realisation of this society, one 'new' on the way to the 'new New'.

The notion of processual utopia helps us to complement the idea of concrete utopian thinking as an element of Critical Theory, as a critical-theoretical
practice. In the last section of the preceding chapter, I explained the meaning of the concept of concrete utopia for Bloch, and subsequently, on the basis
of this meaning, outlined what concrete utopian thinking could be. I advance
the idea of processual thinking in an analogous fashion. Before proceeding, it
should be noted that concrete and processual thinking are not two mutually
exclusive forms of utopian thinking, but are instead fully compatible. I have
distinguished between them only for purposes of clarity.

It is useful to consider the idea of processual utopian thinking independently because it shows directly that utopian thinking is not inherently dangerous or destructive to desirable social change. The idea that utopian thinking, in
the sense of positive conceptualisations of a better future, is indeed dangerous
has been explicitly articulated, among others, by the prominent French critical
theorist Michel Foucault:

> But the idea of a program of proposals is dangerous. As soon as a program
> is presented, it becomes a law, and there's a prohibition against inventing
> [...] The program must be wide open.[50]

Foucault sees utopian thinking as consisting not only in programmes, but in
programmes which eventually become or evolve into laws.[51] As laws, utopian

50   Foucault 1997, p. 139.
51   This quotation of Foucault should not be understood as a comprehensive representation
      of his stance on utopian thinking more generally. In fact, Foucault considers that, espe-
      cially under the circumstances of the postwar era, a viable alternative to socialism needs to

thinking is destructive because it prohibits any deviation from itself, and thus prohibits the creation, development and invention of other, perhaps even more desirable ideas of the good. But why does utopian thinking need to become law, or better, why should we recognise its ideas as fixed, absolute or universally valid? This does not need to be the case. Once we substitute, as the object represented by utopian thinking, a teleological utopia with a processual utopia, utopian thinking does not correspond to a programme, but to something more fluid and open. I call this form of utopian thinking processual thinking, which Thompson too has indicated in his discussion of a 'plan' that is 'purely contingent', a plan that constantly reacts to the contingent emergence of new circumstances.[52] In Thompson's phrasing, this notion 'restores utopian thinking that would not go as far as, but therefore also simultaneously went beyond, the limitations of any reified and programmatic blueprint'.[53] By saying that processual utopian thinking would not go 'as far as' a programmatic blueprint, Thompson means that it does not claim to identify with the true, absolute utopia. At the same time, processual utopian thinking also goes beyond a blueprint: the contingency of its content, which it openly admits to, does not restrict or inhibit human action and thinking in the same way as programmes or laws. Instead of being restricted to the realisation of the absolute utopia, utopian thinking in its processual form is constructive of it. Once we adopt Bloch's notion of processual utopia, then utopia becomes a world that 'could be there if we could only do something for it. Not only if we travel there, but *in that* we travel there the island of utopia arises out of the sea of the possible – utopia, but with new contents'.[54]

---

be constructed, and that intellectuals have a role to play in this construction. See Foucault 2003, pp. 105–14. Foucault, moreover, advances the notion of 'heterotopia', an alternative to a singular utopian blueprint, that does in many respects resonate with concept of 'processual utopia' developed here. See Foucault 1986.

52   Thompson 2016, p. 444.
53   Thompson 2012, p. 83.
54   Bloch 1964, p. 352.

Conclusion

The question that originally motivated this book was the methodology of Critical Theory. How is Critical Theory done? More specifically, how is Critical Theory done with respect to its self-defined objective of facilitating progressive social change? What are the ends, methods, means, practices or tools it should employ to attain this objective? 'Going to the streets', in one or another form, might in fact be the most straightforward answer to this question. I am, however, interested if critical theorists *qua* critical theorists have an additional, somewhat separate role to play in this process. Can their skills, capacities, knowledges, ways of arguing and writing, diagnosing and analysing, reasoning and criticising, abstracting and synthesising be utilised productively above, beyond, and in conjunction with public activism? It is, of course, clear that any effective employment of these more strictly conceptual means will depend on their interaction with public activism itself. The relationship between critical theorists and society, or their position in it, is, despite its significance, not my concern here. My concern is instead solely the form or the nature of critical theorists' conceptual means.

Critique, or more specifically, critique of the existing society, social critique, is likely the foremost of these means. Critical Theory reasserted the central appeal of the Enlightenment that, as Kant summarised it, 'to critique everything must submit'.[1] Hegel and Marx sustained this fondness for critique, and in parallel further developed and transformed it. Hegel renounced Kant's conception of critique, a conception that presupposes the existence of an autonomous subject, and Marx subsequently turned aspects of Hegel's critique on its head. By the turn of the twentieth century Marx's approach to critique was upheld, and yet also repealed. Max Weber, Georg Lukács and finally the critical theorists themselves renounced the instrumentality of the existing practices of critique, but not of critique itself. With Critical Theory, critique became synonymous with its method per se. It is, after all, called *Critical* Theory. In Critical Theory critique has indeed often been complemented by other tools, such as by diagnosis and analysis (for example, in order to posit an aspect of the existing society as wrong, this aspect first needs to be identified among many others). The notion of critique, however, has functioned as the umbrella term, colonising all others.

---

1   Kant 1998 [1781], pp. 100–1.

Over the past few decades, many have recognised the fruits of two centuries of critique as bittersweet. Nietzsche anticipated this sentiment, doubting the purely positive effects of forcing everything to undergo critical interrogation and unmasking. That critique has run out of steam is a claim that today extends across the various political orientations of philosophers. Besides Bruno Latour, Peter Sloterdijk and Slavoj Žižek represent two further voices to have forcefully articulated the critique of critique.[2] Alain Badiou talks about 'the crisis of negation', specifically 'the conception of negation which was a creative one', or, as I have called it, of negation in which the positive or constructive part is supposed to always already be included.[3] Within literary theory, Rita Felski has drawn attention to the limitations of critique, and with respect to the existing sociopolitical circumstances Naomi Klein has contended that 'no is not enough'.[4] Amy Allen and Nikolas Kompridis have directed their scepticism of critique more exclusively at Critical Theory. What is distinct in this strand of disapproval of purely critical practices is its immanent invitation towards utopian thinking as the alternative that could complement critique. Whereas Allen calls for restoration of the 'anticipatory-utopian moment' of Critical Theory, Kompridis's proposal consists in reorienting critique towards 'disclosure', disclosure of the possibilities, yet to be noticed or attained, of another world.[5] It is not entirely clear why utopian thinking is immediately perceived as this alternative or complementing method to critique. Above all, it seems, this suggestion is derived from a mere hunch, even if a very strong one, that Critical Theory's commitment to a radically better future must also have been implanted into its fabric, that its aim of to attaining a specific kind of future must somehow also feature in the ways this objective is to be attained.

I too have approached the writing of my book with these two preliminary judgements, one of critique as unsatisfactory, deficient or even destructive, and the other of utopian thinking as the other possible, immanently available method or end of Critical Theory. The thoughts, research and writing that were spurred by these initial sentiments subsequently sharpened into the question of the ends of utopian thinking in Critical Theory. The ensuing investigation of these ends has been historical as well as critical. The historical trajectory

---

2 In his public lectures and newspaper articles and blog posts, Žižek repeatedly emphasises that the failure of the contemporary left can be traced to its inability to construct an alternative to the present capitalist society. See, e.g. Žižek 2014 and 2016. See also Žižek 2015 and 2017. For Sloterdijk see Schinkel and Noordegraaf-Eelens 2011.

3 Badiou 2011, p. 234.

4 Felski 2015; Klein 2017.

5 Allen 2015, p. 514; Kompridis 2005, p. 334. For an extended version of Kompridis's argument, see Kompridis 2006.

itself is complex, and consists of at least two aspects. The first aspect concerns the actual historical presence or existence of utopian thinking in the writings of critical theorists. In Marx, the figure who exerted most influence on the tradition of Critical Theory, utopian thinking was constitutive of his theorising. In the first instance this is evident from Marx's writings themselves. His ideas of species-being and non-alienated labour unveil the radically different and more desirable nature of human beings, one that would prevail in the future communist society. Some of the assertions of the early Marx give the reader the impression that, in such a society, the self of the one would merge with the selves of the others, leaving one to never be truly on her own again. One's wishes, needs, desires, worries, pains and troubles would coalesce with our wishes, needs, desires, worries, pains and troubles. This fusion of the individual with her community presents, however, only one face of Marx's species-being. Only its other face establishes this concept as a properly utopian one, in the sense of being 'too good to be true'. While one completely identifies with the others, the individual maintains its individuality, its uniqueness, its singular identity. It is this double insistence on the individual being identifying as strongly with herself as she does with her community that infuses Marx's conception of human nature with something strongly appealing. The intensified closeness between individuals does not come at the cost of diminished diversity among them. In fact, the opposite is true: in a communist society, the supposed impossibility of being at the same time one with the others and one with oneself is overcome: 'Only in community [with others has each] individual the means of cultivating his gifts in all directions; only in the community, therefore, is personal freedom possible'.[6] That utopian thinking was indeed constitutive of Marx's writings becomes further evident once Marx's philosophical anthropology is complemented with a list of the institutional characteristics of a society inhabited by species-beings. The foremost of such institutional characteristic is common ownership of the means of production. Marx's utopianism becomes even more visible once we refocus our gaze from Marx's writings themselves to their broader historical context of the mid-nineteenth century. One of the most marked characteristics of this era was nothing but the presence of utopian thinking in its politics. The notion of the communist or socialist society was then very much present. In the sense that this society did differ radically from the existing one, its notion can be described as utopian. Among other political forces, it was the First International that effectively embodied and advocated for socialism. For all the disagreements that

---

6   Marx and Engels 1978 [1932], p. 74.

prevailed among the individual parties of this organisation, eventually leading to its dissolution, this diverse array of Marxist, anarchist, socialist, communist and more liberal member-groups was united in its struggle against the rising capitalist order and in its replacement by a society defending the interests of the workers. Marx was both a theoretician and an activist involved in the activities of the First International and was committed to many of its objectives and ideals. Insofar as we accept my suggestion that these ideals of socialism can be described as utopian, Marx too should be perceived as engaging in the practice of utopian thinking. One could, of course, argue that relative to some of his fellow communist and socialist sympathisers, Marx's vision of communism appears basic and vague, and, moreover, that relative to Marx's corpus as a whole, very few pages – or even lines – are dedicated to spelling out this vision. Yet, neither of these two considerations undermines my argument that utopian thinking presents one essential dimension of Marx's thinking. Both of these considerations fail to take into account the broader historical context to a sufficient extent. The first looks as Marx's writings almost independently of that context, whereas the second judges the existence of Marx's utopianism solely on the basis of a comparison with a small set of his contemporaries. Perhaps the most crucial question to be asked regarding the place of utopian thinking in Marx needs to consider the relationship between his writings and the extent to which utopian vision was already available in the wider political discourse. Perhaps the very fact that such a notion was readily available was one of the reasons why Marx did not dedicate much time to elaborating it.

Through Marx's influence, utopian thinking was instilled in the foundations of Critical Theory. These kernels of utopian thinking were, however, never given the proper chance to grow and develop into a substantial dimension of Critical Theory. While the legacy of early Critical Theory is ambivalent – on the one hand, there is Adorno's thought, lacking basically any positive conceptualisation of communism, and, on the other hand, there are Bloch's writings that brim with utopian expressions – Critical Theory today stands as a non-utopian intellectual tradition. The ambivalence in early Critical Theory is complex, and the designation of Adorno as a non-utopian thinker and of Bloch as a utopian one holds only in certain respects. The main qualification of Bloch's utopian thinking is that it is in no way a straightforward continuation of Marx's. Nor does it correspond neatly to the definition of utopian thinking I have outlined in my introduction, which is, in fact, inspired by Marx's utopian thinking in the first place. Bloch's *Principle of Hope* with its format of a utopian encyclopaedia is often intractable, his *Traces* are as incomprehensible as Adorno's constellations, and his notion of *Heimat* does not inform us much about communism. A comprehensive and nuanced account of the nature, form and kind of Bloch's utopian thinking has not yet been provided by Bloch scholarship. Although this book attempts to provide such an analysis only in a preliminary and provisional manner, it has shown that some aspects of Bloch's utopian thinking are congruent with positive or affirmative thinking. Bloch introduced many neologisms and literary figures in his accounts of a utopian society, formulating them at odds with prevailing grammatical rules, and combining them with criticism of the existing society. All of these modifications ensued in his new variety of utopian thinking. Yet, the foremost object of this new thinking remains utopian society itself. The diversions and detours that Bloch takes in disclosing this utopian society exist and need to be acknowledged. However, they also need to be put aside if we are to recognise the positive or affirmative nature of his utopian language. In contrast to Adorno, Bloch insists that utopian thinking must provide images of what utopia *is*.

My conception of the historical trajectory of utopian thinking in Critical Theory both elaborates on and disputes those accounts offered by the existing scholarship. The elaboration is a very simple one: instead of seeing early Critical Theory to be synonymous with the names of Adorno, Horkheimer and Benjamin, I also include Bloch; there are good historical reasons for this, just as there are reasons for his exclusion. There is, of course, no single correct way to group individual thinkers into intellectual traditions, and my aim has not been to argue that my delineation is in any way superior. But it is precisely the arbitrariness entailed in the labelling of intellectual traditions that should be recognised and attended to. This labelling presents an important factor conditioning the process of knowledge creation and transmission, including simply the exclusion of certain ideas by including certain others. The boundaries of intellectual traditions should thus constantly be renegotiated: the ideas of those thinkers who are deemed to belong to, or to represent them, should constantly be questioned, and of those who lie outside them not consigned to oblivion.

The historical trajectory that ensues from resuscitating the name of Bloch shatters our accepted understanding of what Critical Theory is and does. This shattering consists not only in a certain enrichment and increased complexity. These occur whenever we broaden the set of specific inputs we take into consideration. Rather, the shattering consists in the alternative light thrown by these new considerations onto our interpretation of what was previously there. More concretely: the ideas of Bloch inform our interpretation of Adorno in new ways. The focus on Adorno is partially responsible for today's conviction that early Critical Theory preserved the essential ethos of utopian thinking.

My book has shown why this conviction is problematic, and why it might be more appropriate to see Adorno as abandoning utopian thinking. Although his utopianism has been recognised as very novel – as negative thinking – this practice has thereby allegedly preserved its place in early Critical Theory. If utopianism received a different place – a negative place – this place is still a place, as opposed to a no-place. Negative utopian thinking is, after all, interpreted as utopian thinking, and not as non-utopian thinking. The transformation of utopian thinking that this method or practice of Critical Theory underwent in Adorno's thinking has so far been understood as a slight tweaking, a minor alternation, as opposed to a fundamental reconfiguration or a complete change. This course of claims changes once we bring Bloch into the picture. Bloch advanced yet another novel kind of utopian thinking. By juxtaposing him to Adorno, one is compelled to draw a question mark under the supposedly utopian images of Adorno. Bloch does not provide explicit arguments as to why it is problematic to conceive of these images as utopian. Nevertheless, his writings prompt us to take another proper look at Adorno's negative utopias. I have argued that interpretations of negative utopias as offering another way to depict their positive side have turned into a kind of dogma in Adorno scholarship. Adorno might have said that 'utopia lies essentially in the determinate negations' and that 'the consummate negativity one squarely faces explodes into its mirror-image', but once we actually attempt to understand where and how utopia 'lies' in the criticism of the existing society, or, how the mirror image of the negative 'explodes', we realise that, at worst, it does not at all, or at best, it conceals the positive almost completely from our view.[7] The historical trajectory that ensues from the interpretation of Adorno through the lens of Bloch is thus more radical than the existing one. At its core lies the claim of a radical reconfiguration and suppression of utopian thinking in early Critical Theory: Marx's utopian ferments were not preserved but abandoned. At the same time, my interpretation highlights that the suppression of utopianism was not total: by including Bloch as one of its representatives we can see that Critical Theory branched out in another direction that indeed deserves to be designated as utopian. So far, however, this Blochian branch remains above all entangled in history, whereas the Adornian one grew into a familiar element of the present.

The second aspect of the historical thread of my book highlights additional reasons why the suppression of utopian thinking in early Critical Theory should not be conceived of as total. This part of the book has to do with the reconstruc-

___
7   Adorno in Bloch 1969b, p. 362; Adorno 1980 [1951], p. 281.

tion of the critical theorists' own views on what the ends of utopian thinking in Critical Theory are or should be. In other words: what specifically did Marx, Adorno and Bloch hold the role of utopian thinking in Critical Theory to be? This reconstruction has been impeded by the fact that none of these thinkers explicitly posed this question to themselves. This is the case especially with Marx. At that time, the vision of communism lay on the horizon, and although the degree to which this vision ought to be concretised presented a contestable issue, the non-existence of the vision itself was not conceivable. Further considerations of how, why and in what sense the vision of communism ought to be specified were seized in advance by Marx's idea that such considerations are unnecessary. Inevitably, Marx thought, certain groups in society would move the train of history forward, and, moreover, move it in the right direction. But history did not advance along this route, and culminated instead in a near annihilation of the West. The critical theorists offered one explanation for this turn of history. Their explanation posited that a specific objective condition in history is not a guarantee for how history as a whole would unfold, but that history is, in turn, dependent also on the prevailing ideas and beliefs, their propagation and integration into the social fabric, as well as on the subjects themselves. Adorno was one of the thinkers who fully adhered to this explanation. The problem was that this explanation entailed a further implication that yet again prevented a serious engagement with the question of whether and how utopian thinking could be utilised to facilitate the rerouting of history onto the right track. If utopia lies in the realm that is cognitively inaccessible, inaccessible under any circumstances, and inaccessible especially under the existing circumstances of the utmost falseness and wrongness, how could it then be conceptualised? Adorno concluded that indeed it cannot be conceptualised, at least not positively. Since any attempt at such articulation would result in another mere tool of ideology, Adorno issued the *Utopieverbot* and removed positive utopian thinking from the toolbox of Critical Theory. Adorno was, however, not completely content in imposing this prohibition. His mistrust emanated from the fact that the toolbox of Critical Theory, at least in comparison to Marx's, appeared impoverished. Criticism or negation of the bourgeois ideology on its own seemed insufficient or inappropriate, or even destructive in relation to the very objective of Critical Theory. Adorno, however, never articulated the reasons for this concern, or even the concern itself. It does, however, seem to me that the two have been captured very aptly by the following verses:

One just keeps saying, 'No ... No ... No ...'
Head bowed, hat in hand,

A cringing, cunning little step back,
With each dialectical evasion,
Retreating, receding, 'no ... no ... no ...'
Until one simply disappears ...[8]

By attesting to the ever-diminishing strength and weakened posture of negation, the poem elicits something that could perhaps be described as its annihil-
ating ethos. Its message concerns not only the insufficiency of critique, but also
its utmost futility. At least in some instances Adorno acknowledged this futility,
and he reflected on some alternatives to critique, including utopian thinking.
Yet, by avoiding any direct, open or explicit description of a utopian society,
Adorno set himself a very difficult task, the aspirations of which, as I contended in my criticism of negative utopia, he failed to fulfil. Bloch too contended
that criticism on its own is ineffective and even counterproductive. The reason
for this lies in Bloch's understanding of what human beings are at their core,
of how they act and function. Bloch conceives of human beings as structured
simultaneously by positivity and negativity; there is always something that we
are, but in the midst of this determined presence there also lies an undeter-
mined lack or absence. What is furthermore innate to human beings, in Bloch's
view, is the constant attempt to overcome and fill this lack. This attempt takes
the form of longing, yearning, striving, craving and wishing. Or, as Bloch put it:
'Primarily, everybody lives in the future, because they strive, past things only
come later, and as yet genuine present is almost never there at all'.[9] For Bloch,
the evidence for our living in the future is the existence of cognitive processes
of longing and striving, of looking forward, towards the future. The fact that so
much of our cognition is concerned with the future, Bloch argues, also turns
human beings themselves into beings that exist, live in, or inhabit this future.
These cognitive processes are, on the one hand, positive. They create or produce the content that inhabits or occupies the space of the negative. Yet, on the
other hand, they are constitutive of negativity, their very existence is vital to our
recognition of ourselves as uncompleted beings. This two-sided nature of longing is one reason why the positive and the negative are inseparable, even if the
differentiation between the two has been central to the arguments developed
across this book.

This positive/negative nature of longing is not its only distinct two-sided
characteristic. Another one concerns the directional nature of its productiv-

---

8   Leyner 2012, p. 32.
9   Bloch 1977 [1954/55/50], p. 2.

ity. While subjects, in their efforts to overstep their edges, self-generate the content that is to fill the lack, they are, of course, not its only source. Just like Marx, Bloch too believed that no self exists independently of its environment and of other human beings. This world outside the subject thus also informs and feeds into the productive processes of longing and striving. But not all that lies outside ourselves is equally conducive to enter these processes, it is specifically what Bloch calls the content of hope, something that is allied with fullness and goodness, reaching into the future, that protests and thereby stands in opposition to the emptiness and dissatisfaction confined to the present. The dreams of a better life already available in the world affect and shape the subject's own dreams of a better life, which then condition them and their actions; and these are in turn necessary for the construction of an actual utopia. For Bloch, the depiction of utopia is also the building of utopia. Here we come back to the processual nature of utopian thinking which I discussed at the end of Chapter 5. There I argued that this processuality highlights the fact that an individual depiction of a utopia conceptualised in one moment should always be left open to revision, as it presents only one inroad into the broader process of conceptualising this society. The processuality, however, can also refer to the 'process of building or constructing' this society, whereby its depictions become its participating ingredients. This processual 'tweaking' of the notion of utopian thinking provides one simple yet significant argument as to why dreams, outlines, and visions of a better life, of a more humane way of living together, need to be created. Objects that are concerned with the future, that speak of the future, sustain and supplement subjects' own concerns with the future. One's projections forward and those supplied by others continuously reinforce each other. If critical theorists, generally speaking, do not include or address these projections in their writings, they jeopardise their readers' receptiveness, or access to their writings. If their texts are to have any effect with respect to social change, a link, connection or bridge between the authors and the audience needs to exist. Since utopian thinking is one foundation of this link, critical theorists ought to employ it.

The stakes that Critical Theory takes up in its refusal of utopian thinking as one of its tools might be particularly acute in the current historical conjuncture in the West: the staggering rise of the populist and authoritarian far right parties. The rise in the right populist movements has in fact been paralleled by an increase in popularity of the left ones. The left, however, has been relatively much less effective in gaining public recognition and backing. At least as far as Trump and Brexit are concerned, one common denominator in the explanations of their success appears to be the phenomenon of 'white working class anger'.[10] This is not to say that the working class was the primary or the only base of either Trump's or the 'Leave' camp. In fact, much evidence shows that the average Trump as well as Brexit voter was neither poor nor unemployed, but earning above median income.[11] My point concerning the working class is that those of its members of who did vote for the populist options were animated significantly by rage and discontent.[12] This discontent stems from both the material and normative displacement that this particular social group has experienced.[13] The move to the post-industrial society over the last couple of decades has not been socially all-inclusive, neither in terms of new job opportunities, nor with respect to alternative lifestyles and progressive moral views, including multiculturalism, environmental protection, and gender equality. The values, beliefs and expectations of certain sections of population have become unfounded and delegitimised, carving into their very identities or subjectivities. Or, in Blochian terms: the constitutive lack of these individuals has deepened. Something they maintained or possessed has been taken away, thus increasing the gap which separates them from the realisation of their dreams, hopes and wishes. These hopes and wishes, however, have not been weakened or demolished, or at least, Bloch would have argued that they have not been: dreaming, hoping and longing is the one human activity that *never* ceases. It does not seem too big a leap to argue that the greater these lacks or gaps are, the more likely it is that individuals become receptive to the available material that could readily fill them. This material certainly includes the readily available promises of an essentially better future. Trump's 'Make America Great Again' and UKIP's 'Take Back Control' carried such promises.[14] It is, however, less clear what leftist slogans, ideas, views and manifestos do the same. The recent left populist movements have not only been relatively less successful in obtaining voters' support, but have also lacked a vision of a systematically different and desirable future. Rather than reaching for and insisting on, as well as simultaneously revising its radical heritage of *equality, solidarity and community*, the left has settled closer to the centre. In contrast, the utopian visions of the right are based openly on its extreme, on the principles of *exclusion, intolerance and inequality*. Critical Theory's refusal to contribute to a formulation of a utopian society which, while maintaining the allure and appeal of the right-wing one, would in contrast be based on progressive values, represents a major

10   See Avlijaš 2016; Gusterson 2017.

11   See Sasson 2016; Taylor 2019.

12   See Brown 2018, p. 60.

13   See Inglehart and Norris 2016.

14   See McMillan 2017; Russell Hochschild 2016, pp. 221–31.

risk. Eventually the hopes and aspirations of individuals might be channelled towards and consumed by whatever utopian promises are currently available, irrespective of how deeply problematic these might be.

Besides the historical thread, my book also entails a critical thread, concerned above all with Adorno's negative utopias, and his view of the impossibility to envisage them positively. Whereas I have advanced my concerns pertaining to negative utopias, my criticisms of the view of the impossibility of utopian thinking yet need to be spelled out. I have argued that Adorno's ideas of identity thinking and culture industry have played a significant role in displacing utopian thinking from Critical Theory, in particular by preempting the mere possibility of envisaging in the present the truly desirable society of the future. Adorno instead rendered all utopian conceptualisations as falsely utopian, that is, as mere duplications of the present society. But is that so? Are our visions of a different society in fact not indicative of a different society, but only of the existing one? The answer to this question depends on the criteria we adopt in determining what counts as 'different'. One criterion of Adorno was that of identity thinking itself: whatever content is conceptualised in this form of thinking, it *cannot* be different, it cannot contradict, but merely conform to, what already exists. The viability of this criterion is, of course, dependent on Adorno's highly problematic generalisation that the whole of the existing society is debased and degenerated. Many counterexamples could be provided, both within the society of Adorno's time and in the current one, of practices, values, beliefs and attitudes that do seem to oppose the prevailing normative order. This way of criticising identity thinking does, however, not bring us very far, as we eventually fall back on the initial deadlock question of how we decide on the norms determining which practices or views are sufficiently different from the dominant ones as to be perceived as actually 'different'. Another critique of identity thinking, informed by Bloch's ontology of the Not-Yet, is more productive. The view of reality as not yet fully developed or determined does undermine Adorno's understanding of identity or positive thinking. In an affirmative sentence, Adorno argues, the copula conjoining a subject with its predicate (for example, 'is') says: 'it is so, not otherwise', and furthermore that 'it should not be anything else: the identity would otherwise performed'.[15] The meaning of positive thinking shifts in the context of reality as the Not-Yet. Given that it is as fundamental to reality that 'it is so' as that 'it could be different', no articulation of reality, be it positive or negative, can posit a conclusive identity between the subject and its predic-

---

15   Adorno 1996 [1966], p. 151.

ate. This shift in the meaning of positive thinking is relevant as it, of course, also shifts the meaning of positive utopian thinking: by envisaging a utopian society, one is not excluding other possibilities of good practices and values, one is not denying that the content of the actually existing utopian society of the future will differ from that entailed in one's existing conception of it. Such a reading of utopian visions changes the terms on which the whole controversy regarding their possibility proceeds. The question is now no longer whether we can conceptualise Adorno's 'Other' or Bloch's *Heimat*, but rather, whether we can provide descriptions of societies which in one way or another approach or resemble some dimensions of the radical goodness signified by these concepts. The answer to this reformulated question is more likely to be affirmative. Reconstructing the original question itself clearly indicates the narrowness of Adorno's own position, and calls for the revision of the existing place of utopian thinking in Critical Theory. For once this question of the possibility of utopian thinking will have been settled, the more significant one regarding the actual role of utopian thinking as a tool can finally be properly addressed.

Bloch does not offer a satisfactory answer to this question of the ends of utopian thinking. As Douglas Kellner and Harry O'Hara observe:

> It is his *conviction* that only when we project our future in the light of what is, what has been, and what could be can we engage in the creative practice that will produce the world we all want and realize humanity's deepest hopes and dreams.[16]

Bloch does not only consider that one's own hopes and wishes are interdependent with those that are currently available socially and that they mutually reinforce each other, but that certain projections of the future drive, nourish, energise, inspire, motivate and propel individual as well as collective action. The significance of utopian thinking is, according to Bloch, greater and more complex than the significance of something that functions merely as a necessary input to fill the constitutive lack of the subjects themselves. It is, however, not sufficient to simply use this very specific register of driving and striving to convey the greater significance and complexity of the role of utopian thinking. To achieve that, the knowledges and vocabularies of multiple disciplines would have to be brought together and advanced in a new research agenda.

---

16   Kellner and O'Hara 1976, p. 16. [italics mine].

The question of the role of utopian thinking in social change could initially be approached from a historical perspective: have utopian ideas participated in social upheavals or uprisings, both in those which resulted in redistribution of power and in those that were suppressed? This question in fact does not seem very contentious. Historians tend to agree that utopian ideas of some variety were involved in most revolutionary social transformations. While Bloch himself examined in detail the peasants' revolts in the early sixteenth century, other scholars offer persuasive evidence in support of this claim for later periods of history, including the American and the Russian Revolution, as well as the communist and socialist revolutionary wave in mid-nineteenth century Europe.[17] The more specific question that would need to be considered is *how* these utopian ideas affected the practices and actions of the individuals and of the movement.

Another avenue towards a comprehensive theory of the role of utopian thinking could be opened by focusing specifically on its affective dimension. By this I mean looking not only at the literature that, alongside Bloch's own writings, considers the significance of hope as an affect.[18] Political theory more broadly has in fact recently experienced a revived interest in affect. On the one hand, this revival corresponds to a revision of the long-standing philosophical tradition running from Aristotle, Machiavelli, Hume, Rousseau and Nietzsche that, in examining human beings as rational as well as emotional beings, highlights the role of emotions in politics. Feminist scholars in particular have contributed extensively to this development in political theory.[19] On the other hand, this turn draws heavily on the relevant ideas provided by cognitive neuroscientists. Theorists such as William Connolly, Leslie Paul Thiele, and John Protevi view political action not as an expression of judgements arrived at by the means of reason, but as a complex interaction of various somatic and social processes.[20] In these theories affect is seen as a distinct layer of experience both prior to and beneath language and intentional consciousness, a bodily and autonomic force that shapes one's views, judgements and beliefs. While these theories would need to be advanced further, to consider the complexities that the specific dimensions of radical social change and utopian thinking add to the picture (for example, how would the conclusions of these theories

---

17   See Bloch 1977 [1921]. For the American Revolution see Linebaugh and Rediker 2000; for the communist and socialist revolts Brangsch and Brie 2016; and for the Russian Revolution Adamczak 2011.

18   For contemporary scholarship on hope and affect see Solnit 2016; Aronson 2017; Lear 2006.

19   See Nussbaum 1990 and Ahmed 2016.

20   Connolly 2002; Thiele 2006; Protevi 2009.

change when instead of focusing on the individual we were to focus on a group of individuals, and thus instead of individual actions on collective ones), they could serve as a good starting point.

On the basis of a better understanding of the functions of utopian thinking in social change, we could specify further what utopian thinking as a tool or method of Critical Theory could look like. Drawing on Bloch's concepts of concrete and processual utopia, I have outlined some initial features of such practice. Although this specification is rather provisional it does prove valuable as it currently stands. It gives rise to two significant conclusions that directly undermine another set of influential arguments against utopian thinking, namely those provided by the liberal tradition. Although one objective of my book has been to show that the discrediting of utopian thinking that occurred in the previous century should not be ascribed only to this tradition, I have not argued that liberals do not share in the responsibility for the demise of utopian thinking. The liberal discourse has undoubtedly played an important role in this process, and continues to do so. Utopian thinking is today, above all, deemed as dangerous, and this is an idea that is in these very terms defended most vehemently by thinkers such as Karl Popper. The processual form of utopian thinking I have defended points to some limitations of Popper's view. The processual interpretation shows that utopian thinking is not necessarily related to the notion of a blueprint, a set of instructions which are devised with an intention to be strictly followed and implemented in reality immediately, without any further consideration. Popper's anti-utopian argument that utopia will inevitably lead to its opposite, a dystopia, a violent upheaval, however, presupposes this very programmatic conception of utopia. That is, Popper presupposes that any articulation of a utopian society strives ultimately and solely for its implementation. But if the activity of utopian thinking is engaged in for other motives, then Popper's criticism loses its grounds. Another idea ensuing from the processual perspective further impairs the liberal strand of anti-utopianism. Popper in fact acknowledges that prior to attempting a realisation of utopia through violence, individuals might first endeavour to obtain political support by rational means, by 'convincing' those who do not initially share their conception of a utopia to reconsider. However, achieving an absolute consensus regarding the content of the utopian society is just as little an aspiration of processual utopias as is their immediate, uncompromising realisation. Given that processual utopian thinking builds on the idea that we cannot know the ultimate utopia, but only a multiplicity of its precursors, its aim then cannot be to arrive at a universally shared conception of the former. This, however, does not mean that conversation between alternative utopian visions should be hindered, nor does it mean that *any* articulation of a supposedly good society is to be granted entry to this utopian pool. It rather means that, instead of being focused on reaching an instantaneous agreement between those who disagree, more attention should be paid to understanding the alternatives from their own perspective, which might then in turn render disagreements less strong and conflictual than they might initially appear.

I conclude with the words of one less and one more likely ally of the spirit of this book, John Rawls and Michel Foucault. In his treatise on liberalism Rawls posited that:

> A modern democratic society is characterised not simply by a pluralism of comprehensive religious, philosophical, and moral doctrines but by a pluralism of incompatible yet reasonable comprehensive doctrines.[21]

Whereas the currently existing modern democracies stand very much removed from a world of co-existing, equally worthy viewpoints and values, the world of utopian thinking could effectively prefigure this 'pluralism of incompatible yet reasonable comprehensive doctrines'. Such a pluralistic conception of utopian thinking would focus more on creating an array of desirable futures and substantiating each of them, and less on achieving an accord among them. Foucault made a similar point with respect to the role that a public intellectual could play in relation to activist social movements:

> What is important is not an authoritarian unification, but a kind of infinite swarming of desiring machines – in school, factories, neighbourhoods, in a day nurseries, in prisons, everywhere. It is not a question of trimming or totalizing all these various partial movements, but of connecting them together on the one stem.[22]

Depictions of such a diversity of utopian visions is where the building of Rawls's utopia could start in reality. On such a tree no single utopia would assume a status of exclusivity, and each and every one would always remain open to change. A depiction of such a utopian tree is, by no means, the exclusive task of critical theorists. I have argued only that they too ought to participate in its creation.

---

21   Rawls 1993, p. xvi.
22   Deleuze and Foucault 1973, p. 105.

Bibliography

English Translations Consulted

Theodor W. Adorno

'The Actuality of Philosophy', translated by Benjamin Snow, in *The Adorno Reader*, edited by Brian O'Connor, Oxford; Malden, MA: Blackwells, 2000.

Aesthetic Theory, translated by Robert Hullot-Kentor, Minneapolis: University of Minnesota Press, 1997.

Dialectic of Enlightenment: Philosophical Fragments, translated by Edmund Jephcott, Stanford CA: Stanford University Press, 2002.

History and Freedom: Lectures 1964–1965, translated by Rodney Livingston, Malden MA: Polity Press, 2006.

Lectures on Negative Dialectics; Fragments of a Lecture Course 1965/1966, translated by Rodney Livingston, Malden MA: Polity Press, 2008.

Minima Moralia: Reflections from Damaged Life, translated by Edmund Jephcott, London: NLB, 1974.

Notes to Literature, Vol. 1, translated by Shierry Wever Nicholsen, New York: Columbia University Press, 1991.

Notes to Literature, Vol. 2, translated by Shierry Wever Nicholsen, New York: Columbia University Press, 1992.

Negative Dialectics, translated by E.B. Ashton, London: Routledge&Kegan Paul, 1973.

Problems of Moral Philosophy, translated by Rodney Livingston, Cambridge: Polity Press; Stanford CA: Stanford University Press, 2000.

Ernst Bloch

A Philosophy of the Future, translated by John Cumming, New York: Herder and Herder, 1970.

Heritage of Our Times, translated by Neville and Stephen Plaice. Cambridge: Polity Press, 1988.

Literary Essays, translated by Andrew Joron, Jack Zipes, Frank Mecklenburg and Helha Wild, Stanford: Stanford University Press, 1988.

The Principle of Hope, Vol. I–III, translated by Neville Plaice, Stephen Plaice and Paul Knight, Cambridge, MA: MIT Press, 1986.

The Spirit of Utopia, translated by Anthony A. Nassar, Stanford: Stanford University Press, 2000.

The Utopian Function of Art and Literature, translated by Jack Zipes and Frank Mecklenburg, Cambridge, MA: MIT Press, 1988.

Traces, translated by Anthony A. Nassar, Stanford: Stanford University Press, 2006.

Karl Marx and Friedrich Engels

Marx and Engels Collected Works, translated by Richard Dixon and others, London: Lawrence&Wishart, 1975–2005.

Full Bibliography

Abromeit, John 2011, *Max Horkheimer and the Foundations of the Frankfurt School*, Cambridge: Cambridge University Press.

Adamczak, Bini 2014, *Kommunismus, kleine geschichte, wie es endlich anders wird*. Münster: Unrast Verlag.

Adamczak, Bini 2011, *Gestern Morgen: Rekonstruktion der Zukunft*, Münster: Unrast Verlag.

Adorno, Theodor W. 2003, *Vorlesung über Negative Dialektik: Fragmente zur Vorlesung* (1965/66), in *Theodor W. Adorno, Nachgelassene Schriften*, Section IV: Vorlesungen, Volume 16, edited by Rolf Tiedemann, Frankfurt am Main: Suhrkamp.

Adorno, Theodor W. 2002, 'Adorno an Mann, 1. Dezember 1952', in *Theodor W. Adorno, Thomas Mann. Briefwechsel 1943–55*, edited by Christoph Gödde und Thomas Sprecher, Frankfurt am Main: Suhrkamp.

Adorno, Theodor W. 2001, *Zur Lehre von der Geschichte und der Freiheit* (1964/65), in *Theodor W. Adorno, Nachgelassene Schriften*, Section IV: Vorlesungen, Volume 13, edited by Rolf Tiedemann, Frankfurt am Main: Suhrkamp.

Adorno, Theodor W. 1996, *Probleme der Moralphilosophie* (1963), in *Theodor W. Adorno, Nachgelassene Schriften*, Section IV: Vorlesungen, Volume 10, edited by Thomas Schröder, Frankfurt am Main: Suhrkamp.

Adorno, Theodor W. 1996 [1968], 'Diskussionsbeitrag zu "Spätkapitalismus oder Industriegesellschaft"', in *Theodor W. Adorno, Gesammelte Schriften*, Volume 8, edited by Rolf Tiedemann in collaboration with Gretel Adorno, Susan Buck-Morss und Klaus Schultz, Frankfurt am Main: Suhrkamp.

Adorno, Theodor W. 1996 [1966], *Negative Dialektik*, in *Theodor W. Adorno, Gesammelte Schriften*, Volume 6, edited by Rolf Tiedemann in collaboration with Gretel Adorno, Susan Buck-Morss und Klaus Schultz, Frankfurt am Main: Suhrkamp.

Adorno, Theodor W. 1996 [1965], 'Henkel, Krug und Frühe Erfahrung', in *Theodor W. Adorno, Gesammelte Schriften*, Volume 11, edited by Rolf Tiedemann in collaboration with Gretel Adorno, Susan Buck-Morss und Klaus Schultz, Frankfurt am Main: Suhrkamp.

Adorno, Theodor W. 1996 [1964], 'Parataxis, Zur späten Lyrik Hölderlins', in *Theodor W. Adorno, Gesammelte Schriften*, Volume 11, edited by Rolf Tiedemann in collaboration with Gretel Adorno, Susan Buck-Morss und Klaus Schultz, Frankfurt am Main: Suhrkamp.

Adorno, Theodor W. 1996 [1962], 'Zu einem Porträt Thomas Manns', in *Theodor W. Adorno, Gesammelte Schriften*, Volume 11, edited by Rolf Tiedemann in collaboration with Gretel Adorno, Susan Buck-Morss und Klaus Schultz, Frankfurt am Main: Suhrkamp.

Adorno, Theodor W. 1996 [1960], 'Blochs Spuren', in *Theodor W. Adorno, Gesammelte Schriften*, Volume 11, edited by Rolf Tiedemann in collaboration with Gretel Adorno, Susan Buck-Morss und Klaus Schultz, Frankfurt am Main: Suhrkamp.

Adorno, Theodor W. 1995, 'Adorno an Benjamin 17 December 1934', in *Theodor W. Adorno, Theodor, Walter Benjamin. Briefwechsel 1928–1940*, edited by Henri Lonitz, Frankfurt am Main: Suhrkamp.

Adorno, Theodor W. 1994, 'Adorno an Horkheimer, 2 Oktober 1937', in *Theodor W. Adorno, Max Horkheimer. Briefwechsel, Vol. 1, 1927–1937*, edited by Christoph Gödde and Henri Lonitz, Frankfurt am Main: Suhrkamp.

Adorno, Theodor W. 1990 [1970], *Ästhetische Theorie*, in *Theodor W. Adorno, Gesammelte Schriften*, Volume 7, edited by Rolf Tiedemann in collaboration with Gretel Adorno, Susan Buck-Morss und Klaus Schultz, Frankfurt am Main: Suhrkamp.

Adorno, Theodor W. 1980 [1951], *Minima Moralia: Reflexionen aus dem beschädigten Leben*, in *Theodor W. Adorno, Gesammelte Schriften*, Volume 4, edited by Rolf Tiedemann in collaboration with Gretel Adorno, Susan Buck-Morss und Klaus Schultz, Frankfurt am Main: Suhrkamp.

Adorno, Theodor W. 1977, 'Vernunft und Offenbarung', in *Theodor W. Adorno, Gesammelte Schriften*, Volume 10, edited by Rolf Tiedemann in collaboration with Gretel Adorno, Susan Buck-Morss und Klaus Schultz, Frankfurt am Main: Suhrkamp.

Adorno, Theodor W. 1977 [1951], 'Kulturkritik und Gesellschaft', in *Theodor W. Adorno, Gesammelte Schriften*, Volume 10, edited by Rolf Tiedemann in collaboration with Gretel Adorno, Susan Buck-Morss und Klaus Schultz, Frankfurt am Main: Suhrkamp.

Adorno, Theodor W. 1973 [1931], 'Die Aktualität der Philosophie', in *Theodor W. Adorno, Gesammelte Schriften*, Volume 1, edited by Rolf Tiedemann in collaboration with Gretel Adorno, Susan Buck-Morss und Klaus Schultz, Frankfurt am Main: Suhrkamp.

Adorno, Theodor W. 1981 [1947], *Dialektik der Aufklärung*, in *Theodor W. Adorno, Gesammelte Schriften*, Volume 3, edited by Rolf Tiedemann in collaboration with Gretel Adorno, Susan Buck-Morss und Klaus Schultz, Frankfurt am Main: Suhrkamp.

Alexander, Peter and Roger Gill (eds.) 1984, *Utopias*, London: Duckworth.

Allen, Amy 2015, 'Emancipation without Utopia: Subjection, Modernity, and the Normative Claims of Feminist Critical Theory', *Hypatia*, 30, 3: 513–29.

Avlijaš, Sonja 2016, 'From Brexit to Trump: Why mobilising anger in a constructive way is now one of the key challenges in modern politics', *LSE European Politics and Policy*, available at: http://blogs.lse.ac.uk/europpblog/2016/06/30/brexit-trump-mobilising -anger/.

Ahmed, Sara 2016, *The cultural politics of emotion*, New York: Routledge.

Amjahid, Mohamed and Gero von Randow 2016, 'Utopien: Sehnsucht ohne Ort? Von wegen!', *Die Zeit*, available at: https://www.zeit.de/2016/52/utopien-europa-demokr atie-suche.

Anderson, Raymond H. 2004, 'Czeslaw Milosz, Poet and Nobelist Who Wrote of Modern Cruelties, Dies at 93', *The New York Times*, 15 August 2004, available at: https://www .nytimes.com/2004/08/15/books/czeslaw-milosz-poet-and-nobelist-who-wrote-of-modern-cruelties-dies-at-93.html.

Anderson, Perry 1976, *Considerations on Western Marxism*, London: Verso Editions.

Amberger, Alexander 2013, 'Ernst Bloch in der DDR', *Deutsche Zeitschrift für Philosophie*, 61, 4: 561–76.

Aronson, Ronald 2017, *We: reviving the social hope*, Chicago: Chicago University Press.

Badiou, Alain 2011, 'The Crisis of Negation: An Interview with Alain Badiou', interviewed by John van Houdt, *Continent*, 1, 4: 234–8.

Benhabib, Seyla 1986, *Critique, Norm, and Utopia: A study of the foundations of critical theory*, New York: Columbia University Press.

Benjamin, Walter 1996, *Gesammelte Briefe / Walter Benjamin*, Volume 2, 1919–1924, edited by Christoph Gödde und Henri Lonitz, Frankfurt am Main: Suhrkamp.

Benjamin, Walter 1977 [1942], 'Über den Begriff der Geschichte', in *Walter Benjamin Gesammelte Schriften*, Volume 1, edited by Rolf Tiedemann and Hermann Schweppenhäuser, Frankfurt am Main: Suhrkamp.

Benjamin, Walter 1977 [1928], *Ursprung des deutschen Trauerspiels*, in *Walter Benjamin Gesammelte Schriften*, Volume 1, edited by Rolf Tiedemann and Hermann Schweppenhäuser, Frankfurt am Main: Suhrkamp.

Berlin, Isaah 2013 [1959], *The Crooked Timber of Humanity: Chapters in the History of Ideas*, edited by Henry Hardy, Princeton and Oxford: Princeton University Press.

Berghahn, Klaus L. (ed.) 2011, *The Temptation of Hope*, Bielefeld: Aisthesis Verlag.

Bernard, Andreas und Ulrich Raulff (eds.) 2003, *'Minima Moralia' neu gelesen*, Frankfurt am Main: Suhrkamp.

Bernstein, J.M. (ed.) 1991, *The Culture Industry: Selected Essays on Mass Culture*, London: Routledge.

Blicke, Peter 2002, *Heimat: A Critical Theory of the German Idea of Homeland*, New York: Camden House.

Bloch, Ernst 1977 [1975], *Experimentum Mundi; Frage, Kategorien des Herausbringens, Praxis*, in *Ernst Bloch, Gesamtausgabe*, Volume 15, Frankfurt am Main: Suhrkamp.

Bloch, Ernst 1977 [1972], *Das Materialismusproblem, seine Geschichte und Substanz*, in *Ernst Bloch, Gesamtausgabe*, Volume 7, Frankfurt am Main: Suhrkamp.

Bloch, Ernst 1977 [1969a], 'Universität, Marxismus, Philosophie. Antrittsvorlesung in Leipzig, Mai 1948', in *Philosophische Aufsätze zur Objektiven Phantasie*, in *Ernst Bloch, Gesamtausgabe*, Volume 10, Frankfurt am Main: Suhrkamp.

Bloch, Ernst 1977 [1969b], 'Etwas fehlt ... Über die Widersprüche der utopischen Sehnsucht. Ein Rundfunkgespräch mit Theodor W. Adorno, 1964', in *Philosophische Aufsätze zur Objektiven Phantasie*, in *Ernst Bloch, Gesamtausgabe*, Additional Volume, Frankfurt am Main: Suhrkamp.

Bloch, Ernst 1977 [1968], *Atheismus im Christentum*, in *Ernst Bloch, Gesamtausgabe*, Volume 14, Frankfurt am Main: Suhrkamp.

Bloch, Ernst 1977 [1965a], 'Über ungelöste Aufgaben der sozialistischen Theorie; Ein Gespräch mit Fritz Vilmar 1965', in *Philosophische Aufsätze zur Objektiven Phantasie*, in *Ernst Bloch, Gesamtausgabe*, Additional Volume, Frankfurt am Main: Suhrkamp.

Bloch, Ernst 1977 [1965b], 'Kann Hoffnung enttäuscht werden? Eröffnungs-Vorlesung, Tübingen 1961', in *Literarische Aufsätze*, in *Ernst Bloch, Gesamtausgabe*, Volume 9, Frankfurt am Main: Suhrkamp.

Bloch, Ernst 1977 [1963/64], *Tübinger Einleitung in die Philosophie*, in *Ernst Bloch, Gesamtausgabe*, Volume 13, Frankfurt am Main: Suhrkamp.

Bloch, Ernst 1977 [1962], *Subjekt-Objekt; Erläuterungen zu Hegel*, in *Ernst Bloch, Gesamtausgabe*, Volume 8, Frankfurt am Main: Suhrkamp.

Bloch, Ernst 1977 [1954/55/50], *Das Prinzip Hoffnung*, in *Ernst Bloch, Gesamtausgabe*, Volume 5, Frankfurt am Main: Suhrkamp.

Bloch, Ernst 1977 [1935], *Erbschaft dieser Zeit*, in *Ernst Bloch, Gesamtausgabe*, Volume 4, Frankfurt am Main: Suhrkamp.

Bloch, Ernst 1977 [1930], *Spuren*, in *Ernst Bloch, Gesamtausgabe*, Volume 1, Frankfurt am Main: Suhrkamp.

Bloch, Ernst 1977 [1921], *Thomas Münzer als Theologe der Revolution*, in *Ernst Bloch, Gesamtausgabe*, Volume 2, Frankfurt am Main: Suhrkamp.

Bloch, Ernst 1977 [1918], *Geist der Utopie. Erste Fassung*, in *Ernst Bloch, Gesamtausgabe*, Volume 16, Frankfurt am Main: Suhrkamp.

Bloch, Ernst 1975, *Gespräche mit Ernst Bloch*, edited by Rainer Traub and Harald Wieser Frankfurt am Main: Suhrkamp.

Boella, Laura 2012 'Spuren', in *Bloch-Wörterbuch: Leitbegriffe der Philosophie Ernst Blochs*, edited by Beat Dietschy, Doris Zeilinger and Rainer Zimmermann, Berlin; Boston: De Gruyter.

Boldyrev, Ivan 2014, *Ernst Bloch and his Contemporaries: Locating Utopian Messianism*, London: Bloomsbury Academic.

Bottomore, Tom, et al. (eds.) 1991, *A Dictionary of Marxist Thought*, Oxford: Blackwell Reference.

Bowie, Andrew 2003, *Introduction to German Philosophy: From Kant to Habermas*, Cambridge: Polity.

Brangsch, Lutz and Michael Brie (eds.) 2016, *Das Kommunistische*, Hamburg: VSA Verlag.

Brittain, Christopher Craig 2010, *Adorno and theology*, London; New York: T & T Clark.

Brown, Wendy 2018, 'Neoliberalism's Frankenstein: Authoritarian Freedom in Twenty-First Century "Democracies"', *Critical Times*, 1, 1: 60–79.

Brudney, Daniel 1998, *Marx's Attempt to Leave Philosophy*, Cambridge, Mass.; London: Harvard University Press.

Buber, Martin 1958, *Paths in Utopia*, Boston: Beacon Press.

Buck-Morss, Susan 1977, *The Origin of Negative Dialectics: Theodor W. Adorno, Walter Benjamin and the Frankfurt Institute*, New York: The Free Press.

Chitty, Andrew 1998, 'Recognition and Relations of Production', *Historical Materialism*, 2: 57–97.

Chitty, Andrew 1993, 'The early Marx on needs', *Radical Philosophy*, 64: 23–31.

Chrostowska, S.D. 2019, 'Serious, not all that serious: Utopia beyond realism and normativity in contemporary critical theory', *Constellations*, 26: 330–43.

Chrostowska, S.D. and James D. Ingram (eds.) 2017, *Political Uses of Utopia: New Marxist, Anarchist, and Radical Democratic Perspectives*, New York: Columbia University Press.

Claeys, Gregory 2014, 'Early Socialism as Intellectual History', *History of European Ideas*, 1–12.

Claussen, Detlev 2008, *Theodor W. Adorno: One Last Genius*, translated by Rodney Livingstone, Cambridge, Mass.: Harvard University Press.

Connollly, William 2002, *Neuropolitics: thinking, culture, speed*, Minneapolis, MN; London: University of Minnesota Press.

Cook, Deborah (ed.) 2008, *Theodor Adorno: Key Concepts*, Durham, UK: Acumen.

Cooke, Maeve 2006, *Re-Presenting the Good Society*, Cambridge, Mass.; London: MIT Press.

Daniel, Jamie Owen and Tom Moylan (eds.) 1977, *Not Yet: Reconsidering Ernst Bloch*, New York and London: Verso.

Davies, Laurence 2011, 'Isaiah Berlin, William Morris, and the Politics of Utopia', in *The Philosophy of Utopia*, edited by Barbara Goodwin, London: Frank Cass.

Demirović, Alex 1999, *Der nonkonformistische Intellektuelle: die Entwicklung der Kritischen Theorie zur Frankfurter Schule*, Frankfurt am Main: Suhrkamp.

Dietschy, Beat, Doris Zeilinger and Rainer Zimmermann (eds.) 2012, *Bloch-Wörterbuch: Leitbegriffe der Philosophie Ernst Blochs*, Berlin; Boston: De Gruyter.

Ellul, Jacques 1985, *The Humiliation of the Word*, Grand Rapids, Mich.: Eerdmans.

Engels, Friedrich 1987 [1880], 'Die Entwicklung des Sozialismus von der Utopie zur Wissenschaft', in *Marx/Engels Werke*, Volume 19, edited by Institut für Marxismus-Leninismus, Berlin: Dietz Verlag.

Engels, Friedrich 1975 [1878] 'Herrn Eugen Dühring's Umwälzung der Wissenschaft', in *Marx/Engels Werke*, Volume 20, edited by Institut für Marxismus-Leninismus, Berlin: Dietz Verlag.

Engels, Friedrich 1962 [1885], 'Zur Geschichte des Bundes der Kommunisten', in *Marx/Engels Werke*, Volume 21, edited by Institut für Marxismus-Leninismus, Berlin: Dietz Verlag.

Felski, Rita 2015, *The Limits of Critique*, Chicago: The University of Chicago Press.

Finlayson, Gordon 2012, 'On not being silent in the darkness: Adorno's singular apophaticism', *Harvard Theological Review*, 105, 1: 1–32.

Fortunati, Vita 2000, 'Utopia as a Literary Genre', in *Dictionary of Literary Utopias*, edited by Vita Fortunati and Raymond Trousson, Paris: Honoré Champion.

Foucault, Michael 2003, 'Das Wissen als Verbrechen', in *Michel Foucault, Schriften in vier Bänden. Dits er Ecritcs*, Vol. III, translated by Daniel Defert et al., Frankfurt am Main: Suhrkamp.

Foucault, Michael 1997, *Ethics: Subjectivity and Truth, Essential works of Foucault, 1954–1984*, Volume 1, edited by Paul Rabinow, translated by Robert Hurley et al., New York: The New Press.

Foucault, Michael1986, 'Of Other Spaces', translated by Jay Miskowiec, *Diacritics*, 16, 1: 22–7.

Fourier, Charles 1983, *The utopian vision of Charles Fourier; selected texts on work, love, and passionate attraction*, translated and edited by Jonathan Beecher and Richard Bienvenu, Columbia: University of Missouri Press.

Freeden, Michael, et al. (eds.) 2013, *The Oxford handbook of political ideologies*, Oxford: Oxford University Press.

Freud, Sigmund 1989 [1899], 'The Interpretation of Dreams', in *The Freud Reader*, edited by Peter Gay, New York: W.W. Norton.

Freud, Sigmund 1989 [1908], 'Creative Writing and Day-Dreaming', in *The Freud Reader*, edited by Peter Gay, New York: W.W. Norton.

Freyenhagen, Fabian 2013, *Adorno's practical philosophy: living less wrongly*, Cambridge: Cambridge University Press.

Friedlander, Eli 2012, *Walter Benjamin: A Philosophical Portrait*, Cambridge, Mass.: Harvard University Press.

Fromm, Erich 1967, *You shall be as gods: a radical interpretation of the Old Testament and its tradition*, London: Cape.

Gay, Peter 1989, *The Freud Reader*, New York: W.W. Norton.

Geoghegan, Vincent 2013, 'An Anti-humanist Utopia?', in *Privatization of Hope; Ernst Bloch and the Future of Utopia*, edited by Peter Thompson and Slavoj Žižek, Durham: Duke University Press.

Geoghegan, Vincent 1996, *Ernst Bloch*, London; New York: Routledge.

Geoghegan, Vincent 1987, *Marxism and Utopianism*, London; New York: Methuen.

Geoghegan, Vincent 1987, 'Marxism and Utopianism', *Utopian Studies*, 1: 37–51.

Gusterson, Hugh 2017, 'From Brexit to Trump: Anthropology and the rise of nationalist populism', *American Ethnologist, Journal of American ethnological society*, 44, 2: 209–14.

Geuss, Raymond 2004, 'Dialectics and the revolutionary impulse', in *Cambridge Companion to Critical Theory*, edited by Fred Rush, Cambridge: Cambridge University Press.

Geuss, Raymond 1981, *The Idea of a Critical Theory: Habermas and the Frankfurt school*, Cambridge: Cambridge University Press.

Glazova, Anna and Paul North (eds.) 2014, *Messianic thought outside theology*, New York: Fordham University Press.

Goodwin, Barbara 2001, *The Philosophy of Utopia*, London: Frank Cass.

Habermas, Jürgen 1985, *Die neue Unübersichtlichkeit, Kleine politische Schriften v*, Frankfurt am Main: Suhrkamp.

Habermas, Jürgen 1985, *Der philosophische Diskurs der Moderne: zwölf Vorlesungen*, Frankfurt am Main: Suhrkamp.

Hagedorn, Gregor et al. 2019, 'Concerns of young protesters are justified', *Science*, 364, 6436: 139–40.

Hamacher, Werner 2014, 'The Messianic Not', in *Messianic thought outside theology*, edited by Anna Glazova and Paul North, New York: Fordham University Press.

Harman, Graham 2011, *Quentin Meillassoux: philosophy in the making*, Edinburgh: Edinburgh University Press.

Harrington, Austin (ed.) 2005, *Modern Social Theory: An Introduction*, Oxford: Oxford University Press.

Hattstein, Markus and Michael Theunissen 1992, *Erfahrungen der Negativität – Festschrift für Michael Theunissen zum 60. Geburtstag*, Hildesheim: Olms.

Hegel, G.W.F. 1975, *Logic*, trans. by William Wallace, Oxford: Oxford University Press.

Held, David 1990, *Introduction to Critical Theory: Horkheimer to Habermas*, Cambridge: Polity.

Holz, Hans Heinz 2012, 'Spekulativer Materialismus', in *Bloch-Wörterbuch: Leitbegriffe der Philosophie Ernst Blochs*, edited by Beat Dietschy, Doris Zeilinger and Rainer Zimmermann, Berlin; Boston: De Gruyter, pp. 483–508.

Honneth, Axel (ed.) 2005, *Dialektik der Freiheit: Frankfurter Adorno-Konferenz 2003*, Frankfurt am Main: Suhrkamp.

Honneth, Axel (ed.) 2000 'The Possibility of a Disclosing Critique of Society: The *Dialectic of Enlightenment* in Light of Current Debates in Social Criticism', *Constellations*, 7, 1: 116–27.

Horkheimer, Max 1970, "Auf das Andere Hoffen", *Der Spiegel*, 5 January 1970.

Horkheimer, Max 1968, 'Traditionelle und kritische Theorie', in *Kritische Theorie*, Frankfurt am Main: S. Fisher Verlag.

Hoy, David C. and Thomas McCarthy 1994, *Critical Theory*, Oxford: Blackwell Publishers.

Howells, Richard 2015, *A Critical Theory of Creativity: Utopia, Aesthetics, Atheism and Design*, Houndmills, Basingstoke, Hampshire; New York: Palgrave Macmillan.

Hölscher, Lucian 1996, 'Utopie', *Utopian Studies*, 7, 2: 1–65.

Hudis, Peter 2012, *Marx's concept of the alternative to capitalism*, Leiden, Boston: Brill.

Hudson, Wayne 2013, 'Bloch and a Philosophy of the Proterior', in *Privatization of Hope;*

Ernst Bloch and the Future of Utopia, edited by Peter Thompson and Slavoj Žižek, Durham: Duke University Press.

Hudson, Wayne 1982, *The Marxist philosophy of Ernst Bloch*, London: Macmillan.

Huhn, Tom and Lambert Zuidervaart (eds.) 1997, *The Semblance of Subjectivity. Adorno's Aesthetic Theory*, Cambridge, Mass.: MIT Press.

Inglehart, Ronald F. and Pippa Norris 2016, 'Trump, Brexit, and the rise of Populism: Economic have-nots and cultural backlash', *Harvard Kennedy School, Faculty Research Working Paper Series*, RWP16–026.

Inwood, Michael 1999, *A Hegel Dictionary*, Oxford: Blackwell.

Jacobs, Jack 2015, *The Frankfurt School, Jewish Lives, and Antisemitism*, New York: Cambridge University Press.

Jacobsen, Michael Hviid and Keith Tester, (eds.) 2012, *Utopia: social theory and the future*, Farnham; Burlington, VT: Ashgate.

Jacoby, Russell 2011, 'Karl Popper, Isaiah Berlin, and the Anti-Utopian Refugees', in *The Temptation of Hope*, edited by Klaus L. Berghahn, Bielefeld: Aisthesis Verlag.

Jacoby, Russell 2005, *Picture Imperfect: Utopian Thought for an Anti-utopian Age*, New York: Columbia University Press.

Jacoby, Russell 1999, *The End of Utopia: politics and culture in an age of apathy*, New York: Basic Books.

Jacoby, Russell 1981, *Dialectic of Defeat: contours of Western Marxism*, Cambridge: Cambridge University Press.

Jaeggi, Rahel 2014, *Kritik von Lebensformen*, Frankfurt am Main: Suhrkamp.

Jaeggi, Rahel 2005, '"Kein Einzelner vermag etwas dagegen" Adornos *Minima Moralia* als Kritik von Lebensformen', in *Dialektik der Freiheit: Frankfurter Adorno-Konferenz 2003*, edited by Axel Honneth, Frankfurt am Main: Suhrkamp.

Jameson, Fredric 2004, 'The Politics of Utopia', *New Left Review*, 25: 35–54.

Jameson, Fredric 1974, *Marxism and form: twentieth-century dialectical theories of literature*, Princeton: Princeton University Press.

Jarvis, Simon 1998, *Adorno: A Critical Introduction*, New York: Routledge.

Jay, Martin 1984, *Adorno*, Cambridge, Mass.: Harvard University Press.

Jay, Martin 1973, *The Dialectical Imagination; A History of the Frankfurt School and the Institute of Social Research*, Boston: Little Brown.

Jäger, Lorenz 2004, *Adorno: A Political Biography*, translated by Stewart Spencer, New Haven, Conn.: Yale University Press.

Jeffries, Stuart 2016, *The Grand Hotel Abyss: The lives of the Frankfurt School*, London; New York: Verso.

Kant, Immanuel 1997 [1781], *Critique of Pure Reason*, translated and edited by Paul Guyer and Allen Wood, Cambridge: Cambridge University Press.

Kant, Immanuel 1991 [1784], 'Idea for a Universal History with a Cosmopolitan Purpose', in *Political Writings/Kant*, edited by Hans Reiss, translated by H.B. Nisbet, Cambridge: Cambridge University Press.

Kapur, Akash 2016, 'The Return of the Utopians', *The New Yorker*, 16 September 2016, available at https://www.newyorker.com/magazine/2016/10/03/the-return-of-the-u topians.

Kaufmann, David 2000, 'Correlations, constellations and the truth: Adorno's ontology of redemption', *Philosophy and Social Criticism*, 26, 5: 62–80.

Kellner, Douglas 2005, 'Western Marxism', in *Modern Social Theory: An Introduction*, edited by Austin Harrington, Oxford: Oxford University Press.

Kellner, Douglas and Harry O'Hara 1976, 'Utopia and Marxism in Ernst Bloch', *New German Critique*, 9: 11–34.

Klein, Naomi 2017, *No is not enough: defeating the new shock politics*, London: Allen Lane.

Koch, Gerd 2012, 'Heimat', in *Bloch-Wörterbuch: Leitbegriffe der Philosophie Ernst Blochs*, edited by Beat Dietschy, Doris Zeilinger and Rainer Zimmermann, Berlin; Boston: De Gruyter, pp. 168–89.

Kompridis, Nikolas 2006, *Critique and Disclosure: Critical Theory between Past and Future*, Cambridge, MA: MIT Press.

Kompridis, Nikolas 2005, 'Disclosing Possibility: The Past and Future of Critical Theory', *International Journal of Philosophical Studies*, 13, 3: 325–51.

Korstvedt, Benjamin M. 2010, *Listening for Utopia in Ernst Bloch's Musical Philosophy*, New York: Cambridge University Press.

Koselleck, Reinhart 2002, *The Practice of Conceptual History: Timing History, Spacing Concepts*, Stanford: Stanford University Press.

Kufeld, Klaus and Peter Zudeick (eds.) 2000, *"Utopien haben einen Fahrplan": Gestaltungsräume für eine zukunftsfähige Praxis*, Mössingen-Talheim: Talheimer.

Kumar, Krishan 1987, *Utopia and Anti-Utopia in Modern Times*, Oxford: Basil Blackwell.

Latour, Bruno 2004, 'Why Has Critique Run out of Steam? From Matters of Fact to Matters of Concern', *Critical Inquiry*, 30: 225–48.

Lear, Jonathan 2006, *Radical hope: ethics in the face of cultural devastation*, Cambridge, Mass.; London: Harvard University Press.

Lenin, Vladimir I. 1975, *Lenin Collected Works*, Moscow: Progress Publishers.

Leppert, Richard, (ed.) 2002, *Essays on Music: Theodor W. Adorno*, translated by Susan H. Gillespie, Berkeley: University of California Press.

Levitas, Ruth 2013, *Utopia as Method: The Imaginary Reconstitution of Society*, Basingstoke: Palgrave Macmillan.

Levitas, Ruth 1990 'Educated Hope: Ernst Bloch on Abstract and Concrete Utopia', *Utopian Studies*, 1, 2: 13–26.

Leopold, David 2016, 'On Marxian Utopophobia', *Journal of the History of Philosophy*, 54, 1: 111–34.

Leopold, David 2009, *The young Karl Marx: German philosophy, modern politics, and human flourishing*, Cambridge: Cambridge University Press.

Linebaugh, Peter and Marcus Rediker 2000, *The many-headed hydra: sailors, slaves, commoners, and the hidden history of the revolutionary Atlantic*, Boston: Beacon Press.

Maimonides, Moses 1963, *The Guide for the Perplexed*, Chicago: University of Chicago Press.

Mann, Thomas 2002, 'Mann an Adorno 30. Oktober 1952', in *Theodor W. Adorno, Thomas Mann. Briefwechsel 1943–1955*, edited by Christoph Gödde und Thomas Sprecher, Frankfurt am Main: Suhrkamp.

Mannheim, Karl 1952 [1929], *Ideologie und Utopie*, Frankfurt: Verlag G. Schulte-Bulmke.

Manuel, Fritzie P. and Frank E. Manuel 1979, *Utopian Thought in the Western World*, Oxford: Basil Blackwell.

Markun, Silvia 1977, *Ernst Bloch in Selbstzeugnissen und Bilddokumenten*, Reinbek bei Hamburg: Rowohlt.

Marcuse, Herbert 1977, *The Aesthetic Dimension: Toward a Critique of Marxist Aesthetics*, Boston, Mass.: Beacon Press.

Marcuse, Herbert 1969, *An Essay on Liberation*, London: Allen Lane.

Marcuse, Herbert 1964, *One dimensional man: studies in the ideology of advanced industrial society*, London: Routledge&Kegan Paul.

Marx, Karl 1992 [1932], 'Exzerpte aus James Mill: *Éléments d'économie politique*', in *Marx/Engels Gesamtausgabe*, Volume 4, Part 2, edited by Institut für Marxismus-Leninismus, Berlin: Dietz Verlag.

Marx, Karl 1987 [1891], 'Kritik des Gothaer Programms', in *Marx/Engels Werke*, Volume 19, edited by Institut für Marxismus-Leninismus, Berlin: Dietz Verlag.

Marx, Karl 1981 [1844], 'Zur Kritik der Hegelschen Rechtsphilosophie. Einleitung', in *Marx/Engels Werke*, Volume 1, edited by Institut für Marxismus-Leninismus, Berlin: Dietz Verlag.

Marx, Karl 1979, *The Letters of Karl Marx*, edited by Saul K. Padover, Prentice Hall: New Jersey.

Marx, Karl 1978 [1888], 'Thesen über Feuerbach', in *Marx/Engels Werke*, Volume 3, edited by Institut für Marxismus-Leninismus, Berlin: Dietz Verlag.

Marx, Karl 1977 [1885], *Das Elend der Philosophie. Antwort auf Proudhons 'Philosophie des Elends'*, in *Marx/Engels Werke*, Volume 4, edited by Institut für Marxismus-Leninismus, Berlin: Dietz Verlag.

Marx, Karl 1977 [1848], *Manifest der Kommunistischen Partei*, in *Marx/Engels Werke*, Volume 4, edited by Institut für Marxismus-Leninismus, Berlin: Dietz Verlag.

Marx, Karl 1975 [1871] *The Civil War in France*, in *Marx and Engels Collected Works*, Volume 22, London: Lawrence&Wishart.

Marx, Karl 1968 [1932], 'Ökonomisch-Philosophische Manuskripte von 1844', in *Marx/Engels Werke*, Volume 40 (add. volume), edited by Institut für Marxismus-Leninismus, Berlin: Dietz Verlag.

Marx, Karl 1964 [1894], *Das Kapital, Kritik der Politischen Ökonomie, Vol. III*, in *Marx/ Engels Werke*, Volume 25, edited by Institut für Marxismus-Leninismus, Berlin: Dietz Verlag.

Marx, Karl 1962 [1867], *Das Kapital, Kritik der Politischen Ökonomie, Vol. I*, in *Marx/ Engels Werke*, Volume 23, edited by Institut für Marxismus-Leninismus, Berlin: Dietz Verlag.

Marx, Karl 1961 [1849], 'Lohnarbeit und Kapital', in *Marx/Engels Werke*, Volume 6, edited by Institut für Marxismus-Leninismus, Berlin: Dietz Verlag.

Marx, Karl 1960 [1852], 'Der achtzehnte Brumaire des Louis Bonaparte', in *Marx/Engels Werke*, Volume 8, edited by Institut für Marxismus-Leninismus, Berlin: Dietz Verlag.

Marx, Karl and Friedrich Engels 1978 [1932], *Die deutsche Ideologie*, in *Marx/Engels Werke*, Volume 3, edited by Institut für Marxismus-Leninismus, Berlin: Dietz Verlag.

Marx, Karl and Friedrich Engels 1962 [1845], *Die Heilige Familie, oder Kritik der kritischen Kritik. Gegen Bruno Bauer & Consorten*, in *Marx/Engels Werke*, Volume 2, edited by Institut für Marxismus-Leninismus, Berlin: Dietz Verlag.

Marx, Karl and Friedrich Engels 1959 [1848] 'Programme der radikal-demokratischen Partei und der Linken zu Frankfurt', in *Marx/Engels Werke*, Volume 5, edited by Institut für Marxismus-Leninismus, Berlin: Dietz Verlag.

Mazzini, Silvia 2012, 'Kältestrom – Wärmestrom', in *Bloch-Wörterbuch: Leitbegriffe der Philosophie Ernst Blochs*, edited by Beat Dietschy, Doris Zeilinger and Rainer Zimmermann, Berlin; Boston: De Gruyter.

McMillan, Chris 2017, 'MakeAmericaGreatAgain: ideological fantasy, American exceptionalism and Donald Trump', *Subjectivity*, 10, 2: 204–22.

McNay, Lois 2013, 'Contemporary Critical Theory' in *The Oxford handbook of political ideologies*, edited by Michael Freeden et al., Oxford: Oxford University Press.

Mendieta, Eduardo 2005, *The Frankfurt School on Religion: Key Writings by the Major Thinkers*, New York; London: Routledge.

Moir, Cat 2018, 'Ernst Bloch – Who was he and Key Contribution: *The Principle of Hope*', in *SAGE Handbook of Critical Theory*, edited by Beverley Best, Werner Bonefeld and Chris O'Kane (London: SAGE Publications).

Moir, Cat 2016, 'Beyond the Turn: Ernst Bloch and the Future of Speculative Materialism', *Poetics Today*, 37, 2: 327–51.

Müller-Doohm, Stefan 2005, *Adorno: A Biography*, translated by Rodney Livingstone, Cambridge: Polity Press.

Münster, Arno 2012, *Ernst Bloch: eine politische Biographie*, Hamburg: CEP Europäische Verlagsanstalt.

Nussbaum, Martha 1990, *Love's Knowledge: essays on philosophy and literature*, New York: Oxford University Press.

O'Connor, Brian 2013, *Adorno*, London: Routledge.

O'Connor, Brian 2000, *The Adorno Reader*, Oxford: Blackwell.

Ollman, Bertell 2007, 'Marx's Vision of communism a reconstruction', *Journal of Socialist Theory*, 8, 1: 4–41.

Owen, Robert 1993, *Selected Works of Robert Owen, Vol. 2*, edited by Gregory Claeys. London: Pickering.

Owen, Robert 1971 [1813], *A New View of Society* in Owen, *A New View of Society and Other Writings*, introduction by G.D.H. Cole, London and New York: J.M. Dent.

Paden, Roger 2002, 'Marx's Critique of the Utopian Socialists', *Utopian Studies*, 13, 2: 67–91.

Paddison, Max 1993, *Adorno Aesthetics of Music*, Cambridge: Cambridge University Press.

Pensky, Max 1997, *The Actuality of Adorno: Critical Essays on Adorno and the Postmodern*, Albany: State University of New York Press.

Popper, Karl 1986 (1963), 'Utopia and Violence', *World Affairs*, 149, 1: 3–9.

Pritchard, Elizabeth A. 2002, '*Bilderverbot* Meets Body in Theodor W. Adorno's Inverse Theology', *Harvard Theological Review*, 95, 3: 291–318.

Protevi, John 2009, *Political Affect: Connecting the Social and the Somatic*, Minneapolis, MN; London: University of Minnesota Press.

Rawls, John 1993, *Political Liberalism*, New York: Columbia University Press.

Richter, Gerhard 2007, *Thought-images: Frankfurt School Writers' Reflections from Damaged Life*, Stanford: Stanford University Press.

Rose, Gillian 1982, *The Melancholy Science: An Introduction to the Thought of Theodor W. Adorno*, London: MacMillan.

Rosen, Michael 1982, *Hegel's Dialectic and its Criticism*, Cambridge; New York: Cambridge University Press.

Rush, Fred, (ed.) 2004, *Cambridge Companion to Critical Theory*, Cambridge: Cambridge University Press.

Russell Hochschild, Arlie 2016, *Strangers in their own land: anger and mourning on the American right*, New York: New Press.

Saint-Simon, Henri 1987, *The Political Thought of Saint-Simon*, edited by Ghita Ionescu, Oxford: Oxford University Press.

Sasson, Eric, 2016, 'Blame Trump's Victory on College-Educated Whites, Not the Working Class', 15 November, Available at: https://newrepublic.com/article/138754/blame-trumps-victory-college-educated-whites-not-working-class.

Schiller, Hans-Ernst 2017, *Freud-Kritik von Links; Bloch, Fromm, Adorno, Horkheimer, Marcuse*, Springe: Klampen Verlag.

Schinkel, Willem and Liesbeth Noordegraaf-Eelens, (eds.) 2011, *Medias Res. Peter Sloterdijks Spherological Poetics of Being*, Amsterdam: Amsterdam University Press.

Schweppenhäuser, Gerhard 2009, *Theodor W. Adorno: An Introduction*, translated by James Rolleston, Durham: Duke University Press.

Schinkel, Willem and Liesbeth Noordegraaf-Eelens, (eds.) 2009, *Theodor W. Adorno zur Einführung*, Hamburg: Hamburg Junius.

Solnit, Rebecca 2016, *Hope in the Dark: Untold Histories, Wild Possibilities*, Edinburgh: Canongate Canon.

Sorel, Georges 1999 [1908], *Reflections on violence*, edited by Jeremy Jennings, Cambridge: Cambridge University Press.

Stedman-Jones, Gareth 2015, 'Introduction', in Marx and Engels, *The Communist Manifesto*, with an introduction and notes by Gareth Stedman Jones; translated by Samuel Moore, London: Penguin Books.

Stedman-Jones, Gareth 1991, 'Utopian socialism', in *A Dictionary of Marxist Thought*, edited by Tom Bottomore et al., Oxford: Blackwell Reference.

Talmon, J.L. 1957, *Utopianism and Politics*, London: Conservative Political Centre.

Taylor, Ros, 2019, 'Is Brexit a contest between low-earning Leavers and high-earning Remainers?', 18 March, Available at: https://blogs.lse.ac.uk/brexit/2019/03/18/is-brexit-a-contest-between-low-earning-leavers-and-high-earning-remainers/.

Tiedemann, Rolf (ed.) 2003, *Can One Live after Auschwitz?: A Philosophical Reader*, Stanford: Stanford University Press.

Thiele, Leslie Paul 2006, *The Heart of Judgment: Practical Wisdom, Neuroscience, and Narrative*, Cambridge: Cambridge University Press.

Thompson, Peter 2016, 'Ernst Bloch and the Spirituality of Utopia', *Rethinking Marxism*, 28, 3–4: 438–52.

Thompson, Peter 2013, 'Religion, Utopia and the Metaphysics of Contingency', in *Privatization of Hope; Ernst Bloch and the Future of Utopia*, edited by Peter Thompson and Slavoj Žižek, Durham: Duke University Press.

Thompson, Peter 2012, 'What Is Concrete about Ernst Bloch's Concrete Utopia?', in *Utopia: social theory and the future*, edited by Michael Hviid Jacobsen and Keith Tester, Farnham; Burlington, VT: Ashgate.

Vidal, Francesca 2012, 'Hoffnung', in *Bloch-Wörterbuch: Leitbegriffe der Philosophie Ernst Blochs*, edited by Beat Dietschy, Doris Zeilinger and Rainer Zimmermann, Berlin; Boston: De Gruyter, pp. 189–212.

Vidal, Francesca 2000, 'Sein wie Utopie: Zur Kategorie Heimat in der Philosophie von Ernst Bloch', in *"Utopien haben einen Fahrplan": Gestaltungsräume für eine zukunftsfähige Praxis*, edited by Klaus Kufeld and Peter Zudeick, Mössingen-Talheim: Talheimer.

Webb, Daren 2000, *Marx, Marxism and utopia*, Aldershot: Ashgate.

Wenzel, Uwe Justus 1992, 'Negativistische Ethik?', in *Erfahrungen der Negativität – Festschrift für Michael Theunissen zum 60. Geburtstag*, edited by Markus Hattstein and Michael Theunissen, Hildesheim: Olms.

Wheatland, Thomas 2009, *The Frankfurt School in Exile*, Minneapolis, Minn.: University of Minnesota Press.

Whitebook, Joel 2004, 'The Marriage of Marx and Freud', in *Cambridge Companion to Critical Theory*, edited by Fred Rush, Cambridge: Cambridge University Press.

Wiggershaus, Rolf 1995, *The Frankfurt School: Its history, theories, and political signific-ance*, translated by Michael Robertson, Cambridge, Mass.: MIT Press.

Wuilmart, Françoise 1985, 'Problematik beim Übersetzen von Ernst Blochs "Das Prinzip Hoffnung" ins Französische', in *Bloch-Almanach*, Ernst-Bloch-Archiv, 5: 204–22.

Zimmermann, Rainer E. 2013, 'Transforming Utopian into Metopian Systems: Bloch's Principle of Hope Revisited', in *Privatization of Hope*, edites by Peter Thompson and Slavoj Žižek, Durham: Duke University Press.

Zipes, Jack and Frank Mecklenburg (eds.) 1988, *The Utopian Function of Art and Liter-ature: selected essays*, Cambridge, Mass.; London: MIT Press.

Zudeick, Peter 1987, *Der Hintern des Teufels: Ernst Bloch – Leben und Werk*, Moos: Elster Verlag.

Žižek, Slavoj 2017, *The Courage of Hopelessness: chronicles of a year of acting danger-ously*, London: Allen Lane.

Žižek, Slavoj 2016, 'Why There Are No Viable Political Alternatives to Unbridled Capit-alism', *Big Think*, 27 November, Available at: http://bigthink.com/videos/slavoj-zizek -on-the-failures-of-the-leftist-movement.

Žižek, Slavoj 2015, *The Trouble in Paradise: from the end of history to the end of capital-ism*, London: Penguin Books.

Žižek, Slavoj 2014, 'Only a radicalised left can save Europe', *NewStatesman*, 25 June, Available at: http://www.newstatesman.com/politics/2014/06/slavoj-i-ek-only-radi calised-left-can-save-europe.

Žižek, Slavoj 2010, *Living in End Times*, London: Verso.

Index of Names

Index of Subjects